BROWN

Also by Kamal Al-Solaylee

Intolerable: A Memoir of Extremes

BROWN

WHAT BEING BROWN IN THE WORLD TODAY MEANS (TO EVERYONE)

Kamal Al-Solaylee

HarperCollins*PublishersLtd*

Brown

Published by HarperCollins Publishers Ltd

First Canadian edition

HarperCollins books may be purchased for educational, business, or sales promotional use through our Special Markets Department.

HarperCollins Publishers Ltd
2 Bloor Street East, 20th Floor
Toronto, Ontario, Canada
M4W 1A8
www.harpercollins.ca

Library and Archives Canada Cataloguing in Publication information is available upon request

ISBN 978-1-44344-143-8

Printed and bound in the United States of America
RRD 9 8 7 6 5 4 3 2 1

In loving memory of my mother, Safia, whose brown skin lives in mine

CONTENTS

Introduction *Brown. Like Me?* 1

PART I

Chapter 1 *A Colour, a Vanished Race, a Metaphor* 31
Chapter 2 *Colourism: Fair Is Fair?* 52
Chapter 3 *Trinidad: Guarding the Colour Line* 69

PART II

Chapter 4 *The Philippines: At the World's Service* 93
Chapter 5 *Hong Kong: Workers, Women, Mothers* 117
Chapter 6 *Sri Lanka: In the Shadow of the Philippines* 148
Chapter 7 *Qatar: Between Men* 171

PART III

Chapter 8 *The United Kingdom: British Values* 195
Chapter 9 *France: Another Paris* 219
Chapter 10 *The United States: Undocumented* 243
Chapter 11 *Canada: The Wedge Issue* 270

Acknowledgements 297
Notes 301

INTRODUCTION
Brown. Like Me?

I remember the moment I realized I was brown. My brown face, my brown legs and my curly black hair began to weigh on my mind in a way they never had before. Let me take you back to Cairo, early 1974. For several days, one of Egypt's two state television channels had been promoting the small-screen premiere of *Oliver!*, the 1968 film version of the British musical. It was a big deal in Cairo, and probably an omen for a city whose future poverty levels and income inequality would make Victorian London look like a socialist paradise. I write that with the full benefit of hindsight. I was a nine-year-old boy growing up as part of an expatriate Yemeni family, so I can't say that I knew much about the economy or the distribution of wealth back then.

I can't remember why I decided to stay up so late on a school night to watch a period musical about English orphans, pick-pocketing gangs and prostitutes with teachable-moment altruism. I had but a passing familiarity with the story, and Western musicals were an artistic taste I had yet to acquire. (I caught up with them as part of an education in all things camp and old Hollywood when I came out as a gay man in my early twenties.)

The film aired just a few months short of my tenth birthday. Life in Egypt had returned to normal after three weeks of fighting and humiliating—or so the propaganda machine would have Egyptians believe—the Israeli army in a war that had started on October 6, 1973. The end of hostilities meant a return to regular programming and a break from the rotation of military- and nationalist-themed songs and documentaries. My father, a lifelong anglophile, probably insisted that we children watch this slice of Merrie Olde England—a display of all things English that only a hardcore colonial like him was permitted to find jolly or nostalgic.

About twenty minutes into the film, though, he lost interest. You could always tell when something he longed for turned out to be a dud, because he'd start talking through it. Probably he hadn't realized that this was a musical version of Dickens's *Oliver Twist.* He didn't particularly like musicals, unless they starred Fred Astaire and Ginger Rogers, his childhood idols.

I, on the other hand, trembled on the inside as I watched the film. My world tilted in that moment, and I'm not sure it's been set right since.

Every time the camera zoomed in on the face of the young actor playing Oliver, Mark Lester, I became painfully aware of how different my own face looked. As the youngest child in a large family, I was adored by my older siblings—the sweet baby boy. But the more I gazed at Lester's face, the less I felt any kind of pride in my looks, and my innocence slipped from under me in the process. He was just too beautiful, too angelic-looking. It defied the laws of nature as I knew them then. I don't think I viewed him in any sexual terms, even though my own awareness of my same-sex desire predated that evening by a few years. I saw it as a skin-to-skin and not boy-to-boy attraction. He had what, all of a sudden, I desired.

If my lifelong journey with physical insecurities and differences in skin colours can be traced to a single moment in time, it is that one. Most children in my immediate circle in downtown Cairo looked like variations of me. Sure, some bragged about their very light complexion or their ash-blond hair, but no one came close to Mark Lester in brightness, whiteness, holiness. Looking at him, I felt like a lost soul, forever damned by a dark skin.

To be beautiful—to be adorably mischievous—a person needed to look like Lester. His light, shiny hair and his perfectly proportioned features forced me to rush to the bathroom to look at my own face and tousle my own hair. Probably for the first time in my life, all I saw reflected in that mirror was a black, dandruff-prone and curly mane; a big, flat nose; and ears that looked more clown-like than child-like. The hair could be trimmed or straightened, I consoled myself, and perhaps my nose and ears weren't all that unshapely. But there was one thing I couldn't rationalize away: my brown skin. What was I to do with this dark mass? How could I ever catch up with Lester's whiteness, which was the essence of his impossible beauty? If I scrubbed my face with soap ten, twenty times a day, would it get lighter and whiter? What about the rest of my body? How many showers a day would that be? How do you wash the brown away?

I needed answers. I needed help. I got neither.

I felt cursed with this brownness that I'd inherited from my passes-for-white father and my dark brown mother, who came from a Bedouin sheep-tending family in the southern tip of Yemen. My ten siblings displayed a variety of skin shades—some closer to my father's, some to my mother's. I came in between. Standard brown. Egyptians had coined a word for people like me: *asmarany*. It meant someone with a dark complexion, possibly from sustained exposure to the sun, and probably from working cotton fields or construction sites. There was pride in being sun-kissed—it was a symbol of hard work and stamina. In the nationalist period immediately after the 1952 revolution, which eventually severed the country's ties to the British and Ottoman empires, popular musicians wrote songs about the beauty of *asmarany* people. I recently came across one from the late Lebanese singer Sabah, in which she defended her love for an Egyptian *asmarany* man by insisting that his dark skin was actually the secret to his beauty. The song title translates to "So What If He's Brown-Skinned?"

But I didn't comprehend brown skin in that positive sense that night in 1974, or in the many years that followed. Popular music aside, Egypt was teeming with images that not so subtly equated lighter skin with social refinement and physical perfection—possibly, and with hindsight again, my first encounter with white privilege. It's still difficult to fathom how a country at the heart of the Middle East—one that led the way in pan-Arabism and post-colonialism—would be the custodian of a tradition in which the predominant skin colour was relegated to an inferior social position. To be white or very fair-skinned was to win the genetic lottery, and the few who claimed their tickets ensured that social traditions perpetuated this "understanding." Egyptian cinema, the Hollywood of the Arab world, featured a number of leading men and women whose lighter skin was the most desirable part of their physical package.

Egyptian TV commercials and print advertisements of the time sold a bourgeois, consumer-friendly lifestyle through lighter skin, which they promoted as aspirational for the millions of rich *and* poor locals. I don't recall seeing brown-skinned women or men—certainly no dark brown or Nubian-black models—in any of the advertising I grew up watching in the Middle East. Only *National Geographic*–style travel posters in hotels or airports sold an "authentic" Egyptian experience to Western tourists. With the exception of their white teeth, those smiling faces were enveloped in darkness, as if to fulfill tourist fantasies of an exotic journey into the tip of Africa. From my travels over the past few years, I can safely say that selling whiteness and selling out brownness is a long and still-thriving tradition in the Middle East, the Gulf and Southeast Asia. In Dubai, white, European-looking faces promote everything from multimillion-dollar condos to fast-fashion outlets like Zara and H&M. In the odd instance when advertisers deign to use Arab models, it looks like a generous dollop of white paint has been applied to their faces. Not even white people are *that* white.

Many of these images, I suppose, had entered my subconscious before that night watching *Oliver!* Yet somehow those close-ups of Lester's face served as the catalyst, triggering a lifelong awareness of my skin colour as my gateway to seeing the world and being seen by it. This played out in a variety of social and political contexts over decades and across many countries. Wherever I lived or travelled to, my skin awareness followed, a shadow of my shadow. I don't think I'll ever be able to separate myself from it, but I can unpack its meanings, or at least some of them, with a look back at my own and other people's journeys with brownness.

*

AROUND 1979, WHEN I was in high school and trying (and failing dismally) to experiment with heterosexuality, a beautiful young Egyptian girl made it clear that we couldn't date—and I use that very North American term loosely and anachronistically—because her mother would find me too dark. My skin tones would pollute the gene pool of a bourgeois Egyptian family that took pride in its lighter skin, its biggest asset in the marriage and social markets.

As a teenager, I lived in fear of being given any item of clothing in red. My parents had taught me and my siblings to show gratitude by using gifts from family and friends as soon as possible. But a popular Egyptian saying at the time went something like this: "Get an *asmarany* to wear red and you'll make people laugh at him." In plainer words, he'll look like a monkey's behind. The association strikes me as profoundly racist now, but what really sank in for me at the time was the idea that some colours were off limits for me—not because they didn't complement my skin tones but because they made me look like a beast.

My awareness of being brown would become entrenched a few years later, when I moved to the West. As a foreign student in the United Kingdom in the early 1990s, I was called "Paki" more than once. I often wanted to shout back that I wasn't actually Pakistani. It had never occurred to me that I would be lumped with South Asians on the racial-slur spectrum, because I had thought of myself as lighter-skinned than most of them. They were dark brown; I was light brown. Couldn't these racists tell the difference?

As a Canadian citizen in the aftermath of September 11, I learned to accept racial profiling as part of my everyday reality as a brown male—at least until I reached my late forties and started looking too haggard to be a troublemaker or a jihadist. Terrorism is a young man's business.

When I was a (younger) gay man visiting largely white bars and clubs in North America and Europe, I felt either desired or rejected because of my skin tone. (It depended on the evening and the crowd.) Even during a brief 2008 visit to Buenos Aires, the heart of what I thought was brown Latino country, I apparently went to the wrong bar, the one frequented by Argentines of European descent. I'd never felt more like a pariah in my entire life, and that included the time I went on a London-bound bus trip to visit the British Parliament with a group of Young Conservatives in 1991. Getting ignored in bars didn't rankle me that much in general, but this felt more like invisibility—a complete erasure of every part of me, not just my skin. An Argentine friend told me the next day that I should have gone to a more working-class bar where brown and black gay men, local and international, socialized. Being of a lower class made it acceptable to be of darker skin, too.

As a gay man who came of age in the 1980s, between the AIDS epidemic and the perfect-body cult with its white assumptions, I had already found it hard to avoid pondering how skin colour set people apart from (or invited them into) the inner circles of fabulousness. Whenever the models for crotch-enhancing underwear or phone sex in bar rags weren't white, they were black. *Very* black. Desire came in two colours only, and mine wasn't one of them. And although many white gay men of my generation fetishized darker-skinned males, projecting images of hyper-masculinity on, say, Latinos and Middle Easterners, the latter rarely crossed over from the "ethnic porn" aisle to the mainstream of gay sexuality.

Not all my personal experiences of being brown have carried negative undertones, however. In the winter, my white friends tell me they envy my complexion because it doesn't turn as pasty and washed-out as theirs does. (I never notice the difference and have always thought they were being too self-conscious about their own skin, the poor dears.) In parts of New York, I often take advantage of being perceived as *not black*. I've had no problem hailing cabs late at night in Manhattan or asking for directions from passersby. In the hierarchy of skin shades, being brown occupies the comfortable middle space, the buffer—we are not as privileged as whites but not as criminalized as blacks.

My own shade of brown is not fixed—it gets darker in the summer and lighter in the winter. Like many middle-class people who trace their origins to the Global South, I tend to avoid the sun wherever I go. (I used to wonder why white people went to such great lengths to get a tan. All those hours on the beach, and for what?) I'm over fifty now and have never once sunbathed in a park on a summer day, taken a beach holiday or set foot inside a tanning salon. It's a brown-people thing. And a class one, too. The darker you turn, the more you look like the working masses—or so I've been trained to think since childhood. More than forty years later, I can still hear my sister Hoda admonishing me for playing under Cairo's blazing sun: "You'll look like a *khadaam* [a servant]." Summer or winter, it didn't matter—the sun became a year-round enemy to the lightness of our skin. Whenever my brother Wahby, the darkest of the eleven children, misbehaved or showed his stubborn streak, my mother would chide him with the word *abd*, Arabic for "slave."

If you're brown, it's hard to deprogram yourself from thinking such seemingly superficial but nonetheless existential questions as: Am I too dark? If I get darker, will I lose my social position? If I avoid the sun forever, will I pass for white, or at least southern European? Brown people can turn their in-between skin into a back door to Europeanness and whiteness. They just need to stick to the very southern parts of the continent.

Over the years, I've heard similar stories from several Hispanic, Arab, South and East Asian, and North African friends. We live in our skin, our largest human organ—and possibly the biggest prison of them all.

I recall a Syrian student who refused to join a picnic with other doctoral candidates from the graduate club at Nottingham University (where I was doing my PhD in Victorian literature) because the sun was too bright that particular July weekend. It was the very reason the British students had planned the outing. Another friend of Indian descent invited me to a curry restaurant in her hometown of Leicester, where she proceeded to treat the dark-skinned waiter—Bangladeshi, if I remember correctly—abominably, dismissing my concerns on the grounds that "darkies" like him were used to this abusive behaviour from the community. It was the first time I'd heard the word "darkie." It never left my consciousness. It had a negativity that my then favourite word, "swarthy," didn't. Swarthy implied exoticism, even desire.

In 2004, when I told an Indian friend in Toronto that I'd booked my first-ever trip to Southeast Asia, she asked if I could bring her back some skin-whitening creams. (The Toronto summer sun turned her brown skin a shade too dark for her comfort.) Had I known such concoctions existed, I would have forked over all my allowances and begged for more to get hold of them in the post-*Oliver!* years. I spent three weeks travelling through the gorgeous landscapes of Singapore, Malaysia and Thailand on that trip, but I tracked the journey less by the change in scenery and local cultures and more by the gradual darkening of my skin. I didn't want to be a darkie.

Facing a mirror and examining not just my hair but my exact shade of brown turned into a lifelong preoccupation. You may think that I'm operating at the shallow end of life. But I know I'm not alone. Who hasn't obsessed about their body, hair, face, skin—whatever colour the latter may be? Didn't James Joyce write that "modern man has an epidermis rather than a soul"?

It took time to see beyond the exterior. But over many years, I've identified with and felt strengthened by narratives that transcended appearance, including the civil rights, feminist, gay liberation and social justice movements. I experienced a political awakening from the outside in. And while this book is not a chronicle of that journey, it wouldn't have been written without the realization that my struggles to feel at ease in the skin I'm in reflect global issues and trends that go beyond the personal. Everywhere I looked, every story I heard, all but confirmed the prejudices and advantages that a skin tone can inflict or bestow on individuals, communities and nations. The concept of race as biologically determined may have been banished from all but the most extreme corners of politics, but the experiences of racialization, of being judged—literally, in the case of the US legal system—on the colour of one's skin, continue. And the closer I looked, the more I noticed the unique place that brown skin occupied in the global story of race relations and perceptions.

*

I BELIEVE THERE'S A certain collective experience that unites people of brown skin—brown people—despite their geographic, ethnic, national and cultural differences. We are united (and divided) by the fact that we're not white. Or black. Millions of us may be living in East Asia, but we're not ethnic Chinese either. We are billions of people spread across the world and better known as Middle Easterners, Latin Americans, North Africans, and South and Southeast Asians.

To be brown in the world today is to recognize narratives and life experiences that unfold with striking similarities despite different settings and contexts. These are not exclusive to brown people, but they take place with such frequency and in such concentration among us that we can claim some ownership of them. Uppermost among them—and a particular focus of this book—are the experiences of the brown migrant and immigrant. Although each term refers to a specific group of people—migrants move out of desperation, while immigrants relocate in pursuit of better lives—the lines between the two continue to be blurred as war and ecological disasters ravage parts of the Global South.

We're on the move, uprooted, always elsewhere, a sizable portion of 244 million people living outside our countries of birth (a figure, the UN projects, that will reach 590 million by 2050). You'll find us at airports, border crossings and ports, aboard trains, ferries and cars, with our luggage and boxes held together by duct tape and sheer willpower. Our dreams and trepidations dominate this endless journey. Some of us may have our papers in order as we cross borders, but many of us hope to enter other countries, other worlds, using false claims (visiting family) or on humanitarian grounds (seeking refugee status at point of entry). Some of us are surgeons, university professors, investors, tech wizards and creative artists, but many, many more have found a calling in life by doing the work that affluent local people no longer wish to do. We're here to build high-rises, work in kitchens, clean homes, tend to the young and elderly, pick fruits and vegetables from fields (and stock them in supermarkets), and drive everyone home after a night of boozing.

The brown immigrants trigger conversations and political strategies from which their black, East Asian and white counterparts are spared—at least at this moment in time. Those of us who are Muslim live under constant suspicion for the religion we follow. As the 2015 federal elections in Canada proved, when a political party lags behind in the polls, nothing whips its base into a frenzy of racial discrimination faster than depicting Muslims as a stain on Canadian values.

The association of brown people with transient labour is not limited to the white, developed world. As I will show in this book, the lives of some brown migrant workers reach certain intensity in places as far apart as the Caribbean and the Far East, and even *within* other brown nations. It's hard not to think of the brown South Asian worker without considering the thousands of construction workers from Nepal, Sri Lanka and Bangladesh whose blood and sweat have gone into virtually every building, high- or low-rise, in Dubai and Qatar. It's in Dubai, too, that middle-class immigrants from the Middle East and the South Asian subcontinent have for decades kept the schools, banks, hospitals, hotels, food courts and malls running—without ever being afforded the benefits of citizenship.

We are lured to do the work in good times—until the economic bubble bursts. Then we turn into the job stealers, the welfare scammers and the undocumented. Two days before Christmas 2014, the Malaysian government mobilized its military aircraft to deport hundreds of undocumented Indonesian workers. Other illegal workers in Malaysia come from India, Bangladesh and Nepal, and at least one report estimates their numbers at six million. The boom in the Malaysian economy in the decades prior to the financial crisis of 2008 led to a vast improvement in lifestyle for locals. Millions joined the middle classes (by Malaysian standards), and then farmed out work on plantations and in restaurants and homes to other, less privileged brown people from the region. Many collected garbage or cleaned bathrooms in the upscale malls that earned Kuala Lumpur a spot on CNN's list of the top-five shopping destinations in Asia. In early 2015, Indonesian diplomats formally protested to the Malaysian government after a print ad for a vacuum cleaner featured the tagline "Fire Your Indonesian Maid Now."

Men made up the majority of the deported, but brown women are on the move, too. The brown migrant worker, whether in the West or the Gulf States or East Asia, is best symbolized by the millions of Filipina nannies, caregivers and domestic workers. Their tales of family separation, harsh living conditions, exploitation and physical abuse transcend borders. According to one labour organization, employers and recruiters who underpay or fail to pay domestics walk away with about $8 billion a year in illegal profits. As one domestic in Hong Kong told me, the jackpot was a permit to work for a white family in the United States or Canada. (In the informal poll of worst-possible destinations that I conducted with a group of domestic workers, also in Hong Kong, Saudi Arabia topped the list.)

But even in open, tolerant Canada, assumptions about skin colour and specific lines of work are made. I learned that while taking my dog for a walk a few days after moving into my condo building in midtown Toronto. A resident stopped me to ask if I had a business card. I couldn't understand why until it dawned on me that she thought I was a dog walker. Her mind couldn't conceive of the possibility that I was also a resident. She read my skin tone as my identity: worker, and low-paid at that. Many of my aging neighbours rely on a revolving cast of caregivers, helpers and cleaners—most of whom are brown. They hail from the Philippines, Central or South America, and occasionally Somalia or Ethiopia. I see and say hello to so many of them every morning, but I've never once learned their names and have often mixed up which caregiver works for which neighbour on my own floor.

I suspect I'm not alone. How many of us know the name of the Colombian or Nepalese cleaning lady we see only when we work late in the office? Brown people are everywhere and yet somehow remain invisible or nameless. But life and the global economy would come to a halt if the mass relocation of these workers—cleaners, domestic workers, security guards, maintenance staff, cooks, pedicurists, construction workers, farmhands and cashiers who ask for your loyalty card when you pay for toothpaste and toilet paper—were to stop. We keep the world running as we ourselves are run out from one spot to another. The words "work permit," "legal status" and "permanent visa" are music to our brown ears. The notes get discordant when we hear "minimum wage or below," "dormitory-style accommodation," "withholding passports" or "deportation." Our lives unfold as a constant battle to move from the second set of words to the first, to lend legitimacy and a home base to our journeys.

We know (or at least hope) that legitimacy brings with it political recognition and social acceptance. Others in the Western world have reached a similar conclusion.

*

BROWN PEOPLE ARE INFLUENCING politics on both sides of the Atlantic, destabilizing established power systems and forging new alliances (or strange bedfellows, as the case may be). Our presence in these societies can sometimes split populations into two camps: those who want us out or silenced, and those who welcome us, even if grudgingly, to settle scores against the first camp. Again, the 2015 Canadian federal election, still fresh and likely forever imprinted on my mind, serves as a prime example. When a Muslim woman fought for (and eventually won) her right to be sworn in as a citizen with her face behind a niqab, her story dominated media coverage and changed the tenor of the campaign for all three major parties. Some voters in Quebec switched their support to the Conservatives for what they perceived to be the party's strong position on creeping Islamism in the country. The Conservatives had relatively little political traction in the province up until that point. Several Liberal (and liberal) commentators who would normally have come out against the niqab used the government's politicizing of the issue as a symbol of its race-baiting strategies and suddenly stood in solidarity with the defiant woman.

In the United States, discussions of race tend to revolve around relationships between the black and white communities, which leaves the masses of brown citizens out of the conversation altogether. In 2014 and 2015, three cases of white police officers killing unarmed black men (Michael Brown in Ferguson, Missouri; Eric Garner in Staten Island, New York; and Walter Scott in North Charleston, South Carolina) turned a single racial encounter—white police officers against black men—into a symbol of race relations in the country. Latinos and brown people from Arab and Muslim countries make appearances in other areas of the race debate: immigration and terror, respectively. Does racism in, for example, the nation's police forces manifest itself against blacks only? Do Latinos, Arabs, and South and Southeast Asians get a free pass from an increasingly militarized police in the United States? Ask any brown taxi driver in New York City about racially tinged encounters with the NYPD and you'll get a very different answer. When staff in a Texas school called the police to report a brown, Muslim fourteen-year-old boy, Ahmed Mohamed, on suspicion of terrorism for bringing a homemade digital clock to class, can there be any doubt that his skin colour and faith had placed him outside what society considers normal—encourages, even—in young men? Why do Americans still see race in such black-and-white terms when the truth is that their society is becoming largely brown?

My questions take nothing from the historically complicated relationship African Americans have with white institutions and structures of power. And I'm certainly not arguing for a few extra seats at the police-brutality table for brown people. (We are probably relieved to be left out in this instance.) Instead, I'm trying to see why some brown experiences in America get excluded from general discussions of race, especially given what the demographics tell us about today and what they predict for the future. The browning of America is not a manifestation of supremacist paranoia but a numerical fact.

Let's look, briefly for now, at the Hispanic community in the United States. As of July 2015, it was estimated that fifty-five million Americans identified as Hispanic/Latino. The community grows at a rate of about 2.1 percent a year, a seemingly modest ratio but one that hides a more impressive piece of data. On average, about fifty thousand Latino children turn eighteen every month in the States. That's fifty thousand votes a year up for grabs from a demographic that generally skews younger: over 60 percent of Latino Americans are under the age of thirty-five. In California, Latinos officially outnumber whites (14.99 million to 14.92 million, according to figures from the US Census Bureau). In economic terms, Latino buying power sat at about $1.6 trillion in 2015. Advertisers and marketers who have been circling the community for years are swooping in now that a large number of middle-class Latinos take part in the consumer culture of their white neighbours.

The statistics for immigrants to the United States from South Asia are equally staggering. Between 2000 and 2010, South Asian Americans became the fastest-rising major ethnic group, according to numbers collected by the Asian American Federation from the 2010 census data. The rate of increase is estimated at 81 percent decade over decade (that is, 1990 to 2000 and 2000 to 2010). Even if the total number of South Asian Americans seems small (3.4 million), relatively high birth rates within that community and elevated immigration levels from the region are set to swell the ranks. And these figures don't include South Asians living in the States illegally or those who didn't complete the census because of any number of immigration-related infractions.

If we are to better understand racial politics in North America, we will need to see the brown population as central to how we live race today and what that means for the future of everything, from how detergents are sold to how votes are won.

We can no longer afford to occupy the margins of society, to check the "other" box on a form. The Democrats know that Latinos—despite their varied ethnic backgrounds and political affiliations—constitute a major voting bloc. Barack Obama's November 2014 deportation amnesty, if it survives ongoing legal challenges, may turn out to be his greatest gift to his successor from the pool of Democratic presidential hopefuls. (About 71 percent of Latinos backed Obama in the 2012 elections.)

Among those covered by Obama's executive order were tech workers in Silicon Valley who came to the United States from India on a temporary working visa known as the H-1B. About 130,000 IT workers of Indian background enter the US on that visa every year to work in the STEM (science, technology, engineering, math) fields. (Their dependants may come to the States on an H4 visa, staying as long as the H-1B visa holder retains his or her legal status.) In 2013, Infosys, an India-based IT services provider, assigned 509 workers to Apple sites in California. According to *Computerworld* magazine, 499 (or 98 percent) of those workers were listed as Asian. The remaining ten identified as either black or white. Is there a shortage of workers in these high-tech industries? Or are tech companies lobbying for these visas to drive down wages—the brown worker as technically savvy scab? The answer likely depends on your political leanings or where you get your news fix. And whether the visa is a symbol of the borderless global trade in talent or the facilitator of a brain drain in the Third World (or even a new form of indenture) is a debate we'll continue having as long as the Industrial North and the Global South exist. The fact remains: the overrepresentation of brown workers as the foot soldiers of the tech industries will influence the political map of the United States when those guest workers morph into permanent residents—and voters—as many of them eventually do.

Increasingly, the balance of power in America looks to be in the hands of brown populations.

Indeed, demographic projections from the US Census Bureau suggest that white people will lose their majority status by about 2043, making America the first major post-industrial nation where minorities will be the majority. Minorities in this sense include blacks, Hispanics and Asians (Chinese, Indian, Arab, etc.). By 2060, Hispanics alone will count for one in three Americans, or about 34 percent of a projected population of 420 million.

In Canada, the Latin American community is more recent and significantly smaller than its counterpart in the United States, but its rate of growth—and its economic clout—continues to rise. Fast. It now represents about 1.2 percent of the population, and its numbers increased by 25 percent between 2006 and 2011, to reach just over 380,000 people. Unlike South Asian, Chinese and Caribbean people, Latinos began to immigrate to Canada primarily in the last decade of the twentieth century and the first ten years of this one. So while the numbers may be small, the overall growth rate is astonishing, and in line with immigration patterns of more established communities in their early arrival histories. About a third of Toronto's Hispanic community landed in that city between 2007 and 2012. Mexico, Colombia and El Salvador top the list of countries of origin.

Although the community is yet to leave its footprint firmly on the Canadian economy and culture, it's one that businesses, including banking, are lusting after. As recently as 2011, the *Globe and Mail* described the Hispanic presence in Canada as "all but unknown and ignored," and "practically invisible." The Toronto Hispanic Chamber of Commerce (THCC) has been working to change this perception, and its biggest draw is not the volume but the quality of immigrants. While the debate around immigration in the United States tends to focus on an uneducated or poorly paid labour force, the THCC stresses the entrepreneurial nature of its members, a reflection of the generally higher educational levels of immigrants to Canada from Central and South America. About half of THCC's members come to Canada with a university degree or professional diploma. In 2013, the THCC estimated that the economic impact of its members' businesses was somewhere between $50 million and $74 million.

By comparison, the South Asian community now constitutes the largest visible minority group in Canada, ahead of East Asians and blacks. According to the 2011 Canadian census, this community represents about 4.9 percent of the population (1.6 million people). The numbers may in fact be larger if you include newcomers whose status was in limbo or under review at the time of the census. Statistics Canada believes that immigration from Asia in general—and that includes the Middle East—was the largest source of newcomers to Canada between 2006 and 2011. It reports that immigration from Africa is also rising, but points out that Algeria and Morocco top the list of countries of origin among new arrivals. In other words, brown nations dominate virtually all immigration sources in Canada. And demographic projections suggest that the trend will continue, since the median age of visible minority immigrants is younger: 33.4 compared with 40.1 for whites. At a median age of 30.02, Arab Canadians are the second-youngest ethnic group after blacks; they're followed by South Asians, at 32.8. By 2031, one in four people in the Greater Toronto Area will be of South Asian descent. Take a walk in downtown Toronto or parts of its suburbs and you'll see that the browning of Canada's largest city is well under way.

Racial and ethnic categories—and how they are defined—have a major impact on almost every aspect of political governance. Governments depend on identifying their constituencies. And that road begins with collecting data. Canada's census asks respondents to name the ethnic or cultural origin of their ancestors. Respondents are free to list more than one country or ethnic group. By contrast, the US census asks respondents to choose first from a set of five racial categories before providing more specific information on their ethnicity. The five racial groups are: White, Black or African American, American Indian and Alaska Native, Asian, and Native Hawaiian and Other Pacific Islander. The Census Bureau is quick to point out that these "generally reflect a social definition of race recognized in this country and [are] not an attempt to define race biologically, anthropologically, or genetically."

Clearly, this methodology can result in some inaccuracies in capturing the racial and ethnic diversity of the country. Hispanics, for example, are allowed to choose from any racial group in the above list of five, while Arabs and North Africans are grouped under White. The arbitrary nature of classifications by race, particularly for Arabs and Latinos, suggests that the number of brown people may be higher even if it appears statistically lower—a potential problem for brown people who want to see a more accurate reflection of America's population in data collected by their government.

Ethnic advocacy groups in the United States and Canada pore over census data for a very compelling reason: demography is political destiny. It's also an economic bargaining chip. In Canada, all three major political parties are fighting for the hearts and minds of immigrants, particularly South and East Asians. For most of their tenure (2006–15), the Harper Conservatives were congratulating themselves on rewriting the standard biography of the left-leaning, urban immigrant into one that supports a more conservative social and political agenda. The 2014 municipal elections in Toronto may have attracted worldwide attention because of the notoriety of the city's crack-smoking former mayor, Rob Ford, and his protector-brother, Doug, but the result—a more moderate conservative candidate, John Tory, won by a small margin—was a clear indication that the immigrant vote had reached a critical mass. The battle for the mayor's office was decided on the outskirts of the city, where large and largely neglected immigrant, brown, East Asian and black communities reside. The city's largest suburbs—Rexdale and Mississauga in the west end and Scarborough in the east—are now dominated by masses of the working immigrant poor. Progressive politicians in Canada have a lot to learn about the brown wave if they want those immigrant votes. Fielding brown or ethnic candidates will no longer be enough to get new Canadians to check their names on the ballots.

*

THE NUMBERS AND STATS tell one part of the story of being brown in one part of the world, North America. But numbers alone can't and don't reveal the personal, the emotional, the stories, the heartbreaks and triumphs behind this or that percentage of brown clout or political capital.

This is where this book comes in.

I propose that we think of brown as a continuum, a grouping—a metaphor, even—for the millions of darker-skinned people who, in broad historical terms, have missed out on the economic and political gains of the post-industrial world and are now clamouring for their fair share of social mobility, equality and freedom. Past colonial powers (France, Britain, Italy) must now resolve the paradox of having former subjects living among them, transforming themselves from nameless individuals with swarthy skins into neighbours, co-workers and friends. Brown is the colour of the five million Muslims in France, most of whom come from the former North African French colonies. Brown is the colour of the Pakistani and Indian immigrants to the United Kingdom who arrived as the Raj gave way to post-partition chaos and violence.

Brown is the colour of the uprisings that have taken over the Arab world in the first half of this decade. It's the colour of hundreds of thousands of Egyptians—young and old, illiterate and digitally savvy—saying "Enough" to a life of poverty and political oppression. Most of their revolutions have been usurped, silenced or devastated by ruling parties and widening ethnic tensions between Sunnis and Shiites, but the essence of that moment, its idealism, lives on. Brown is yet another Mediterranean ghost ship carrying hundreds of Syrian or North African asylum seekers who were faced with a choice between staying put or possibly perishing en route—and still chose the latter. It's the wave of refugees knocking at Europe's doors in the summer of 2015. The thwarted revolutions in Syria and Libya, as well as the ongoing instability in Iraq, have led to the displacement of about seventeen million people, according to 2014 figures from the International Organization for Migration. A population almost half the size of Canada's is scattered across refugee camps, shelters, no man's lands.

Brown represents hundreds of Nepalese, Indian and Bangladeshi construction workers dying daily—literally, an average of one a day—to build arenas and infrastructure for Qatar's 2022 World Cup. Brown is the thousands of Latin children smuggled by their own parents or travelling alone across the US–Mexico border in hope of finding a life away from drug wars, marauding militias and extreme poverty. Some are killed when they're deported back to Central America.

We are not a distinct ethnic group but myriad large ones with more in common than we have acknowledged before. Eugenicists have been kept up all night worrying about our birth rates and concocting ways to sterilize our fecund kind before we contaminate the purity (and beauty) of white people. Blacks in East Africa and parts of the Caribbean resented us for being a market-dominant minority. And for that, they exiled us, forcing us to seek refuge anywhere that would have us. Some moved to North America, others to the Gulf States. Our stories and histories have spread worldwide, and we've created diasporic communities to protect and showcase our heritage and, most of all, our food. Everyone loves our food—biryani rice, falafel, couscous, tacos—and in many ways, we're identified with what we prepare in our kitchens or serve others in our "ethnic" restaurants. Our bodies, too, are sometimes consumed as a slice of exotica or sexual adventurism, a tradition that has existed in bafflingly perfect harmony with our supposed physical inferiority since the heyday of racialist science.

For much of our history, we've been defined by others—as the brown race, as the weaker tribe, as the civilization-ready subjects of empires. But the time has come for us to self-identify as we wish. There's strength in numbers and comfort in knowing that one's experience is not isolated or an aberration. Whenever I get pulled aside when crossing the US border, I find it reassuring that I'm not the only brown face. I see the Iraqi or Pakistani business traveller, the Colombian student, the Sri Lankan chef or the Indian family with three or four or five children, and I know that while our stories are different, we find ourselves singled out because of our brown skins and histories. We don't talk to each other, but we do exchange knowing glances. It's our lot as brown people to be treated with suspicion when we cross borders.

Often we're asked to speak on behalf of a billion people and their faith—any brown Muslim knows what that feels like. Sometimes the calls for us to speak, to justify actions taken by a tiny fraction of our communities, are posed in good faith, as when a friend asks me to explain, say, the origins of the Sunni–Shiite hostilities. Every Irish person who's ever been asked about the history of the Troubles between Catholics and Protestants probably can relate to this. Other times the calls to speak have an accusatory tone, particularly when coming from right-wing media outlets in the US and Canada. With the rise of so-called lone-wolf attacks in Western cities, the pressure on the average brown person of Muslim origin to explain the incomprehensible has increased. Many friends find this to be problematic, and I agree—but only to some extent.

We carry the burden of our skin colour everywhere we go. Pretending that it's otherwise is intellectual dishonesty. I can talk about terrorist attacks in faraway lands—a satirical magazine in Paris, a coffee shop in Sydney—because the narrative of the radical jihadist has been thrust into my world by Western media and by the perpetrators of these heinous crimes. It has become part of my story whether I choose to tell it or not. Hispanic and Filipino migrants tell me that they experience a similar thing. If one Filipina maid is caught stealing or "acting immorally" in the Gulf, all are under suspicion and expected to account for such aberrant behaviour. Similarly, long-established Mexican-Americans are drawn into debates on illegal immigration as if they're to blame for any new influx. Many of them have not set foot in Mexico for generations, and all are culturally more American than Mexican, but as sociologists tell us, hyphenated people—like those of mixed race—are usually seen as belonging to the subordinate and not the dominant group. Italian and Irish Americans have lost that hyphen, and have worked their way toward whiteness and the mainstream; for us, the hyphen is imprinted like a birthmark on our skin. Our transition into the collective is still in progress.

But perhaps we need that hyphen. In Europe—particularly France and Britain—colonization serves as the brown people's overarching story. In North America, browns don't have the history of slavery that gives black people their defining narrative. Brown people need a grand story. As this book will show, there's no one definitive account but a continuum of story arcs.

I know that the tale of a young brown boy watching a beautiful white actor and feeling adrift is not an isolated incident. I also know that my history of migrating from a developing country to the West echoes in the experiences of millions of other immigrants, asylum seekers, refugees, temporary workers and their extended families. I want to tell you their stories because I believe they complete mine and yours. You may be brown, white, East Asian, aboriginal or black. Male or female. Gay or straight. Some or none of the above. However you choose to identify, these stories are in essence about us, all of us—about the world we've inherited, created, fought for or against. We're all in this together, regardless of skin colour or country of origin. To write about brownness is to write about whiteness. To experience brownness is to recognize blackness, as a colour and a political experience. To be brown is to know how many shades of brown a community can live with, and which ones are allowed to triumph (over the rest). To talk about brown people means involving other Asian communities that live so close to them.

However, I am deliberately privileging the brown experience as my lens for exploring the world. Write what you know, they say, and I know this. I *know* this brown life because I've lived it. We don't hear enough from brown people—certainly not from the disenfranchised and itinerant among them. They never stay in one place long enough to gain political clout or leave behind more than fragments of their histories.

This book is not intended as a travelogue, but I'd like to invite you along on the many journeys I've taken in pursuit of stories and personal testimonies of what being a brown person really means. How is this experience similar to the experiences of other racialized groups? In what way does it partake of or challenge white or black hegemony, particularly in North America? Our stopovers will include Doha, Qatar, where a Sri Lankan driver in his fifties has emerged as a father figure to a generation of his countrymen who must adapt to heat, long working hours, isolation and a complete lack of privacy. We'll visit the Philippines and Hong Kong, where domestic workers and employees in the service industry negotiate their lowly status in a world of Chinese and expat families, as well as in businesses that can be friendly or hostile (or even violent). Many of the maids I met in Hong Kong are raising other people's children, leaving their own in the care (or neglect) of others. If the children they look after were to pick up Tagalog, it would become the world's new lingua franca. I stop in Colombo, the capital of Sri Lanka—and of the skin-lightening industry in South Asia—where a cosmetic surgeon talks candidly about the appeal and dangers of his profession. And where a former domestic worker spent hours every single day for almost a month helping her only child land a similar job in a country neither mother nor daughter knew much about.

In Paris and London, I meet people of, respectively, North African and South Asian descent whose Muslim faith has pitted them against the classic narrative of the Republic or the made-up one of British values. In the United States, I spend time with undocumented workers during a summer when presidential hopeful Donald Trump has used them to whip up his base of angry, under-employed white Americans. (In my own Canada, I saw how a decade of Conservative rule tore apart the country's reputation as a fair and progressive society, largely by casting its Arab and Muslim populations as enemies of the state.)

Those who shared their journey with me illuminated and enriched my own story, and my understanding of my skin and place in the world. I glimpsed my reality in theirs, even though my position as a university professor and author in Canada has bestowed on me all sorts of privileges, but specifically class.

In general, I focus my reporting on big cities because I believe that the brown continuum as I propose it here is an urban one. Brown people are both visible and invisible in the city's colleges, plazas and office towers. Some of us show up to attend classes or cut multimillion-dollar deals, others to clean offices and get them ready for the next day.

That's part of the paradox and reality of being brown in the world today.

PART I

CHAPTER 1

A Colour, a Vanished Race, a Metaphor

The sidewalks and patios of downtown Bangkok are bursting with shoppers and traffic-stopping selfie-takers on a hot mid-December evening. Terminal 21, a travel-themed mid-level mall, offers an air-conditioned respite from the outdoor hustle. On this particular night, I'm looking for a getaway as I avoid an outdoor Christmas party hosted by the students at the Wattana Wittaya Academy, an elite boarding school for girls. The academy and I have had our differences, but by and large we've learned to get along. My temporary base in Bangkok overlooks the school's yard, and I've already got accustomed to—or decided to find charming—the wafting sounds of Christmas carols as early as 6:30 a.m. in the lead-up to the holidays. The morning assembly's motivational speeches became white noise after a few days. But I draw the line at a whole evening of "White Christmas," even in Bing Crosby's supple voice.

I stop at a local T-shirt stand called Over the Sky for some basics to get me through a few weeks of winter heat. Although the tiny kiosk miraculously holds a stock of over forty or fifty designs in all sizes, items come in a limited number of colours: white, green, blue, black and brown. I opt for a series of T-shirts with geometric patterns, trying on a handful in different colours. The sales assistant's English is limited, but he can still be quite vocal when my pick doesn't match what he has in mind for me. He also offers his honest opinion on which colours look better on me: black, blue and (in the right shade) green. He just doesn't see me in white or brown. White highlights my grey hair, while brown washes me out. He dramatizes the latter observation by putting a brown shirt on his own brown skin and uttering, "Same, same," a phrase so popular in Thailand that a nearby store sells T-shirts with these very words printed on them.

He has a point, though, and it's one that I've known on an instinctive level for some time. Brown is just not my colour—when it comes to clothes. I like it on floors, credenzas and window blinds, but I can count on one hand the number of brown clothing items I've bought in the last, say, ten or fifteen years. As a child, I hated the colour red. But as a middle-aged man living in the West, I felt that brown clothes on brown skin would make me look more "ethnic" when all I craved was to blend in, to be less visible. My mind associates the colour with feces. Why would I want to wear the colour of shit? Am I being too unreasonable, too self-loathing? I know that many other brown people tend to avoid wearing the colour too close to their faces for similar reasons. (Brown pants and skirts are acceptable for some, but they must be paired with another colour on top.) What's in the colour brown, and how does it affect us, all of us, psychologically?

*

IN THE WORLD OF colour psychology—a field that veers between catering to the academically arcane and serving the market needs of corporate branding and home decor, with a stopover in New Age wonderland—brown is always the bridesmaid and never the bride.

It's not the main attraction or a standout in an artist's palette, but it is a solid background colour that, according to the website Empower Yourself with Color Psychology, suggests hard work, industriousness and reliability. It's a colour you can count on to get the job done. Little wonder, then, that UPS chose brown (Pullman Brown, to be exact) for its courier business. If you're sending something across international or state borders, the thinking goes, you want to go with a company whose corporate colour suggests reliability and efficiency. The founder of UPS, James Casey, initially fancied delivery trucks in yellow, but according to company lore, Charlie Soderstrom brought brown with him when he became a partner in 1916. It would be impossible to keep yellow trucks clean on the dirt roads of early twentieth-century America, Soderstrom reasoned, while brown hid dust and grime nicely. Brown, now the company's nickname, will always deliver.

On the other extreme end of that efficiency scale are the Storm Troopers, the paramilitaries who facilitated the rise of the Nazis in Germany in the 1920s and early 1930s. They became known as Brownshirts after the colour of their uniforms. The headquarters for the Nazi Party in Munich was called the Brown House. Electoral maps of Germany in the 1930s used the colour brown to mark districts won by the Nazi Party. Proving the main tenet of colour psychology—that colour goes beyond aesthetics and into meaning—brown subliminally established a relationship between the working class and military might on one side and the Nazi Party on the other. And yet the party may have chosen its official colour not by design but by accident—surplus brown army uniforms from Germany's colonial forces in Africa were available at bargain prices in the 1920s.

Designers generally use brown as a background colour. They consider it ideal for floors, especially in darker hues, because it hides dirt (just as it does on parcel delivery vans). Although it suggests warmth to many, brown is one of the least preferred colours in the Western world, asserts Empower Yourself with Color Psychology. (Bizarrely, it shares this sad category with colours that designers normally describe as "brilliant" or eye-catching: yellow and orange.) It's difficult to understand why brown remains the runt of the colour litter, particularly when you think of its association with nature. Like green, it sends a strong environmental message: the colour of earth, of trees. Think of logs about to go into the fire, a walk in the woods or, depending on the shade of brown, a sandy beach.

In the Western world, decades of environmental consciousness and activism have done little to promote brown as a colour that's at one with the natural world. A probable exception is the brown paper bag as an alternative to plastic. The colour green, by contrast, has come to define the ecology movement, with political parties across the Western Hemisphere taking their name from it. I suspect that a left-leaning, environmentally conscious party known as the Browns would not have the same political resonance. I also wonder if the colour's association with ethnic and migrant groups that multiply ferociously and—as they move to a middle-class, consumer society—leave a bigger environmental footprint puts it at odds with an ecology movement that's largely represented by white activists and scientists. Unless you live in the Land of Oz, green carries none of the associations with skin colour or racial groupings that brown does.

Perhaps too much brown undermines the message. As colour psychologist Karen Haller notes, despite its ruggedness, brown can elicit feelings of "heaviness" and "lack of sophistication." And yet in fashion, brown often symbolizes luxury, excess, desire—especially in silk and satin fabrics. In women's clothes, brown business suits suggest strength but with a hint of earth mother to soften any "ball-buster" connotations. Still, fashion editors advise women to break up the brown by wearing it in combination with another colour. Again, it's not a colour that's allowed to dominate. Men in brown suits run the risk of looking cheap if they don't select the cut and the shade carefully. A brown suit in a light shade that's one size too big telegraphs certain messages: borrowed, hand-me-down, struggling immigrant about to go to an interview for a telemarketing job. In *Saturday Night Live* sketches set in the world of 1960s game shows, male contestants are often dressed in brown suits to emphasize the "period" feel.

The tan suit that President Obama wore for a White House briefing in late August 2014 elicited many class-based responses (some hilarious and some racist) in both mainstream and social media. On the "anniversary" of the suit's debut, *Esquire* ran a satirical follow-up on the "worst suit in presidential history." Talk of a Sears suit and borrowing his father's church suit served as code for the black president's outsider status—the message was that he didn't belong in Washington, even after six years on the job. The more serious commentators pointed out that the tan suit, even in the dog days of summer, didn't strike a grave enough tone for a briefing on such issues as ISIS and Vladimir Putin.

Toronto-based Anna Romanovska teaches colour theory at Ryerson University's School of Fashion and has worked as a theatre costume designer in her home country of Latvia. She believes brown has stodgy and drab connotations and has avoided it in her designs. "If you want someone to disappear on stage, dress them up in brown," she tells me, pointing out that brown absorbs light, while bright colours reflect it. She has dressed many supporting characters in brown to deflect attention from them and direct it at the actors in the leading roles (and the light-coloured costumes).

For most people, however, brown elicits visceral reactions on very different ends of the pleasure/disgust meter. It's associated with chocolate and cocoa beans, as well as fancy coffee drinks like lattes and macchiatos—little symbols of luxury or authenticity. Think a rustic free-trade coffee shop, an emblem of gentrification from Cairns to Cairo, with its wooden tables, bowls of brown sugar and selection of preservative-free, home-made chocolate-chip cookies. Dieticians recommend brown rice and other unbleached grains over white varieties for their nutritional and organic qualities.

But brown also invokes more repulsive images: it's the colour of feces and sewage. It represents our discomfort with and social awkwardness around bodily functions. No wonder we call obsequious people brown-nosers. The phrase is a one-two punch, capturing social opprobrium while also revealing our unease with exposing or getting close to our own anatomy.

Brown's association with certain smells has often tested my own racial biases and tendency to fall back on stereotypes. When I lived in England in the 1990s, the laziest (and by that I mean probably the least offensive) racial slur to toss at an Indian or Pakistani person was to say he smelled of curry. Something about a brown skin evoked the strong smell of a spicy dish. I fell for it. I noticed the scent of Indian food whenever I visited the family home of a Pakistani friend, and I came to associate his national identity with the smell of the food his family cooked. This link hit home when, in the early stages of our relationship, a German boyfriend told me that my sweat emitted a certain odour that probably came from eating lots of Indian and Arabic food. In fact, I ate little of both cuisines, since they required too much preparation and I was living in student housing with a communal kitchen at the time. Still, I felt so self-conscious that I made sure not to eat any remotely spicy food in the seventy-two hours immediately before seeing him.

I know I shouldn't have taken a throwaway comment so seriously, and now I look back and laugh it off, but that exchange represents how the colour brown—on my skin, in my wardrobe, in the minds (and noses) of others—can elicit strong reactions. Despite its neutral role in home decor, it vaults from background to foreground in the social and political arenas. That history goes back to the early days of colonialism, when European men first came into contact with people whose skin colours and facial features, not to mention cultures and religions, differed from theirs. Colonialism may have been chiefly about acquiring land and resources, but among its lasting legacies is a still-thriving tradition of categorizing people according to their physical characteristics, with skin colour as the most salient feature. Sociologists and biologists refer to it as the science of human taxonomy, but it's best understood in terms of power and dominance.

In the eighteenth century, when European sovereign nations ramped up their expansionist missions, brown people entered Western consciousness as a different and newly discovered race within a then-burgeoning field of race science. Much of that science has since been debunked as merely furnishing imperial powers with excuses to dominate "weaker" races, and most of the scientists and anthropologists associated with it are, deservedly, long forgotten. However, the creation (and subsequent dismantling) of the brown "race" offers some sobering lessons to our modern world. In the early eighteenth century, Europeans' ability and willingness to emigrate was seen as evidence of their superior physical and mental powers, and of their rightful claim to the rest of the world. Today, when brown people dominate modern migration patterns, both the context of their movement and the very meaning of it have changed. Modern-day migration is a way not of mastering the world but of serving its economic needs—not to liberate and conquer but to be enslaved and submit—since the vast majority of brown people migrate out of desperation.

A look back at highlights from two centuries of debates on race and ethnicity in Western science and culture provides a certain historical context—and a vital link to where we stand today.

*

LOOKED AT IN TERMS of human evolution, using skin colour to categorize people into distinct racial groups is a relatively recent endeavour. Historians of race, and in particular of what's now known as scientific racism, identify Carolus Linnaeus, an eighteenth-century Swedish zoologist and botanist, as the first to create a four-part racial scheme with a corresponding colour system: Europeans were white, Africans black, Asians yellow and Native Americans red. From the 1730s until his death in 1778, Linnaeus turned his attention to classification of animals, insects, plants—and humans.

Later in the eighteenth century, German anthropologist Johann Blumenbach added a fifth racial group to Linnaeus's existing four: browns, or what he called the Malay race. (He called the four other groups Caucasian, Ethiopian, Mongolian and American.) The Malay race covered a large swath of what we would now call South Asia, East Asia and the Pacific, stretching from Thailand and Malaysia to the Pacific Islands and Australia.

As Nell Irvin Painter explains in her thoroughgoing *History of White People*, Blumenbach was both ahead of and representative of the racialist thinking of his time. He asserted the superiority of the white, European race not just in physical strength and standards of beauty but in moral character and temperament as well. In introducing the brown race in the revised edition of his influential *On the Natural Variety of Mankind* in 1781, Blumenbach (who, like many of his contemporaries, was a skull collector) filled the middle space between the "beautiful" whites and the "ugly" Mongolians. The idea of a brown group of people as a "buffer" race starts with him, and while much of his work is now discounted, this particular aspect shows remarkable resiliency, even if the specifics and contexts have changed. In a large number of societies, being brown still means occupying that middle space, on the cusp of whiteness and on the edge of blackness.

It was Blumenbach who first parsed the role of climate on skin colour, explaining how and why darker people lived in hot climates, while lighter ones prevailed in colder regions. He chided European women for risking the brilliant whiteness of their skins, earned after months of indoor winter life, by spending too much time in the summer sun and becoming "sensibly browner." To be brown marked not just a change in skin colour but a deviation from the standard of beauty that absolute whiteness demanded. Blumenbach's work employed scientific terms and theories to deliver aesthetic pronouncements. Beauty is whiteness, and whiteness is scientifically proven to be beautiful. As Painter puts it, "Race begat beauty, and even scientists succumbed to desire." It wouldn't be the last time in modern Western history that science was pressed into servicing the political and racial assumptions of the day.

Throughout the late eighteenth century and into the mid-twentieth, a host of European and American anthropologists, race scientists and natural historians followed in the imposing footsteps of Blumenbach, providing grist for the colonialist and segregationist mills. The organization of humans into colour-coded groups positioned along a sliding scale of physical and moral characteristics supplied a counter-revolutionary narrative—just what imperial nations wanted to hear to silence opposition to their missions.

Christoph Meiners, a friend and contemporary of Blumenbach's, was far less rigorous in his methodology, according to Painter, but he advocated the enslavement of what he believed to be inferior races. After his death in 1810, Meiners's name disappeared from history and science books until the 1920s. The Nazis revived his fortunes when they latched on to his "scientific" conclusion that Germans had the most delicate skin and the purest blood among the superior race of Europeans. Meiners's wobbly research supplied the foundation for an ideology of racial genocide.

What's remarkable in all this is how the parameters of being brown kept expanding and contracting, depending on changing ideological and political contexts. The brown race was a revolving door of nationalities and nomads. Egyptians, for example, came in and out of it. Ethiopians were black to Blumenbach but brown to some of his successors. In the early twentieth century, Scottish folklorist and historian Donald Alexander Mackenzie and Australian-British brain anatomist Grafton Elliot Smith championed the idea of a "Mediterranean" race from which all modern humans had descended—a theory that contested the established one about the African roots of *Homo sapiens.* They described this new group as a "swarthy" darker-skin race that stretched from the Middle East to Britain, with ancient Egypt at its nerve centre. British people with darker complexions than their peers, Smith suggested, could trace their origins to this expansive race. While popular, Mackenzie's and Smith's theories didn't gain much traction with the scientific or military communities. A Britain that had declared itself *the* empire was hardly going to accept the suggestion that its people shared genetic roots with its colonial subjects, its inferiors.

Many historians consider American eugenicist Lothrop Stoddard's work locating the brown race within specific parts of the world to be the most extensive exercise in racial mapping.

However, Stoddard's classifications come wrapped in an overtly racist and alarmist rhetoric, even when measured against the period's inflammatory standards. In *The Rising Tide of Color Against White World-Supremacy* (1920), Stoddard defined the brown race as those who live in North Africa, the Near East, the Middle East, Central and South Asia, and parts of the Pacific—calling them "nearly as numerous and much more wide-spread than the yellows," or East Asians.

Stoddard's work resonated because it came at a turning point in US race relations, when Americans were reacting to an influx of immigrants from Italy, Eastern Europe and Greece—people European in origin but considered inferior, in part because of their darker skin. The debate on race had moved on from the immorality of slavery in a free republic to how the country must remain the rightful property of a white, Nordic European race, despite successive waves of immigration from all over the globe. Stoddard championed the Immigration Act of 1924, a series of laws that limited the immigration of Southern and Eastern Europeans, and prohibited entirely the immigration of Arabs and Asians.

Another American, Charles Davenport, led a new eugenics movement that emerged as a reaction to the racially diverse wave of immigration to the United States between 1890 and 1920. He received funds from prominent philanthropists and foundations (including the Rockefeller Foundation and the Carnegie Institution) to establish the Eugenics Record Office, which was tasked with "register[ing] the genetic backgrounds of the American population and distinguish[ing] between good and defective lineages." And although he was speaking metaphorically when he talked about building walls to protect America, he conceived of his "science" as literally the country's last defence against non-white newcomers. "Can we build a wall high enough around this country, so as to keep out these cheaper races," he wrote, "or will it be a feeble dam . . . leaving it to our descendants to abandon the country to the blacks, browns and yellows and seek an asylum in New Zealand?"

The rise of Nazism and Fascism in Europe in the 1930s put critics of scientific racism into overdrive. A new narrative to debunk the racialists emerged in such books as *We Europeans: A Survey of "Racial" Problems*, published in 1935 by British biologist Julian Huxley and anthropologist A. C. Haddon, who argued that science offered only a "limited definition of race." American anthropologists Gene Weltfish and Ruth Benedict contributed to the conversation three years later with *The Races of Mankind*, which posited that any scientifically based differences between racial groups were at best superficial and did not provide the physical or moral grounds for the superiority of one race over another. Benedict's mentor at Columbia University's storied anthropology department, Franz Boaz, had already dismissed as inaccurate any suggestion of differences in the brains of white and black people in his influential work *The Mind of Primitive Man*, first published in 1911. His studies, however, gained new momentum in the years before and after the Second World War.

By the end of the Second World War and into the early 1950s, the tide began to shift. As imperial powers loosened their grips on subjugated nations, it became clear that the colonialist assumptions of race- and colour-based human classification went against the liberationist ethos of the era (not to mention recent scientific advances in biology and genetics). The very notion of race—let alone one defined by skin colour—lost credibility. Ashley Montagu, who followed in the footsteps of Benedict and Boaz, argued that race is nothing but a social construct, a concept that endures among social scientists and anti-racism activists. Montagu helped draft the United Nations' 1949 Statement on Race, as well as a similar document for UNESCO a year later.

*

IN THE PAST TWO decades, sociologists started to favour a more nuanced approach: to use "ethnicity" as a more politically neutral term than "race" for understanding who we all are. In their handy 2012 guide, *Race and Ethnicity: The Basics*, Peter Kivisto and Paul R. Croll offer a summary of three working hypotheses that negotiate the relationship between race and ethnicity.

The first of the three hypotheses, which they quickly dismiss, views race and ethnicity as two distinct groupings. In this way of thinking, "ethnicity" refers to those who left their homelands voluntarily (say, Italian or Irish Americans), while "race" refers to people whose migration or extermination (my word) has been traumatic (as it was for, respectively, Africans and Native Americans). This is a very American-centric view of the human experience that creates more problems than it solves. In this scheme, both Asians and Latinos are considered a race, even when their immigration history is closer to that of Italians than Africans.

A second hypothesis sees race and ethnicity as overlapping. Here, race is viewed as a natural and permanent category. A person is either black or white, Asian or Native American. Ethnicity, on the other hand, is more fluid and historically defined. It's also claimed by the groups themselves, whereas race is normally forced upon them. While there are a lot of merits in this hypothesis—especially in recognizing the benefits of self-determination—Kivisto and Croll believe it falls short of capturing the complexity of human experience. Italian and Irish immigrants to the United States and Canada in the nineteenth and early twentieth centuries were seen as undesirable by the Anglo-Saxon and Nordic majorities. And yet within about a century, they have claimed a space for themselves as part of the white majority, moving from the ethnic to the racial while also moving up the ethnic social ladder. Later ethnic groups from the Caribbean or South Asia occupied a place formerly held by immigrants from Southern Europe. The same process applied to Jewish immigrants from Eastern Europe at about the same time. Most of them will now be considered—and consider themselves to be—white. As historian David Roedigar illustrates in his book *Working Toward Whiteness*, this process hinged on a socio-economic movement from the working to the middle classes.

Skin colour, of course, was also a major factor. Many of these groups didn't have to "pass" for white because they were by and large white ("invisible minority," as a later term would have it). They simply restored ties to the dominant white racial group that had been severed by some eugenicists and advocates of a Nordic America.

Kivisto and Croll's final hypothesis—the one that most current sociologists favour—is that race is a subset of ethnicity. In this model, "ethnicity" becomes an umbrella term that encompasses language, religion, geographic origin *and* race. It reduces the role of, but does not completely eradicate, race as an element in determining the parameters of any given ethnicity. Sociologist Steve Fenton argues that it frees our understanding of who we are from the centuries of "discredited science and malevolent practices" that are inherent in the term "race." To me it's a reasonable hypothesis, but by no means does it eliminate the violent aspect of racial encounters. Even recent history has shown that differences based on race can be supplanted by ethnic ruptures that range from skirmishes (Quebec) to cleansing (Serbia) to genocide (Rwanda).

Still, for brown people who formed the majority of the colonized, the shift away from racial to ethnic was welcomed and encouraged. We felt less like an inferior race and more like people with agency. Our inferiority was not a scientific fact but a political fiction written by representatives of the systems that oppressed us. But it would be the last time in history when brown people formed a social or anthropological bloc (as disadvantaged as that bloc might have been). The brown race was divided. It vanished from popular books, racist propaganda and "scientific" papers as each region charted its own course in the modern world. In theory at least, the globe was carved out not along racial lines but economic ones: the Industrial North and the Global South, the developed and developing worlds, and so on.

You may think that these economic divisions represent some progress in how groups of nations identify each other—that they offer a more neutral demarcation system than race. It hasn't worked out that way. The labels may have changed, but people in brown nations continue to occupy a similar low place in the hierarchy of power and influence. You'll find us in the developing, Global South and Third World aisles of the world's supermarket. Whether they're located in a racial or economic model, browns have a long way to go. Is there a case for what sociologists call "lumping"—identifying groups by a wider set of signifiers? Can we reunite the brown people without reviving the essentialist thinking that begat the brown race?

I believe so. And there has never been a better time to examine what it means to be brown in all its contradictions. The headlines of 2015—from Donald Trump's race baiting to the Paris terrorist attacks to the ongoing Syrian refugee crisis—prove that brown bodies continue to endure, and inflict, serious suffering.

In the US and Canada, living while brown elicits a peculiar kind of racial animus that differs from the one that dogs the black community, especially its young men. Anti-brown racism is a brew of cultural incomprehension, religious fear and economic insecurity—with some good old-fashioned colour-based discrimination thrown in.

If anti-brown racism were to be analyzed in a lab, you'd find traces of suspicion based on more than two centuries of the kind of Orientalism that has cast people with swarthy skins as shifty, duplicitous and dangerous, whether they come from the jungles of India or the deserts of Arabia. We were cast as wily when we tried to free ourselves from colonialism and as devious when we collaborated with it.

Lab results will also reveal droplets of ambivalence, particularly in a Western context. Brown people seem close to the mainstream, so normal, and many of us are light enough to pass for a tanned white person. And yet we worship different gods (too many gods), wear strange face covers and write from right to left—all of which designates us as strangers still. We're hired in different parts of the world for our skills and often recruited (or dragged) from our home countries as temporary or seasonal foreign workers, but the welcome mat is pulled from under us if we want to transition from guests into permanent residents, or if we wish to be united with our spouses, children or parents. Our labour is in demand, our families less so. This happens in Asia and Africa as it does in Europe and North America. The recruitment and then expulsion of Asians in East Africa and the collective slave-driving of Filipinos in Singapore and Hong Kong bear testimony to this.

Even when we don't compete for low-paid jobs, ambivalence remains in the picture. Like the Chinese specifically and East Asians in general, brown people who do well in North America are held up as a model minority—the kind of citizens who (unlike African Americans, as the thinking goes) work hard, value education and don't ask for handouts or play the victim. In other words, white populations have designated us as a buffer group between themselves and the black community—a process that has only gained momentum in the neo-liberal interpretation of race relations. In this model, the elevation of brown (and Chinese) people as full participants in the market economy is cited as evidence that the system is colour-blind, that racism no longer exists. In a market-driven model, writes Arlene Dávila in *Latino Spin: Public Image and the Whitewashing of Race*, her analysis of the Hispanic community in the US, "citizens who are entrepreneurial can reign supreme, unencumbered by the pettiness of race, ethnicity and gender."

And yet this very ideology, almost as a sleight of hand, turns around and singles out, for example, Arabs or Muslims as outsiders to a value system based on criteria that move with the political winds. Two works that nearly bookend the first decade of this century—Vijay Prashad's *The Karma of Brown Folk* (2000) and Moustafa Bayoumi's *How Does It Feel to Be a Problem?: Being Young and Arab in America* (2008)—explore the dichotomous nature of white America's response to its darker citizens. Both books draw on the work of black writer and activist W. E. B. Du Bois, who wrote in *The Souls of Black Folk* (1903) what it was like to constantly be asked, in indirect ways, "How does it feel to be a problem?"

Prashad asks of South Asians, "How does it feel to be a solution?" A solution to America's long and torturous history of race relations, to be exact. He explores the contradictions that led to the elevation of middle-class South Asians as a model minority—a role model to blacks and other groups lagging behind, including Mexicans and other Hispanics—while the working class among them (taxi drivers, fast food workers and clerks at convenience stores) continue to experience the worst in racial discrimination and violence. Toward the end of the decade, when America's attention had focused almost entirely on the Arab population, there was very little of that "solution" magic left for Bayoumi to conjure. Brown people of Arab descent have been branded a problem for America's security and a test to its faith in itself as a melting pot of possibilities and dreams.

Brown is also slippery and potentially indefinable. Who counts as brown and who doesn't can sometimes be a matter of self-identification (or self-denial). Two black friends have suggested to me that the relatively light skin tones of Syrian refugees explain why Canadians have opened their wallets and homes so generously. Black refugees don't fare as well because they're not "almost white." My father would have had a breakdown had anyone called him brown. In his mind, he was a light-skinned man who just happened to have been born south of the Saudi desert. "Your mother," he'd tell me, "is brown." Many light-skinned Mexicans, Egyptians, Iranians and others I know spend much of their time and money enhancing the physical and economic features that align them to whiteness: lighter hair colour, the right kind of makeup, non-ethnic clothing (at least in public), unaccented English. They try to wash the brown away by reversing the layers of the coconut. In the classic coconut model, a person acts white on the inside while remaining brown on the outside. The reverse model hides the inner brown under a layer of white accoutrements and signifiers.

Brown groups are often conflated with and mistaken for each other. A report from a South Asian–American group suggested that between 2010 and 2014, a rise in xenophobic and racist rhetoric in the country's political discourse was echoed by an uptick in hate crimes and violence against a wide group of brown people. The report focused on South Asian, Muslim, Sikh, Hindu, Middle Eastern and other Arab communities. During the four years studied in the report, many Hindus and Sikhs (and Christian Arabs) were assaulted, both verbally and physically, and even killed for what the perpetrators assumed to be their Muslim identity. (Eighty percent of hate crimes described in the report were motivated by anti-Muslim feelings.)

The implied "all brown people look the same" mentality explains why, when it comes to casting supporting and minor characters with dark skin in films and on TV, authenticity takes a back seat to availability or versatility. What matters most is the right shade of brown. Indian actors get cast as Arabs and Arabs as Indians. The proliferation of terrorism-themed films and TV shows since 9/11 has been a boon for brown supporting actors of all ethnicities. And sometimes it goes beyond supporting parts and into lead roles. In *Rosewater*, comedian Jon Stewart's directorial debut, Mexican actor Gael García Bernal plays an Iranian-Canadian.

We can be grateful for the fact that at least an actor from the brown continuum got the part. As another comedian, Aziz Ansari, reminded us, Hollywood was still indulging guilt-free in a bit of brownfacing (casting white actors in ethnic roles and simply darkening their skin with makeup) not that long ago—1988's *Short Circuit 2*. And the practice of whitewashing historical figures from the Global South continues. The casting of Ben Affleck as CIA agent Tony Mendez in *Argo* or Gerard Butler and other white actors as ancient Egyptians in *Gods of Egypt* suggests that, to the film industry, our stories (or the Hollywood version of them) can be told only if we're excluded from leading roles.

This is where writing about brownness gets tricky. My friends have been challenging me on my criteria, asking me to produce my guest list for the brown party.

No, I don't go around carrying a colour swatch with all the shades of brown and measuring people's skins against it to determine who qualifies and who doesn't. To me, brown is not a literal definition but an experiential one, and context determines everything. It's about falling outside the black-and-white binary in North America. In Europe, brownness follows the legacy of colonialism and the compatibility (or lack thereof) of different cultures with Western liberal values. In much of Asia and the Arabian Gulf, it's about who does the work that locals spurn.

And while I didn't set out to exclude any group in writing this book, I knew I couldn't include all of them. The focus on telling stories from the point of view of immigrants and migrant workers meant that, for example, aboriginal people in North America didn't fit, politically or thematically. Although there's an overlap between their experiences and those of people on the brown continuum, I felt that trying to tell aboriginal stories within the parameters I had established would be historically inaccurate and insensitive. Aboriginal people have been, and still are, at the receiving ends of (im)migration waves to their native lands.

In deciding who to write about and who to leave out, I created a simple formula: Has the cultural, national, regional or religious community you come from reached a crisis point in the *host* country? Is that country, be it in North America, the Caribbean, Asia or Europe, experiencing some kind of moral panic about your presence in its midst? If you answered yes to both questions and you're not European white, African American, aboriginal or East Asian, then congratulations (or is it commiseration?), you're brown. Perhaps you can and do pass for white when you feel like it. Good for you, and shame on you. Millions can't and don't. They carry their brownness everywhere they go, and sometimes lose their lives because of it.

Hundreds of construction workers are dying every year in the Gulf States because their skin colour and economic desperation (and the two are related) matter little to their Arab employers, whose wealth has confused their moral compass. Indonesian and Filipina maids are beaten, exploited, raped and forced to give up their children because their ethnicity, class position and skin colour make them less than human. Muslims in both Europe and

North America experience the worst of racial profiling and are the subject of dog-whistle politics that have tested the limits of civil liberties and human dignity. Presidential hopefuls cavalierly describe millions of Mexicans as murderers and rapists, regardless of facts or evidence. The list of anti-brown discrimination goes on.

When I attended a meeting of a social justice group in Phoenix in the summer of 2015, I noticed a collage painting with the words "Brown Is Beautiful." It got me thinking. Brown may indeed be beautiful, but the general picture ain't pretty. I believe, however, that it's necessary—imperative, even—to stop treating the various experiences in the brown continuum as isolated and to begin to see the common threads in them. Those who believe that we will join the Irish, Italians and East European Jews in overcoming racial discrimination and working our way to whiteness have forgotten (or chosen to ignore) the pesky colour question.

Our brown skin will always act as an impediment, even if we cream and laser-peel our way out of it. Sometimes you really can't wash the brown away.

CHAPTER 2
Colourism: Fair Is Fair?

In the winter of 2009, Myanmar's consul general in Hong Kong sent a letter to the media and his fellow diplomats to explain his country's official position on the Rohingya people, an ethnic Muslim minority in the predominately Buddhist state. Myanmar—which continues to be run by a semi-civilian government even after the junta was dissolved in 2011—has always maintained that the Rohingya people originated in neighbouring Bangladesh and therefore should not be considered an indigenous ethnic group. To prove this point, the high-ranking envoy cited the difference in skin tone between the Rohingya minority's "dark brown" complexion and the majority's "fair and soft" skin. Rohingyas were also "ugly as ogres," he asserted, while true Myanmar people were a "good-looking" bunch.

And just in case the recipients of this missive thought he'd made up the connection between skin tone and beauty, he offered himself as exhibit A: "My complexion is a typical genuine one of a Myanmar gentleman and you will accept that how [*sic*] handsome your colleague . . . is."

The letter received attention from local and international media, in part because of its narcissistic and undiplomatic tone and in part because it perpetuated Myanmar's rationale for the exclusion and abuse of the Rohingyas: they just don't belong there. These 1.1 million Muslims, whose roots in Myanmar go back generations, have been denied not just basic human rights but their very existence. A 1982 law stipulated that only ethnic groups whose ancestors had settled in Myanmar before 1823 could claim citizenship. This left the Rohingyas more or less stateless in a country they called home. A series of conflicts in 2012 and 2013 led the Rohingyas to seek shelter in refugee camps with "appalling" and "apartheid-like" conditions, reported international observers.

In the spring of 2015, their plight attracted global headlines when several Asian countries (Indonesia, Malaysia and Thailand, among others) either refused or were slow to accept thousands of Rohingyas who had taken to the Andaman Sea and the Bay of Bengal. These people chose to subsist for weeks on fishing boats—or more accurately, floating coffins—rather than continue living in the refugee camps and under the military's control.

Much has been written about the marginalization and potential eradication of the Rohingya people in the context of a rising tide of intolerance among the Buddhist majority, particularly toward Myanmar's small Muslim population. Little has been said about the difference in skin tones, referenced in the envoy's letter, which propels, at least in part, the dynamics of this particular conflict. The majority has drawn a colour line between itself and the minority within its borders, separating the dark from the light. As is always the case with colour lines, ethnic and economic factors overlap. In much of the world, light skin is associated with power and privilege, while dark skin signifies marginalization and disadvantage. Myanmar has taken this form of discrimination to extremes, but variations of the basic principle can be found on other micro and macro levels—from how you treat your hair to who you choose to marry to how you identify on census forms.

I got a taste of how that applies to the marriage market while having a quiet meal by myself at a family-run Indian restaurant in Bangkok. Upon noticing that I wasn't wearing a wedding ring, the restaurant's matriarch asked if I had a wife and children "back home." (I had already told her I came from Canada, where I worked as a university professor.) I didn't feel the need to share my sexuality with her, so I responded with a simple no. She disappeared for a few minutes and came back with a photo album of "beautiful and ready" Muslim brides of Indian heritage. All, she insisted, were fair and light-skinned. "For you, Professor. You must find fair women." The fact that a few weeks in Bangkok's sun had turned my own skin a few shades darker didn't register with her. She stopped short of saying, "Do it for your children," but implied that a fair-skinned wife could bring me good fortune and social prestige. I had the money and the job that many brown men would envy. I now needed the perfect accessory: a light-skinned wife.

This is the world of colourism, or shadism (and I will use the terms interchangeably, since I can't discern a clear-cut difference between the two among scholars)—a close relative, but not a replica, of racism. Although both colourism and racism are based on the presumption of white superiority, each marches to a different drum, racially speaking. We understand racism as the manifestation of personal and institutional discrimination by members of one group against another, while colourism operates *between* groups and *within* each one. Members of an ethnic community (say, South Asians) may harbour racist thoughts about African Americans based on the belief that brown skin trumps black. But the lighter-skinned among them may also discriminate against dark-skinned individuals or groups in their own community. In the introduction to *Shades of Difference: Why Skin Color Matters*, Angela P. Harris argues that colourism is helping us understand how the colour line is redefining and reframing debates on a catalogue of racial experiences. Alluding to the economic inequalities that create and perpetuate certain racial hierarchies, she writes: "If the study of racism alerts us to the 'big picture' of class struggle, the study of colorism shows us the fine-grained details of how everyday body practices . . . help to make and remake racial difference."

Brown and black people alike have experienced the scourge of racism while shouldering (or passing on) the burden of shadism. Our lives are colour-struck. Still, the economic basis of both racism and colourism offers brown people advantages that continue to be denied to blacks. To understand how this plays out, we need to look at the history and evolution of colourism, and what it says about the changing face and order of demographics based on skin tones, particularly in white-majority societies. A brown advantage may emerge—at least for the light browns.

*

COLOURISM OPERATES ON A global scale. Virtually every society, explicitly or implicitly, has maintained the belief that a lighter skin is preferable to a darker one. Even within the grand and grim narrative of slavery in the United States, differences in skin tones and degrees of pigmentation often separated the free from the enslaved. In *The Color Complex*, their classic study of discrimination among African Americans based on skin tone, Kathy Russell, Midge Wilson and Ronald Hall suggest that even after the end of slavery, "variations in skin color and features have divided the educated from the ignorant, the well-off from the poor, the 'attractive' from the 'plain.'"

Colourism defies simple categorization or enumeration because several aspects of it cannot be objectively quantified or rendered into a demographic statistic. Because of its subjective nature—who are you calling dark-skinned?—as well as its association with self-image, colourism precludes ethnic grouping along such lines as birthplace, history or language. A white doctor friend, whose help I sought in my (failed) search to find Toronto dermatologists who would speak on the record about their skin-lightening practices, described me as "fairly dark" in an email to a colleague. Only two months earlier in Hong Kong, another white friend had questioned why I thought of myself as brown in the same sense that Indians or Sri Lankans did. "But you're so light-skinned," he said.

Even proponents of diversity and inclusive hiring in the North American media and entertainment industries will have to concede that when it comes to jobs with visibility—actor as opposed to screenwriter and anchor versus segment producer—people with very light skin are favoured. Lightness means visibility in a literal sense. This happens whether the actor or anchor happens to be black or brown. Look at CNN and compare the skin tone of Don Lemon with that of the average black protestor in the riot-affected communities from which he has reported. Rihanna? Beyoncé? Are they really as "black" as their choice of musical genres (hip-hop and R&B) suggests? The difference in skin tone between candid photos of Beyoncé and those officially released by her publicity machine can be staggering. The entertainment powerhouse who sang at the inauguration of American's first-ever black president—a light-toned, mixed-race black man, to be clear—presents herself a few shades lighter in the latter set.

When Viola Davis became the first African American to win an Emmy for best lead actress in a drama, the conversation among my friends quickly shifted from why it took so long to how a truly dark-skinned black woman got cast in the role in the first place. As light-skinned academic and broadcaster Melissa Harris-Perry told journalist and polemicist Touré in his book *Who's Afraid of Post-Blackness?*, "The whiter you can make yourself the more likely . . . they'll put you on television." Touré himself writes that in their obsessions with light skin colour, African Americans "aid white supremacy by valuing light skin over dark—lionizing a visual likeness to whiteness."

The same goes for a host of Latino TV presenters and stars. Two or three generations ago, mainstream American viewers associated the Hispanic community with images of the Latin lover with his swarthy skin and thick but sexy accent—think Desi Arnaz from *I Love Lucy* or Ricardo Montalbán of *Fantasy Island*. Today, most Hispanic roles go to women like Sofía Vergara, Eva Longoria and America Ferrera, to a large extent because they can pass for white when they want to. Such is the lightness of their skin and the industry's endorsement of shadism, implicit or otherwise.

The advertising industry follows the same model. Take a close look at the "inspirational" ads by makers of soaps or plus-sized clothing. While these commercials go out of their way to present a rainbow of ethnicities and a range of sizes, very few women in them can be described as dark brown or African black. Most brown and black models flaunt a beige skin colour that comes from a mix of makeup and extreme lighting that makes the women look radioactive. These examples give credence to the note of panic struck by Kimberly Jade Norwood, a professor of law and African American studies, who wrote that "millions of people of color not only hate the skin they live in but they also long to be lighter in skin color." Unless colourism is acknowledged, she adds, "the rising black and brown majority will continue to associate power and privilege with white skin and that association will continue the colour caste hierarchy currently entrenched in American society."

Colourism first gained traction in fields that included a focus on the African American experience, such as law, sociology and race studies—writer Alice Walker reportedly coined the term "colourism" in 1982—but a more global approach to the phenomenon has been gaining momentum in the past decade. The new approach focuses on brown people, who exhibit the greatest variation in skin shades (from the very light and almost white to the very dark and nearly black). Experts in race and demography issues are turning their attention to South and East Asia, the Middle East, and Central and South America, since these locations offer previously unexamined articulations of colourism, each with a different historical and racial context.

In India, sales of prescription and over-the-counter skin-lightening creams have surpassed those of tea and Coca-Cola. While women remain the main target of the skin-lightening industry, products tailored to men's "more rugged" skin vie for shelf space in pharmacies and supermarkets. A report by Global Industry Analysts put the value of the skin-lightening industry at about $10 billion in 2015, with a burgeoning new market in Africa. In 2012, a World Health Organization report estimated that 77 percent of women in Nigeria use products to lighten their skin. Lebanese dermatologists are treating an increasing number of patients from the Arabian Gulf. These medical tourists flock to Beirut in the summer for supervised skin-lightening treatments—in part because Lebanese doctors are seen as better qualified than local ones, and in part because of privacy concerns. Four out of ten women in the Philippines use skin-lightening products, not necessarily to look European but to conform to the ideal of the "Asian beauty" with her porcelain skin. (In China, the obsession with lightness has reached a nutty level—literally. Pistachio nuts are bleached white, washing out all traces of brownness, to "cater to the mass consumer idea of 'the brighter, the better,'" writes Norwood.)

In Central America, people take a slightly different approach to skin whitening. There, governments have attempted to whiten the gene pool of their people by encouraging the immigration of Europeans, as well as procreation between their lighter- and darker-skinned citizens—a process known as *blanqueamiento* (whitening). In Brazil's "racial democracy" with its three hundred official colour designations, skin tone often determines an individual's access to jobs or housing. In a haunting in-depth exploration of Brazil's "chromatically wildly diverse" colour lines, Stephanie Nolen, the *Globe and Mail*'s Latin American bureau chief, explains that the first census after the end of slavery (1890) "asked not about race, but about colour: Citizens were asked if they were white, brown, black, yellow or *caboclo*—a Portuguese word for those with some indigenous ancestry."

While classification according to skin colour may have saved Brazil from the perniciousness of the racial purity movement that swept Europe and the United States in the first half of the twentieth century, it did little to address inequalities inherent in the system. Further, this "We're all Brazilian" mindset suppressed real discussions of race and racism, since (the thinking went) neither existed in the first place. The facts say something else: to be white situates you at the top of the racial hierarchy, and to be dark brown or black places you at the very bottom. Black and mixed-race Brazilians earn, on average, 42.2 percent less than whites. Passing for white (or for brown if you're black) to grab a bigger slice of the economic pie suggests that colourism is about survival. Black Brazilians have a life expectancy five to six years shorter than that of their white compatriots. Young black men die at "dramatically higher rates," reports Nolen.

Some scholars believe that the United States is beginning to adopt a Latin American model for discussing race and identity in response to the increasing diversity of its population. The focus is shifting from shades of black—light black versus dark black—to a pigmentocracy, the social ordering of citizens along a colour spectrum. It's another member of the shadism and racism family.

Whiteness remains at one end of this spectrum and blackness at the other. In between there exists a mass of skin tones and much movement from one spot to another, depending on economic or social mobility. Sociologists Eduardo Bonilla-Silva and David R. Dietrich, writing in *Shades of Difference*, suggest there's some evidence that a triracial system will replace the biracial one that has dominated American history since the seventeenth century. The new system, in order of pigmentation (and attendant privileges), will consist of (1) whites, (2) honorary whites and (3) the collective black. Whites include assimilated white Latinos, urban Native Americans and some people of Asian origin. Honorary whites include light-skinned Latinos, Middle Eastern Americans, and people of Japanese, Korean and Chinese origin. The collective black includes dark-skinned Latinos, West Indian and African immigrants, Vietnamese and, of course, blacks.

Who belongs where will remain fluid and ethnically complex. Arab Americans have traditionally been regarded as honorary whites—as I pointed out in the introduction, American census forms consider them white—but, write Bonilla-Silva and Dietrich, "their treatment in the post-September 11 era suggests their status as white and American is very tenuous." Bonilla-Silva and Dietrich have placed Filipinos in the collective black category, one assumes, because so many are stuck in low-paid migrant jobs. But as a people who place emphasis on education and career, they're likely to jump over the coming few decades into that middle category, which acts as a buffer between whites and the collective black.

But I wonder if this triracial system accommodates class distinctions as comprehensively as it tries to capture skin-tone variations. A light-skinned West Indian surgeon in a New York City hospital, for example, can use her education and income to hew herself closer to the white or honorary white group. A similarly light-skinned West Indian who works as a minimum-wage cleaner or a chef in the same hospital may find herself among the collective black, where income is low and precariousness more common. Pigmentocracy can upend and uphold the racial-economic status quo. As Bonilla-Silva and Dietrich acknowledge, it may even be more effective in maintaining white supremacy because it places whiteness at the top of the system. Even the honorary whites will depend upon the first group's wishes. "*Honorary* means that they will remain secondary, will still face discrimination, and will not receive equal treatment in society."

Pigmentocracy entered the world of American political coverage in early 2015, when pundits found themselves debating how brown a brown state governor should be in an official portrait. A blogger had posted on Twitter a photo of Bobby Jindal, the ultra-conservative governor of Louisiana and (at that time) Republican presidential candidate, next to what was said to be an official portrait of the politician. The photo shows Jindal, who is of Indian heritage, as the dark brown man he is; the portrait, however, lightens his skin to almost white and also airbrushes any hints of ethnicity from his features. If I saw the portrait without the accompanying photo, I would have assumed it was of a young Warren Beatty or Pierce Brosnan circa *Remington Steele*. The only true brown in the portrait is the leather of the governor's shoes.

My friends on Facebook jumped on the story as it broke on the blogosphere, using it as proof of the governor's self-loathing or racial denial. A few weeks earlier, a commentator on CNN had described Jindal's reaction to the *Charlie Hebdo* murders—he repeated unfounded claims that parts of France are "no-go zones" for non-Muslims—as an example of the governor trying to "wash the brown off his face."

Jindal's chief of staff soon tweeted back a picture of the real official portrait, saying that the one posted by the blogger was a private work of art loaned by a supporter. It hangs outside the office, according to Jindal's staffer, and therefore matters less. The "official" portrait shows Jindal's face in a darker but rather unnatural tone that's more orange than brown (in fairness, the light above the portrait may have changed the tone; it certainly seems to have lightened it). But regardless, the incident showed the impact of colourism: those who want political power sometimes see themselves (or allow others to capture them) as lighter in skin tone, or closer to the honorary whites.

But skin colour is just one of the phenotypic signals of racial identity; hair, nose, eyes and lips reveal as much about a person's ancestry as skin tone does. Cosmetic surgeries to fix the shape of the nose or reshape the skin around the eye (blepharoplasty) are now as common as products to straighten curly hair or, for that matter, whiten skin. While patients usually go under the knife with ample warning about the risks involved in any surgery, skin whitening remains shrouded in misconceptions, controversies and uncertainties, both medical and social.

*

"**THE DARK COLOUR** is superior, but people here don't like it."

Dr. Nimal Gamage, a US-trained cosmetic surgeon in Sri Lanka, boils down the colourism debate to this one fact. The doctor makes regular appearances on local television programs to warn viewers, women in particular, about the dangers of commercial skin-lightening creams. I reached out to him shortly after arriving in Colombo, because within less than forty-eight hours, my head was spinning with the many blatant instances of colourism I saw in his country. I'd travelled to Sri Lanka to see why so many of its workers leave, but I was quickly distracted by the range of brown in its people. Every time I visited a restaurant or store that catered to Western or rich Arab tourists, I saw front-line staff with lighter-than-average complexions. The waiters and reception staff at the popular hotel I stayed in fit that description, but cab drivers, cleaning staff and merchants in local stores tended to be darker-skinned. So did the mass of commuters, public school students, and street beggars and touts.

In the more-refined neighbourhood of Cinnamon Gardens, whose elegance was captured by Canadian novelist Shyam Selvadurai in a 1998 novel of the same name, you rarely saw middle-class women walking down the street without an umbrella to block the sun. I even noticed a difference between women waiting for public transport and those driving their children to and from schools and daycare centres: the former were invariably dark, the latter fairly light.

And true to form, Sri Lankan soap operas, a national obsession, featured an assortment of actors whose skin tones reflected the roles in which they were cast. Darker actors play villains or servants, while those with fairer complexions are cast as romantic leads. At the English bookstore inside the Crescat shopping centre off Galle Road, wedding magazines take up more than one shelf, and faces of ever-so-light-skinned brown women stare at me from each cover. I buy one, and when I browse through it in my hotel room, two patterns emerge immediately. First, advertisements for hair and beauty salons feature women of lighter skin, but real-life wedding photos tend to show a wider range of complexions. Second, men are more likely than women, in both advertising and editorial, to be darker-skinned. In fact, a section called Glamorous Couples paraded the magazine's only almost-black person, a groom.

Dr. Gamage, I need your help. Over the years I've witnessed variations of light and dark casting in Egyptian media, but it's never been as explicit as it is in Sri Lanka. TV commercials show women overcoming unemployment, loneliness and shyness after applying lightening cream, reducing the big narrative of colourism into a single thirty-second storyline.

With input from his wife, Kusum, Dr. Gamage and I try to explore this national obsession, over drinks and snacks at my hotel lounge. But even the semi-retired surgeon—he says he's on a one-year self-given sabbatical—can't quite put his finger on where his country's fascination with light skin begins. He concedes it may have something to do with British colonialism, but adds that colourism predates and has outlasted that period in Sri Lanka's history. "It comes from people growing up having strong ideas about beauty. Fairer people are [perceived to be] prettier," Dr. Gamage suggests. "They are also seen as coming from higher social status, because they are not exposed to the sun. There's less damage to their skin from the sun." The decades-long civil war (1983–2009), which pitted the Sinhalese majority against the Tamil minority, also hardened attitudes toward darker-coloured people. While many Sinhalese pride themselves on the fairness of their skin, they've cast Tamils as a generally darker group of people—an "other," in ethnic and skin-tone terms.

As Kusum tells me, so much of colourism is socially determined, and one of its biggest enablers is the institution of marriage and the celebration of it in lavish weddings. Sri Lankan families have been known to take bank loans or re-mortgage their homes to provide their children with dream weddings that confirm their social position or signal their arrival at a new one. Dr. Gamage normally sees a huge increase in business in the months leading up to the spring wedding season, particularly from women signing up for his "Cosmetic Plan for Bride to Be" package. It includes tumescent liposuction; removal of fat from arms, chin and back; fat grafting to change the proportions of the face; and laser treatments and specially formulated creams to make the skin fairer.

I find it strange that a doctor who warns against whitening creams in the media also recommends procedures that achieve similar results. But Dr. Gamage insists there's a vast difference between medically supervised and personalized treatments on the one hand and over-the-counter, mass-produced creams on the other. He recommends avoiding the latter, which are believed to contain poisonous mercury and other cancer-causing substances (carcinogens). He uses products with natural and antioxidant ingredients.

Besides, he's a realistic person who knows that skin-lightening is a tide that can't be stopped—at least not in its spiritual home of Sri Lanka and India. "Our people worship the fair skin," he says, as if to minimize his own role in keeping that religion alive. For a private clinic, skin-lightening is good business. After three initial laser treatments, patients must return at least once a month for fifteen-minute touch-ups, and they must maintain the look using creams sold exclusively at the clinic. As Dr. Gamage himself says, "Once you start it, you become a slave to it." Failure to stick to this regimen can be dangerous—exposure to the sun not only turns people's skin dark but also makes them susceptible to forms of skin cancer (since both the laser treatments and the cream suppress the melanin that protects the skin from UVB rays). He advises people who can't change their lifestyle—police officers, army personnel and anyone else who is expected to work outdoors—not to start the journey because they'll never reach their destination of lighter skin.

In fact, his website includes several references to the sun as the enemy of both dark *and* healthy skin. In "How to Be Fair," he writes: "Staying away from the sun is very important to keep your skin fair. It is very important to remember that even a very fair person can become darker with continued exposure to the sun. In addition to that, sunlight will make you age faster and make your skin tone uneven and increase your risk of skin cancer and melanoma." Avoiding the sun in Sri Lanka is like avoiding breathing—a physical impossibility—but the very wealthy minimize exposure by working indoors and limiting their socializing to the evening hours.

To Dr. Gamage—who worked for many years in California and has dealt with communities from South Asia and Latin America—Sri Lankans and other brown people who pray at the altar of whiteness have missed the fact that darker skin is healthier and ages better than white skin. That's why, he says, aging white people generally look wrinklier and older than their brown or black contemporaries. Melanin protects the skin from the harmful effects of ultraviolet rays, which is why skin cancer levels in the Global South remain significantly lower than those in the Industrial North. (Australia and New Zealand may be located within the Global South geographically, but in economic and demographic terms, they belong to the Industrial North. Skin cancer rates in Australia are elevated.) As scores of white and fair-skinned Europeans and North Americans chase the sun, brown and black people generally spend their lives avoiding it to keep their skin as light as possible.

While the desire for lighter skin may come from a place of insecurity or unhappiness in one's own body, some commentators agree that it can have positive associations. For example, lighter skin helps some people gain confidence, enabling them to land better jobs or take control of their careers. Dr. Gamage points out that many Sri Lankan domestic workers in the Gulf spend part of their savings at the end of their contracts on skin-lightening procedures. They believe that lighter skin can help them secure better-paying jobs on their next trip—particularly in the Gulf area, where skin tones play a role in determining income, a topic I'll explore in depth in part 2.

Dr. Samer Ghosn, a dermatologist and derma-pathologist, also sees patients from the Gulf in his clinic in Beirut, Lebanon. Seventy to 80 percent are women who carry passports from the United Arab Emirates or Qatar, or South Asians who have lived in the region for decades. They travel to Beirut in the summer to avoid the heat and sun at home, and to seek treatments to lighten their skin. What starts as a routine examination often morphs into something deeper.

"Many a time, our dermatologic consultation consists of a psychiatric consultation," says Dr. Ghosn during a Skype interview. "I try to explain to people about the charm of every colour—to explain to them how marketing and commercials want them to be consumers." The doctor's advice usually falls on deaf brown ears, but he still refuses to treat patients with the laser chemical peels they've read about on websites targeting South Asian women. "In dark skin, such procedures are associated with lots of side effects . . . lots of post-inflammatory pigmentation. You might get darker after it." For the peels to work, the patient must avoid the sun completely—a tall order even in the Gulf, where the fall and winter months tend to be milder than in Sri Lanka.

"If they insist," Dr. Ghosn says, "we can always give them creams that make their skins a little bit lighter—anti-aging creams with vitamin C and many other molecules that can help the skin get lighter without harm." These creams don't change the skin tone considerably or immediately, but they may lighten it by one or two shades with repeated use.

While Arab and South Asian tourists in Beirut pursue the dream of lighter skin, Lebanese people themselves are in the middle of a significant cultural shift in how they use their skin as social capital. Only a decade or so ago, well-off Lebanese people would have taken great pride in their pale or light skin. It marked their difference from the working classes, and it hewed them closely to the European and Mediterranean countries to which they've traditionally aspired. Not as much anymore, says Dr. Ghosn. A tanned and visibly darker skin among Lebanon's expanding leisure class signifies wealth and, well, leisure. "If you're darker in colour in Lebanon, it means you can afford to go to the beach, relax under the sun." In other words, do all the things that brown tourists from the Gulf avoid.

No wonder colourism remains a problematic concept—one that, in many aspects, is harder to contain than racism. It changes depending on the cultural context, even as it continues to remain deferential—beholden, even—to whiteness. Let's get one thing clear, though: those sun-loving Lebanese would not be happy if their skin turned dark brown and made them look closer in tone to the Sri Lankan domestics who shop for those over-the-counter creams in Hamara Street in downtown Beirut. There's such a thing as too dark.

Some brown people have become very good at this game, betraying both their desire to emulate whiteness and appropriate its privileges *and* their fear of darkness, whose disadvantages they loathe. A visit to Trinidad took me inside a country whose official narrative depends on a conspiratorial silencing of differences along the black-brown-white continuum. If Sri Lanka had me colour-struck with its shades of brown, Trinidad left me wondering if being a buffer group was ever in our best interests.

CHAPTER 3
Trinidad: Guarding the Colour Line

Roopdian Rampersad offers me a glass of Ciroc, a vodka infused with amaretto. He swears by it and takes it neat; I've never tried it, but something tells me on the rocks may be the wiser choice. It's just before 5 p.m., and drinking on an empty stomach will go to my head—a head that for the past two hours has been trying to keep up with the I-did-it-the-brown-way business stories of this seventy-five-year-old Indo-Trinidadian patriarch.

We're sitting in his family room, an extension off the main living room, with its mismatched sofas and chairs, a corner dining table that doubles as a diaper-changing station and a giant TV for the grandchildren to watch their stash of animated movies, DVDs of which are strewn about the room. Today it's not the ubiquitous *Frozen* but the original *Cars* that the youngest granddaughter insists on playing. She has seen it about two hundred times, her grandmother tells me. I detect a note of exasperation, but you can tell she dotes on the girl—and on her brother, who is finally waking up from his afternoon nap and showing the telltale signs of either crankiness or the terrible twos.

I feel like I've seen this movie before. Not *Cars*, but this family drama. It's a scene that plays out daily in many brown households, in both the diaspora and the home countries, where generations of the same family live together and grandparents turn into child-minders. I've seen it in my own immediate family over the years, in Yemen and in my late aunt's house in Liverpool, England (a place she shared with her son and his children). Indian communities rarely hire other brown nannies or help, preferring instead to keep the childcare in the family.

The all-purpose room—in the central Trinidad town of Chaguanas, once known for its sugar estates and farmland—is the nerve centre of the Rampersad business empire. Nowadays, the lanes off the main road are largely swamplands or patches of neglected fields punctuated by gated mini mansions. The sugar and cocoa estates have been gone for a long time, replaced by an array of local businesses, temples and mosques. I could hear the clanking of tools in a neighbouring tire shop, also owned by the Rampersad family, and at around 3 p.m., the call to Asr (late afternoon) prayers from a mosque inexplicably located at the end of this long country road.

Roopdian and his wife make no concessions to the symphony of tools in the workshop or the amplified prayer call by pausing or adjusting their voices. Business and religion, even when it's a religion other than their own, flow seamlessly into the life of this extended Hindu family. As such, they strike me as typical of the Indo-Trinidadian community that dominates the central and southern parts of this Caribbean island. Small businesses of every imaginable kind—from food sheds selling Indian delicacies to auntie-and-uncle clothing stores to (numerous) mobile phone kiosks—jostle for space on the very narrow main road in this neighbourhood. My guide, Collin, a former schoolteacher who now runs a family business, tells me that this part of the island with its busy commercial streets exemplifies modern-day Trinidad, but it also carries on an older tradition of the various faith communities *within* the Indian diaspora living and letting live. But what about relations between those in the Indo-Trinidadian community and other citizens?

I decided to visit Trinidad because I wanted to know what it is like to grow up brown in a country whose politics have been dominated by a black narrative. I also wanted to test a personal theory—that brown people get the benefit of a lighter skin when compared to or competing with black or African communities on their home turfs. I'd never visited a country where blacks form a majority, so I wondered how my brownness would make me feel in this context. Would I relate to the lives of brown people there? South Asian (and Indian, in particular) people have shared lands and social turmoil with black communities in East Africa, South Africa and the Caribbean. I realize that each country or political situation has its own dynamics, but some themes do recur in the brown-black encounter, particularly in the Caribbean and East Africa. In both these settings, the brown community is often perceived to be the market-dominant one, with racial relations following a familiar path: resentment escalates into violence against brown people or gives way to nationalist policies that exclude them or turn them into the enemy of black independence, an obstacle to self-determination. Grand-scale expulsion, as happened in East Africa, is a third, more extreme response.

But I've also become aware while writing this book that brown communities can exhibit a toxic form of racial prejudice, particularly against people of darker skins. We seem to have internalized the worst of colonial-era skin-tone classifications, long after they've been discredited. In Trinidad, brown hostility to the black community stems from decades of power struggle between the two and colonial manipulation of both. To give one crucial example, Trinidad's embrace of creolization—the process by which new identities are born out of synthesizing traditions from the Old, Indigenous and New Worlds in the colonies—was premised on the exclusion of the Indian community. Imagine a multicultural project that embraces all ethnicities but one. Then imagine being that one excluded ethnicity. How do brown people remain invested in their community when they are constantly reminded of their outsider status? And how can they show good faith and willingness to cooperate when some of their own views remain mired in racial stereotypes?

For Roopdian, Chaguanas sets the scene for his family's struggle not to be left out of Trinidad's story or its economic transformation. Here, three generations of Rampersads—including Roopdian's nine surviving siblings, his five children and their own offspring—have staked a claim on Trinidad as both their homeland and their national, political identity. Roopdian's grandfather came from India to this Caribbean island in the early twentieth century, having been lured by the British government with promises of money and opportunities that sound eerily similar to the enticements used to attract Filipino and Sri Lankan workers to Gulf countries today. An estimated 144,000 men and women from India made their way to Trinidad and Tobago between 1845 and 1917, when indenture was abolished. Other Indian and South Asian nationals were indentured into nearby islands and states, including Guyana, St. Vincent and Grenada—mainly to replace the newly freed slaves whose own ancestors had been shipped from West Africa two centuries earlier. (Prior to the arrival of Columbus in 1498, the indigenous Taino and

Kalinago people lived on the island for centuries. The Spanish conquered Trinidad in the late 1500s and ruled until 1797, when the British seized the island. In 1889 Tobago was amalgamated with Trinidad, creating the united colony of Trinidad and Tobago. It gained its independence in 1962. I call the country Trinidad throughout in part because that's the more familiar name, and in part because it's where my reporting takes place.)

Roopdian can't recall what prompted his grandfather to leave his community and move to Trinidad. "Probably for work or money," he says. However, it's not the grandfather's arrival that haunts this family but the mysterious circumstances of his journey back to India many decades after the end of his five-year indenture period. The same man who uprooted himself and started anew in the Caribbean returned to India at some point in the early 1930s, severing all ties to Trinidad, including any contact with his wife and children. For decades, Roopdian's older brother Sat tried to reconnect with the man he had known briefly as a child. Sat even made his way to India in the early 1960s to explore his grandfather's life before and after Trinidad. All attempts to track his whereabouts or to find out if he was still alive failed. Sat's death in 2013 snuffed out the last connection to the original indentured Rampersad.

As they got older, Roopdian and his siblings lost their bonds to India and became more firmly attached to Trinidad. Roopdian's transformation from a brown minority living among a predominately black majority to a Trinidadian citizen materialized as his business took off in the late 1950s. He was in his teens and early twenties, and his coming of age coincided with the Indo community's political and economic maturation. After decades as subordinates to white colonizers and then black nationalists, Indo-Trinidadians had emerged as a dominant force in social, economic and cultural terms.

With another of his brothers, Roopdian left central Trinidad and headed north to the city of Port of Spain to start a customs brokerage business. For a fee, the brothers would clear customs for wholesale merchandise imported from or exported to Trinidad. The job included loading and unloading containers, warehousing goods and distributing them to wholesalers. Their biggest investment was an American-made truck that Roopdian drove up and down the island. The truck sits in the driveway of his Chaguanas home to this day, a symbol of his go-getting younger self and a reminder to his children and grandchildren of the Rampersad (and by extension, brown) tradition of hard work and thrift. (And, Roopdian insists, it drives better than the new models he's burned through over the years.)

At around this time, many Indo-Trinidadian families began to take over local businesses, moving from their traditional enclaves in central and south Trinidad into the black-dominated Port of Spain in the north. Tensions between the Indian and black communities rose as a result. "Black people did the more laborious work," Roopdian recalls, referring to tasks like unloading shipping containers onto trucks—the literal heavy lifting. Afro-Trinidadians had developed a reputation for being physically imposing, and there was an understanding on the island that Port of Spain "belonged" to them, says Roopdian. Many blacks resented being employed in lowly positions by Indian citizens, whom even the country's "father" and first prime minister, Eric Williams, referred to as "transient" and not true Trinidadians—nearly 120 years after their arrival on the island.

"We had run-ins," Roopdian adds, refusing to elaborate on the nature of these encounters. He admits only to name-calling, with each community putting the other down using racially charged language: blacks were called "niggers," while Indians got stuck with "coolies" (a word from the original Tamil that refers to wages paid to people doing manual labour). The two communities, one brought to the island as slave labour and the other as indentured labour, were free people now, but their history of subjugation set them on a collision course that continues to this day in Trinidad.

Even though a 2011 UN demographics study places the two groups at a statistical tie, with the Indo-Trinidadian community slightly ahead (at 37.6 percent to the Afro-Trinidadian community's 36.3), the country as a whole would strike a casual observer or a tourist as predominately black. That was certainly my impression of the capital city of Port of Spain.

Trinidad likes to think of itself as the embodiment of multiculturalism long before the concept entered North American and European consciousness. In addition to the two major ethnic groups, the island has been home to migrants from China, Syria and many European countries, including Spain and France. (Most plantation owners were in fact French.) The government buildings next to my Port of Spain hotel display murals and sculptural engravings that emphasize tolerance, diversity and harmony. But the symbols of black culture, from calypso music to the annual Carnival, dominate this representation. You can spot the odd depiction of Chinese musical instruments or South Asian dancers, but the story of the country, even in this creative attempt at racial integration, is the story of its Afro-Trinidadian citizens. To be brown in Trinidad is to be a majority and a minority at once—to occupy a space in the national dialogue that is powerful economically but marginalized culturally.

In this landscape, multiculturalism means adhering to the dominant black culture. "I still don't see equality," says Darrell Baksh, a Toronto-born academic of Trinidadian origin, during a stroll along Port of Spain's Ariapita Avenue, home to the high-end bars and restaurants that middle-class Trinidadians frequent.

"I see the Indian culture second to black culture. Black culture is understood as the mainstream." Baksh was working on a PhD on how local music—including chutney, a genre that originated within the Indo community—underscores issues of identity and nationalism on the island.

Being a distinct and separate group forced members of the Indian community to look inward for support. "We've connected because of family relations," Roopdian recalls. "We didn't know anything about India." The various groups of the Indo-Trinidadian community—Muslim, Hindu, Christian, from different geographical regions within India—bonded with each other through the common grounds of family and the experience of indenture. Admittedly, tensions sometimes developed along the lines of class, caste and even skin colour—dark versus light brown, as I show later in this chapter. But despite all the factors that pulled the community apart, physically and culturally, its members were united by their past (indenture) and present (tensions with the black community). The story of Indo-Trinidadians is one where power and class intersect with skin colour—brown skin colour. But unlike Tanzania or Uganda, Trinidad hosts two groups of people who have migrated from or been forced out of their ancestral homes, leaving them to duke it out on a third and faraway land.

*

MISUNDERSTANDING AND DISTRUST BETWEEN the Indo- and Afro-Trinidadian communities began almost as soon as *Fatah El Rizk*, the first ship carrying indentured labour from Calcutta, docked in Port of Spain in 1845. The African community had been emancipated since 1838, and as the long-accepted version of the history goes, planters faced a massive labour shortage. In the past two or three decades, historians of the Caribbean—including Viranjini Munasinghe, author of *Callaloo or Tossed Salad?: East Indians and the Cultural Politics of Identity in Trinidad*—have advanced the revisionist theory that the newly emancipated refused to work on the plantations for what the colonial masters were willing to pay. This forced European planters and British emissaries in the Caribbean to look for a "new system of slavery."

Moving labour from one part of the empire to another could solve that problem, and it had the added advantage of avoiding negotiations with neighbouring countries in the Southern Hemisphere or competing empires (French or Dutch). India seemed like the most likely source of new labour. Not only was it overpopulated and suffering under poverty levels that the British couldn't dream, and had no intention, of alleviating, but its people had acquired a reputation as both hardworking *and* docile—in other words, efficient and controllable. In addition, the tropical heat of the Caribbean wouldn't affect the productivity of Indians, who grew up in a similar climate.

It was meant to be a simple and natural solution, except that the black community viewed the Indian indentured workers as scabs used by crafty planters to drive wages down. The two groups indulged in stereotypes almost from the start. Blacks were said to be lazy and violent, Indians devious and money-oriented and transient. Their temporary status gave them no right to equal treatment, or so the thinking among the black community went. The original indenture agreement stipulated that each labourer had to work a minimum of five years. At end of his contract, a worker was given a choice: a return passage to India; money to stay behind and continue working on plantations; or a grant of five acres of farming or agricultural land. About a quarter of the indentured chose to take the passage to India; the rest settled in Trinidad, suggesting their adaptability or their grim prospects back home. Either way, the workers formerly known as indentured began accumulating land and turning small profits.

In the Afro-Caribbean narrative of Trinidad, the post-indenture land grant gave brown people an unfair advantage, since no similar arrangements were made for the freed slaves earlier in the nineteenth century. This reading often underplayed the fact that while Indians may have signed on to indenture, it doesn't mean that migration was entirely of their own choosing. Many workers were trapped in cycles of underemployment, famine and environmental disasters that made leaving India for an unknown land the more appealing, or only, alternative. In many ways, not much has changed in nearly two centuries; modern-day migrant labourers from South and Southeast Asia are often motivated by a similar note of desperation.

The indenture system itself developed after several attempts to bring in workers from China or Europe had proven unsuccessful. The harsh tropical climate may have played a role in why people from both races failed to meet the productivity test. However, the racialist ideology of the nineteenth century also made it difficult for planters to import white people from Europe as labourers. How can people from a continent that has claimed the top spot in racial hierarchy, beauty and moral fortitude be employed in work previously undertaken by blacks? It made more sense to import people whose skin colour differed from that of their masters. If blacks would not do the work for the wages offered, then people from the next group down, the brown race, would. Not only would this solve the labour shortage, but it would keep wages down and increase the bargaining power of the planters. If this sounds familiar to us in North America today, it's because a similar logic is at play in the Temporary Foreign Worker permits that many neo-liberal governments love to issue. At least that's how unions see it.

The resentment blacks felt toward the Indian arrivals meant that the two ethnic groups led largely separate lives, marked by the occasional physical or rhetorical "run-ins" (to use Roopdian's understated expression). The separation took a physical form as well, with the Indians "confined" to the lower central and southern parts of the island, while blacks congregated in the north and the urban centre of the vast Port of Spain. Each community also adopted different national identities, with Mother India and Mother Africa as the spiritual homeland of each. The path to racial consciousness differed for each community, too.

The path to greater racial awareness for Afro-Trinidadians followed the American model of black consciousness and the Black Power movement, helped by editors of Afro-Caribbean newspapers, who used their publications to promote social change and the uplift of the black community. The end of the First World War marked a turning point in the racial awakening of the black community, as soldiers from the British West Indies Regiment returned home "bitter, radicalized and more race-conscious than before," and took part in the labour unrest and anti-colonial violence that swept Trinidad and other parts of the Caribbean in the 1920s. By the 1950s, a full-fledged Black Power initiative based in the Caribbean had branched off the Civil Rights Movement in the US. In his analysis for the *UNESCO General History of the Caribbean*, Tony Martin argues that African consciousness treated its Indian counterpart with "benign neglect" or incorporated it into a larger struggle against the colonial regime. Indian consciousness, Martin suggests, focused on the African as the adversary, sidelining the British or European planters who used the Indians as a "buffer" between themselves and the increasingly agitated blacks.

At the heart of this white-brown-black colour line was a racial belief in the superiority of browns over blacks—a belief built in part on contemporary European racialist theories and in part on the colonial connection between India and the United Kingdom. This connection led many Indo-Trinidadians to act as if they occupied a special place within the empire—a position not as high as whites but not as low as blacks. Brown was the acceptable middle ground. Affluent black Trinidadians have even taken to describing themselves as brown because the colour serves as a "category of middle-class status," writes anthropologist Aisha Khan in her essay for *Shades of Difference*.

The Black Power movement in the 1960s and early 1970s extended an invitation to the Indian community to join the project of post-colonial nation-building. Many Indians rejected the offer because, historian Bridget Brereton writes, "it subsumed their ethnic identity under a blanket term always primarily associated with people of African descent." The roots of this resistance could be traced to the caste system (in which lighter skin was held in high regard) and had something to do with the geographic origins of the initial indentured labourers, who mostly came from the northern regions of Bihar and Uttar Pradesh (where lighter skin prevailed). Later waves drew on labour from the southern parts of pre-partitioned India, including the darker-skinned Madrasis. Skin tone turned into another way of differentiating among people in the Indian community—or discriminating against them.

Although Eric Williams, Trinidad's first prime minister, wanted to create a multicultural, hybrid community with no Mother India or Mother Africa but a Mother Trinidad and Tobago, his People's National Movement aligned itself with the black movement, often at the expense of Indians. The country's first Indo-Caribbean prime minister, Basdeo Panday of the United National Congress, was not elected until 1995, more than thirty years after independence. Any jubilation at the political ascendency of Indo-Trinidadians was short-lived, however, as his reign lasted a relatively brief six years and may have triggered the worst spate of crimes against the community.

In the first decade of the twentieth-first century, and particularly between 2002 and 2007, a wave of kidnappings for ransom swept through Trinidad, with most of the victims coming from the Indo-Trinidadian merchant and business class, and the alleged perpetrators (few cases were brought to justice) coming from the black community. As I was walking with my guide, Collin, the one-time teacher, on my first full day in Port of Spain, we ran into a former student whom he hadn't seen for over a decade. The student was now running his own IT business outside Port of Spain, but he said he'd kept his visits to the capital city to a minimum ever since he was kidnapped there in 2005. "I was victim number eighty-two," he told his old schoolteacher, adding that he was lucky to be held in captivity for just two weeks. His family paid his ransom—these ranged from half a million to five million Trinidad and Tobago dollars (about US$80,000 to US$800,000)—and he was let go, largely unharmed physically but emotionally scarred.

I could tell he was nervous from the way he kept looking around during our brief conversation, which took place outside a very safe hotel with several security guards and doormen milling about. It occurred to me that almost all the hotel employees, as well as the cab drivers waiting for customers, were black. Perhaps that did make him less comfortable. As Rebecca Prentice explains in her anthropological study of the kidnappings, some working-class Afro-Trinidadians had little sympathy for the suffering of the kidnapped or their families, citing their ability to pay the ransom and linking this crime epidemic to the underground drug-and-gun trade, which purportedly uses the textile industry as a front. There's no proof of the latter theory, although off the record many Indo-Trinidadians have placed the blame for the rampant drug-and-gun culture on Syrian-Trinidadians. (The first victim of kidnapping in 2002 was the son of a Syrian business tycoon.)

The kidnapping spree highlighted the economic disparities and racial tensions on the island, and the vulnerability of the brown community despite its political and economic ascendency. Most brown families chose to settle the matter by paying ransoms, since they viewed the largely black police force as unsympathetic and incapable of getting their loved ones back alive. As Kavyta Raghunandan explains in her study of hyphenated identities in Trinidad, the country's origins as a colonial society established "a stratification . . . based on a class-race-colour hierarchy which some argue has set the foundation for present-day race relations and ethnic competition in Trinidad."

My own encounters with two Indo-Trinidadians at the prime of their professional lives gave me contrasting readings of the class-race-colour continuum in Trinidad. Samantha, a Trinidadian businesswoman of Indian heritage, confirmed Raghunandan's proposition, while Jason, a legal aid attorney and law school lecturer, asserted that his country was too complex to be distilled into one racially divided narrative.

*

THE WHEEL HOUSE PUB in Chaguaramas, a peninsula and the site of a former US naval base, offers a diverse menu for a fairly homogenous clientele. You'll find your classic English pub food—fish and chips or steak and kidney pies with mashed potatoes and gravy—as well as some Italian pastas, Indian curries and Jamaican patties. On a Saturday afternoon in mid-November, customers were either white, middle-class North American or European tourists who had docked their sailboats in the marina and were taking a break in one of Trinidad's prime (and safest) spots, or Afro-Trinidadian men who likely worked in the area and had dropped by for a lunchtime beer. The tourists congregated on the patio, soaking in the hot weather; their glasses of white wine and mugs of beer glistened in the sun and warmed up faster than they could drink them. The black men huddled around the serving area indoors, carrying on conversations among themselves and with the only waitress in the joint. This black-and-white, inside-versus-outside division was interrupted when Samantha and I grabbed a seat on the patio. Like the two brown people we are, we compromised by finding a table outside but under a huge canopy that blocked the sun. That's what I love about hanging out with fellow brown people: no need to explain why we prefer sitting in the shade.

I'd been in Trinidad for just under a week by that point and could tell that I was getting darker by the day, simply from walking down the streets of Port of Spain or travelling around the country for interviews. Skin colour and race, and the associations each brings to socio-economic and cultural status in Trinidad's contemporary society, were the topics of my conversation with Samantha, before and after lunch. I'd insisted on meeting her because I wanted to see how skin colour, being brown, affects women on the island. Do they experience it differently from men? If so, in what ways? Samantha had a lot to say, mostly from her personal experience but also as a member of the Association of Female Executives of Trinidad and Tobago, which has been working on breaking barriers in the business and corporate worlds for women of all races.

It's hard to tell where Samantha places herself on the racial divide in Trinidad. Her maternal grandmother had mixed Spanish and black (creole) blood, while her grandfather was descended from indentured Indian workers. Her father's family is also Indian. Samantha describes herself as an Indo-Trinidadian because, she says with no apology, "I don't want to be identified as black." To be seen as black is to be treated as poorer, less financially independent. However, she's the first to admit that identifying herself as an Indo woman doesn't amount to much more than curiosity and an abandoned family-tree project. "I wouldn't wear anything ethnic," the casually dressed businesswoman says, adding that she never applies the bright red lipstick that some women of Indian heritage believe complements their skin tones.

Samantha's refusal to follow the Indian-heritage playbook stems from her years of studying and working in the United States. She returned to Trinidad about ten years ago to look after her ailing mother. Despite having a master's degree in business administration and more than two decades of work experience, Samantha found herself thrust into the traditional role allotted to women: serving others. She lives with her mother and looks after a number of commercial and residential real estate holdings for the family business, but when her brothers visit she's expected to defer to them, even serving them food. (She tells me that one of her brothers had bankrupted five businesses over the years, but that didn't stop him from lecturing her on business matters.)

Even when she briefly dated a white Dutch man a few years ago, Samantha was surprised to find herself automatically looking after him. She and her mother both tended to him in a way that went beyond local hospitality customs. I ask if her relationship with a white man was an issue for her family and friends. The opposite was true, she insists. In the hierarchy of desirable partners, white people—locals or expatriates—are seen as the top prize. No family would turn down a white suitor (or a light-skinned Syrian or Lebanese, who get lumped in with whites). And although douglas—mixed-race children of Indians and blacks—are common in Trinidad, middle-class and affluent Indians are often unhappy when their children want to marry a person of Afro-Trinidadian descent. Hindu families in particular adhere to notions of purity of race that place blacks at the bottom of desirable racial groups. Samantha admits that she would not entertain any proposals from black men. It's easy to dismiss her position as intolerant (or terribly unromantic), but she put on the record what many Indo-Trinidadians have been socialized to believe but not say out loud—at least not in a country that invests so much of its energy in maintaining that a colour line doesn't exist.

Samantha's pick of neighbourhoods to visit or do business in follows along economic and racial lines, and even determines her beauty regimen. She prefers to get her hair done in the affluent western parts of the island (West Moorings and St. Ann's) because the stylists use high-end salon products and provide better service. It's the part of the island where white Trinidadians and expats live in gated communities, and its main streets are considered safe enough that you will see families going for strolls at night. In her more mixed (and therefore less privileged and more crime-ridden) borough of Arima, Samantha buys her own hair products in advance and takes them with her to the salon.

I look at her immaculately coiffed dark hair and guess that her last appointment was in West Moorings.

There's something universally ethnic about the way men and women spend so much of their time and money maintaining their hair's smoothness and ironing out any curls. Both black and brown people share that experience. But in the Caribbean, smoother hair also means pure Indian heritage, whereas curly hair, or even hints of curliness, suggests black bloodlines. The colour line strikes again.

Jason, a thirty-four-year-old attorney-at-law, lecturer and labour-rights activist, has a view of Trinidad that is starkly different from Samantha's. Trinidad is so mixed, in his opinion, that he doesn't see how anyone can say they're pure anything, much less maintain this purity. It seemed an odd position to take after he and I had spent a long and mostly rainy day exploring the southern tip of the island, a largely rural landscape dominated by Indian businesses, families, temples and the Indian Caribbean Museum, which is dedicated to documenting the experience of this community in Trinidad and elsewhere in the region. (The museum's docent guided us through its collection in a way that suggested either she believed passionately in its mission or this shrine to all things brown didn't get many visitors.) This is a part of the island that has remained purely and proudly Indian.

Jason insisted that we stop in the town of Debe, whose biggest tourist attraction is a series of food sheds along a main road. Indo-Trinidadians stop there at any time of day for a bite to eat. When we got there at 11 a.m. or so, the post-breakfast, pre-lunch snack time had already started. Of the dozen or so sheds, one in particular seemed to be drawing the largest crowd. Krishna's Food Centre sells delicacies that originated in India or were created in Trinidad by the early indentured labourers. It's not a stretch to imagine workers from the sugar or rice plantations that once existed nearby preparing the same dishes at the end of a long day toiling in the fields. Almost everything is fried, and to my delight, the stand offers such vegetarian options as baiganee (fried eggplant in batter) and katchorie (fried split peas, very falafel-like).

Jason tells me that the sheds do brisk business on Friday and Saturday nights, when Indo-Trinidadian families descend on them from all parts of the island before browsing through local stores that sell Bollywood DVDs and soundtracks, spices or kitchen supplies. You can call it Little India, but that historically contested description illustrates the push-pull dynamics among Indo-Trinidadians. They want to be seen as both Caribbean and Indian in a society that often asks them to choose one or the other—or at least expects them to overplay allegiance to Trinidad at the expense of a connection to Mother India.

In the Catholic household in which Jason grew up, his family thought of India as "some exotic land, a vast country far, far away." On Sunday afternoons, the family would gather in the living room to watch a Bollywood movie on state television. "I felt no connection to that world," Jason insists. And neither did his parents. His earliest memory of India as a political or cultural subject was his A-level history class, the History of the People of Trinidad and Tobago. It was there that he first read up on the story of indentured labour alongside the history of slavery. His private school and his family home, both in the heart of Port of Spain, exposed Jason to students from black, Indian, Chinese, Syrian and European backgrounds. So much so that he is now reluctant to identify himself as anything but Trinidadian. Period. No hyphen needed. To prove his point, Jason tells me how little he had in common with brown students from the Caribbean when he studied law at the University of the West Indies in Barbados. "I didn't identify with them at all," he says, adding that he sought the company of other Trinidadians regardless of race or skin colour.

Trinidadian politicians and the manufacturers of the multicultural glue that holds the country together would consider Jason a poster boy and his experience exemplary. This is a country that celebrates every major cultural or religious festival. The list of national holidays includes Indian Arrival Day, Emancipation Day, Diwali, Eid al-Fitr, Christmas and, of course, Carnival. But what politicians say and how they govern can be two completely different realities. Jason acknowledges that when it comes to politics, the country is built to be divided along colour lines, with brown and black people fighting each other for survival. "The parties can assure themselves of victory by polarizing groups of people and pitting them against each other," he says. "How people live on a day-to-day basis is not reflective of how they vote. The two major political parties use the doctrine of divide and conquer, subconsciously forcing people to vote along racial lines."

Later in the day, I recount the story of the kidnap victim I met in Port of Spain and ask Jason about the national stereotypes of the resourceful, wealthy Indo-Trinidadians and the poor and crime-prone Afro-Trinidadians. His sigh betrays frustration with and disbelief at how generations of Trinidadians have created and perpetuated such stereotypes. "I can't believe I'm hearing this," he vents. In the legal aid clinic where he sometimes works, assisting clients with issues from domestic assault to petty convictions, Jason sees equal numbers of people who "appear to be" Indian or African. Both groups can get into trouble or be victims of it. It's the economics and not the racial identity that matters. Trinidadians with better incomes insulate themselves against most legal issues and crime by living in gated communities and avoiding contact with criminal elements.

However, even Jason concedes that "there's a perceived advantage" to being lighter-skinned, both in and out of court. "If the average person was to look at someone with a lighter complexion, she or he may assume that the light-skinned person comes from a certain economic bracket." Generally speaking, this perception works in favour of Indian people. On a personal level, Jason says that he notices skin colour only when he travels outside the country. In Trinidad, he's become sort of colour-blind: "I don't differentiate; I don't discriminate." He applies that philosophy at work and at home, regardless of racial or religious lines. Jason's wife is Hindu, but their two-year-old son, Callum, is being raised a Catholic. As Jason says, Callum will have Hindu cousins, uncles, aunts and grandparents, and he may well identify with Hinduism later in life. If that happens, his son will seek a stronger connection with his Indian heritage, since that is part and parcel of the faith.

When I repeat Jason's assertion that people in this country don't see colour, Darrell Baksh all but laughs it off. Race and skin colour underscore virtually all social and political interactions in Trinidad, he insists. "Indians judge their own people. Fairer is better," he says. Whenever Darrell flies to Toronto for the holidays, members of his immediate family will invariably note that his skin has gotten darker from the Trinidadian sun. The fact that he looks healthy or has gained weight after being almost anemically thin in Canada doesn't factor into the discussion. Some even wonder aloud why he's spending so many years researching a musical genre with a past in old traditions and a future than hinges on a culture more black than brown.

*

ON MY FINAL NIGHT in Trinidad, I joined Jason and his family at a gathering hosted by Ashad, the only Muslim Indo-Trinidadian I got to meet during my visit. Ashad and Jason attended the same high school in Port of Spain and have remained close friends ever since. My initial plan was to see if members of the minority Muslim community held views that differed from those of the dominant Hindus. But as soon as Ashad invited me into his home, the reporter in me gave way to the brown middle-aged man who has been away from his family for decades and just wants to enjoy some family time. I put my notebook down.

The entire evening could have taken place in our family home in Cairo in the 1970s or early 1980s. This extended family—again, the son, his wife and their only daughter live with the grandparents in the same house—felt and looked very familiar. But it was a family that held on to traditional values and eschewed the more liberal aspects of creolization—the men were served first, for example, and the women ate only once the men had had their fill. And yet, as I joined the women around the dining table once the men had decamped for the living room, I heard stories of their involvement in the annual Carnival and I noted that all were financially independent—or at least working for a living. (Ashad's wife ran a beauty salon in the home's converted garage.) The guests that night were Catholic, Hindu, Muslim and Presbyterian, representing the main faiths in the country. I did notice that no one from the black community joined us, even though everyone present mentioned having a close friend or co-worker from the other side of the colour divide. Perhaps, I thought, Jason is right after all. Despite the dominant influence of a colour line, Trinidad can't be reduced to a single assertion or observation.

But as I left I noticed that the house was in a gated community of mainly brown families, with further protection provided by a guard dog, a Rottweiler. (A docile one, but still a Rottweiler.) The isolation and overprotection undercut my briefly held conversion to Jason's vision of Trinidad. They were a physical manifestation of the way the colour line works: separating blacks from browns, and vice versa.

PART II

CHAPTER 4

The Philippines: At the World's Service

The lineup at Manila's United Nations light rail station snakes all the way from the platform, down three flights of stairs and across at least a block of Taft Avenue, a major thoroughfare in this capital city of about 1.7 million residents. (Manila is one of sixteen cities and one municipality that make up Metro Manila, which has a population of nearly twelve million.) Guidebooks and websites written with the young and the adventurous in mind advise visitors to avoid the LRT system during rush hour. Roughly speaking, that will be from seven in the morning to ten in the evening. Almost every hour of the day is rush hour here.

Even by Manila's standards, the crowd at the United Nations station seems exceptionally dense on this Tuesday afternoon in January. A security guard at a café on the ground level of the Times Plaza building on United Nations Avenue believes most commuters are on their way home from the training centre on the third and fourth floors of this heaving business complex. The Magsaysay Center for Hospitality and Culinary Arts (MIHCA) forms part of the Magsaysay enterprise, which trains young Filipinos for a range of careers, from bartending to seafaring.

There's a certain irony in locating the headquarters of this career factory on a street named after the world assembly. You won't find the world in Manila, but Manileños, as citizens of Manila are known, can be found in many of the countries that make up the United Nations. And the various campuses of the Magsaysay Center have earned a reputation as trusted and employment-focused gateways to a national Filipino fantasy: landing a job in the service or hospitality sector outside the country. MIHCA has established itself as *the* finishing school for the hundreds of thousands of maids, cooks, bartenders and waiters in hotels, on cruise ships and in high-end and franchise restaurants around the world. Its recruitment slogan, placed alongside pictures of towel-carrying maids and cocktail-serving bartenders, captures the aspirational nature of service head-on: "Live Your Dream. Aspire MIHCA."

For a few hours this afternoon, I learned why exporting labour has become the Philippines' chief economic and political strategy and its main reputation on the world stage, sometimes leading to dicey international encounters. The execution of Filipina domestic worker Flor Contemplacion in Singapore in 1995 for the murder of another domestic and a local child pitted the two countries against each other, forcing important changes in the regulation of overseas migration in the Philippines. In 1998, the country's then president, Joseph Estrada, vigorously protested a Greek publisher's plan to include the word "Filipineza" in a dictionary as synonym for a domestic servant or helper.

Neither national pride nor stories of European insensitivities to brown migrants seem to preoccupy students in instructor

Roger Ballesteros's class in the housekeeping services program, a full-time, five-month course that includes five hundred hours of OJT (on-the-job training). It's one of seven streams from which prospective students may choose. Housekeeping and the seven-month culinary arts program are the most popular ones on the curriculum. Students can add to their bag of service tricks by enrolling in the shorter Barista 101 (three weeks on the "art and science of coffee preparation") or the two-week Flairtending 101 (think Tom Cruise behind the bar in *Cocktail*). Bartenders with flair draw crowds on cruise ships, I'm told.

This particular day is the second in a week-long module on making beds. The lesson starts in the classroom every weekday morning and moves in the afternoons to a glassed corner of the centre, designed to replicate a twin room in a five-star hotel. In today's class, each student will learn the art of making a bed in just under three minutes.

Since it's early in the training, Ballesteros has paired students and given each team five minutes to fluff the pillows, take off and tuck in a loose bedsheet, tidy up the bedskirt, add another sheet and cover the whole thing with a duvet. Later classes will go over dusting, vacuuming and bathroom cleaning, laying the foundations for a related segment on laundry and household chemicals (detergents, air fresheners, cleaning liquids, etc.) that these students will start in a few weeks. By the end of this module, students should be able to clean any hotel room or cabin on a cruise ship from top to bottom in twenty-five minutes or less, depending on the size. Suites and executive rooms may take longer.

Ballesteros worked his way through the hospitality industry, from bellboy to management, in a thirty-four-year career spent entirely in the Philippines—a rarity in this sector. The time has come, he tells me, to share his professional knowledge and prepare the next generation of Filipino housekeepers and hotel staff.

Although his time-keeping methods may suggest a taskmaster, Ballesteros runs his class with an avuncular touch. He knows that almost all his students want jobs outside the country, and he takes pride in sending them out into the world as ambassadors of Filipino-branded hospitality, which goes way beyond mere service with a smile. Students here are trained—indoctrinated, even—to defer to and please guests. I've never heard the words "Thank you, sir" uttered more frequently or with as big a smile as I have while visiting the centre.

German, Italian and Japanese cruise ships have become the biggest employers of the centre's graduates. The students' rigorous training, command of English and servility attract potential employers. No one at the centre refers to servility as a learning outcome (at least not explicitly), but it's easy to get more than a whiff of it in Manila's restaurants, bars and shops. To Filipinos, service is a calling, a passion—not a joe job. Leisure cruises are big business in the West and Asia, targeting an aging and retired population with time on its hands and money in its cargo shorts, and Filipinos have risen to the challenge, churning out generations of staff to cater to passengers' every whim.

In some parts of Asia, the demand for hospitality staff outpaces the supply. High-end restaurants in Singapore routinely close sections and turn away customers to maintain service standards in the face of chronic labour shortages. Singapore's Manpower Ministry estimated that there were 6,400 unfilled jobs in the food-and-beverage service sector in September 2014. The Philippines tops the list of nations from which Singapore imports workers in that field. For now at least, it looks like students in the culinary arts program have a shot at a decent job in Singapore, assuming they abandon their fascination with cruise ships and get over the city's reputation for exacting standards in service. Filipinos already working in the hospitality industry describe

Singaporeans as anything from tight-assed to sadistic. (The ghost of Flor Contemplacion still haunts Singapore-bound Filipinos, even the young ones I talked to informally.)

But cruise ships remain the number-one choice of almost everyone at the centre. I ask Ballesteros to explain the appeal of working on them. I would have thought that students would view a lifetime of cruising seas and oceans without any of the privileges of being a passenger more a punishment than a preference. "They want to see the world," he tells me, "and they can earn much more there than land-based contracts." He has one eye on our conversation and the other on the timer on his mobile phone so he can ensure that the two students making the bed in front of him do not go over the five-minute limit. Ballesteros explains that it's part pursuit of adventure on the high seas and part hand-me-down fantasy. None of the students have left the Philippines or been aboard a ship before, but they've heard friends and neighbours—and strangers on radio and TV—tell tales of seeing the world while making a living and (as is always the case) sharing their paycheques with their families.

A handful of students nod in agreement with their instructor's views. "You're not tied to one boss or one country," says a young man with classic nerdy-chic glasses; in any other context, I would have cast him as a hipster who is more likely to stay in boutique hotels than clean rooms in them. Another says that leaving her family for extended periods of time gives her the perfect balance between independence and duties to parents or siblings.

There's roughly a fifty-fifty split of men and women in the hospitality program, while men dominate in the culinary arts classes. Virtually all are in their early to middle twenties at the oldest. In fact, the program doesn't accept applicants over thirty-five. Service is for the young. Filipinos often talk of how being young and attractive can mean the difference between a dream life and a nightmare existence in working abroad. Although the Philippines considers English an official language, command of it varies among students in the centre, depending on social background and level of education. By the time they graduate, all trainees will be comfortable enough to conduct a basic conversation with a hotel guest or a passenger on a ship. Language classes are offered to those who need it, at an extra (but small) cost.

At Ballesteros's request, two students who are clearly this cohort's strongest demonstrate an art form that I, never having been on a cruise ship, didn't know existed: folding towels into the shapes of animals. Mae and Kim fold, twist and arrange two towels to make them look like an elephant. They and other students then tackle a new set of towels, turning them into rabbits and dogs. Towel folding was covered in the previous week's module, and students whose work today falls short of standards aboard luxury liners receive an exasperated look from their instructor.

"But what's the point of spending so much time setting up towels in animal shapes when guests are likely to pull them apart to wash their hands or faces?" I blurt out. The question is out before I realize that I'm essentially suggesting he's training them to do something that's a waste of time. "It's there to please the guests," Ballesteros responds instantly. I should have known. These brown men and women aim to please their future Japanese, Western and Arab masters.

Pleasing the taste buds of strangers is the order of the day over at the culinary arts program, where my tour continues. Starting with basics like knife skills, butchery and sanitation, future chefs and wait staff learn how to prepare and serve a variety of Asian and Western meals. Today's lesson is soup, specifically a purée of celery, creamy carrots and mushrooms. Filipino cuisine hardly makes a showing on the course list, I note. The goal, I'm told, is to cater (literally and metaphorically) to the appetites of other nationals and not the domestic market.

The Philippines as a nation takes pride in providing the people power necessary for the economic development of the world outside its borders. As I watch the culinary arts students wiping off a kitchen counter, I have an image of the brown worker as the world's global servant, a permanent downstairs resident to affluent upstairs citizens of various skin colours and ethnicities. Hundreds of thousands of Filipino maids, room service attendants, chefs, receptionists and bellboys keep the world's hospitality industry ticking along, on land and at sea. Others build the salons and spa retreats that employ their brown compatriots as masseurs and physical therapists. Ever since the late 1960s—more on that history in a moment—when the government began thinking of its people as its biggest export and revenue source, a debate has been raging in the Philippines about the social and economic impact of the migrant worker. Can a country incorporate the identities of those who have left it behind, sometimes for decades or on a permanent basis, into its nation-building project in the same way it does their remittances into its GDP?

Speak to any young Filipino of even modest educational background and you'll get one of two views. The first is that working abroad leads to career and salary boosts that benefit the migrants and their dependants in monetary and emotional terms. The second sees it not as an option but as the harsh economic reality of present-day Philippines, a poor country with massive wealth gaps between the rich and the desolate. Workers sign up to a life of servitude and, as some commentators insist, new forms of slavery. What blacks were in the eighteenth and nineteenth centuries to the United States and Indian indentured labourers were in the nineteenth century to British and French imperial powers, Filipinos have become in the late twentieth and early twenty-first centuries. This time, however, their masters don't govern one nation or preside over a single European imperial project. Globalization is their new master. While in broad strokes Filipinos are no different from Sri Lankan or Indonesian workers, they stand apart in sheer numbers and in the way their government has turned their labour into a tightly regulated and overprotected national industry.

When you have more brown people than you know what to do with, why not ship them out?

*

ALTHOUGH THE WHOLESALE EXPORT of Filipino workers began in earnest in the 1970s, the history of labour migration in the Philippines goes back centuries, to the country's earliest encounters with colonialism. Historians of migration suggest that native sailors (then known as *indios*) took part in Spanish-run expeditions to the northern and southern regions of the Pacific as early as the 1570s. Manilamen, as these sailors came to be known, would become a fixture of American, Japanese and British vessels throughout the first half of the nineteenth century. As Filomeno V. Aguilar Jr. points out in *Migrant Revolution*, his vital collection of essays about Filipino migrant workers, US colonialism of the Philippines in 1898 ushered in a new phase in the country's labour history, as locals were recruited to work on American navy ships and on sugar plantations in Hawaii. The Philippines' current reputation as the country with the largest number of seafarers (with Indonesia and China in a distant second and third) builds on centuries of tradition and the professionalization of maritime life. The export of plantation workers in the early twentieth century gave way to service-oriented labour in the Philippines in the late 1960s and early 1970s.

A collision of factors inside and outside the Philippines helped seal the migration deal of the century. When oil prices shot up after the 1973 crisis, the economies of the Gulf countries (Saudi Arabia, the United Arab Emirates, Kuwait, Bahrain, Qatar and, to a lesser extent, Oman) experienced unprecedented growth. Many of these countries had just entered the world stage a few years earlier, when Britain handed over control of its former colonies to Western-friendly royal families and governments. Work on major infrastructure projects, as well as an expansion of residential and commercial sites, meant importing virtually all the necessary labour, from supervisors and logisticians to cleaners and cooks to prepare food for the thousands of workers housed dormitory-style on the cities' outskirts. Work was plenty but workers few.

Enter the Philippines.

Aguilar Jr. suggests that both private and government employers preferred non-Muslim workers from South and Southeast Asia over other Arab and Muslim workers. The predominantly Christian Filipino workers, for example, were less likely to meddle in or stoke sectarian tensions between Shiites and Sunnis, or to take part in Arab politics, especially the Palestinian-Israeli conflict. (The Philippines is Asia's only largely Christian nation, with Catholicism as the main denomination.) But many Filipinos believe another factor has been at the heart of their popularity among other South and Southeast Asian citizens: their fairer shade of brown (compared to the very dark brown of, say, Bangladeshi, Indian and Sri Lankan workers). Command of English is another reason for preferential treatment. In general, Asian workers stood out ethnically and were therefore easier to monitor and keep control of than their Arab colleagues, who could blend in with the local populations of the Gulf. Authorities can instantly spot runaway South Asian construction workers if they're found outside the sites they are bused to daily.

This burst of economic activity in the Gulf was replicated in other countries in Southeast Asia, with Singapore, Hong Kong and Malaysia in particular experiencing both a growth in GDP and chronic labour shortages, particularly in lower-paid, unskilled sectors. Internal migrants (those travelling from the countryside to urban centres) gravitated toward the industrial and manufacturing sectors, leaving jobs in domestic service and sanitation to less fortunate Asian nationals. A Filipina maid or nanny in Singapore or Malaysia was a symbol that her—and domestic work still is a predominantly female profession, with women representing 83 percent of those workers abroad—employers had solidified their position as middle class. Many historians of the Filipino culture of migration also point out the colonial legacy of employing servants of a different race; in effect, many affluent Asians were restaging scenes from their childhoods but casting themselves in the role of their (former) British masters.

At the time of this boom in Asian and Gulf economies, many Western countries with long histories of settling newcomers eased or dismantled their European-based immigration policies. Canada, Australia and New Zealand no longer identified European or white heritage as the main qualification for immigrants wanting to start a new life within their borders. This ushered in waves of immigration from the market-dominant Asians in East Africa and the Caribbean, as well as newcomers from Southeast Asia. The brown advance on the New World begins with this set of colour-blind immigration reforms.

In these countries and elsewhere in Western Europe and the United States, women began to enter or return to the workforce in unprecedented numbers, disrupting men's monopolies on several professions. Many women sought hired help to deal with domestic chores that patriarchy and tradition had assigned them. The 1980s in particular witnessed the return of the domestic servant to middle-class households in several Western democracies, decades after their postwar disappearance. Again, Filipina workers filled that labour gap, performing roles—nanny, cook, cleaner—that had traditionally come within the purview of the "lady of the house." It was a win-win situation. Western and Asian women held on to their gains within the market economy while maintaining the facade of bourgeois domesticity. Filipina domestic workers earned enough to remit a few dollars to their families back home to help them through a deteriorating and corrupt economic and political system—the very thing that had driven the women to seek work abroad in the first place.

Which brings us to living conditions inside the Philippines in the 1970s, when the current wave of migration began. While the country's political and economic situation was complex, several commentators place the blame for what went wrong at the feet of one man: former president Ferdinand Marcos, who came into power in 1965 and controlled the nation for twenty-one years, nine of them under martial law. The sharp rise in oil prices in 1973 derailed an economy that had already begun to suffer from the twin blows of increased population and unemployment on the one hand, and political unrest from left-leaning activists and Muslim separatists on the other. For the first half of the 1970s, the economy grew at 2 percent annually, a respectable performance in its own right but one that paled in comparison to the rates of growth in Singapore or Malaysia at the same time.

Worse, the Marcos government squandered that modest growth on lavish re-election campaigns and quelling internal attacks from the political left and right. From 1972 until 1981, Filipinos lived under martial law—nearly a decade during which Marcos's regime ramped up its political and economic cronyism, giving select members of the president's inner circle a monopoly on the nation's industry and resources. Political opponents were silenced, tortured or killed. In 1983, opposition leader Benigno Aquino Jr. was assassinated at what was then Manila International Airport (it's now named after him) seconds after returning to the Philippines from three years of political exile in the US. His death at what many observers suspect were Marcos's orders laid the foundation for the revolution that would ultimately depose the dictator in 1986.

The political uncertainty during Marcos's reign and the fact that economic benefits accrued to only a tiny minority of the population—those catering to Marcos and his shoe-hoarding wife, Imelda—forced both working- and middle-class Filipinos to seek positions abroad. To Marcos, exporting his countrymen and -women was a way of capitalizing on the Philippines' overpopulation while simultaneously relieving his government of the need to spend on development projects and social assistance for the masses. Migrant workers would remit money from their salaries, the thinking went, to care for the poor and vulnerable in their families or immediate communities. Aguilar Jr. sums up the societal function of this mass exodus brilliantly: "If Philippine society was ever a cauldron about to boil over, overseas migration has taken the lid off and released the pressure."

And migration's role in taking the pressure off continues to this day. Despite rosier economic data and relatively more stable political conditions, the Philippines remains a staggeringly poor country, especially when compared with the more robust economies of its ASEAN (Association of Southeast Asian Nations) neighbours. According to the country's Centre for Migrant Advocacy, one-quarter of the population, or about twenty-three million people, lives on less than US$1.35 a day. An estimated 10.5 million Filipinos (out of a population of nearly one hundred million) temporarily or permanently work outside the country. For young people in the Philippines, migration may well be their only hope. In the second quarter of 2015, unemployment among

Filipinos aged fifteen to twenty-four stood at 16 percent, more than double the national average of 6.4 percent. Government surveys of school-age children have revealed that 40 to 50 percent expressed a strong desire to work abroad. The number increases for children or close relatives of migrants, who often act as informal recruiters for members of their family. The education system, with its emphasis on maintaining command of the English language, is partly designed to facilitate employment abroad. The curriculum more or less inculcates in others the value of service.

Nationalist and upper-middle-class Filipinos have taken strong positions on the transformation of the country into the world's largest human-resources department. Charges of a brain drain resurface every few years in the national media. While unskilled labourers are seen as dispensable, trained professionals are not—those lost to other countries have put human development on hold and lives at risk. As demand for caregivers and nurses in Western nations has increased—an example of how an aging population in the developed world affects life in developing countries—many locally trained doctors have chosen to go back to school to obtain nursing degrees in order to land jobs in overseas hospitals or private clinics.

This flow of migrants continues despite headline-grabbing stories of the exploitation, abuse and even murder of Filipino workers, particularly in the Gulf and Middle East. An estimated twelve thousand Filipino workers were trapped in Syria in the spring of 2011, in the early months of the uprising that turned into a full-fledged civil war. The majority have since been repatriated, but many lost either their lives or their savings. The migrant Filipino worker has been compared to both a modern-day pilgrim and a slave. Yet there's no consensus among Filipinos on who's enslaving whom—and how voluntary this so-called voluntary migration really is when you take into consideration the socio-economic realities of today's Philippines.

*

WALK THROUGH THE INTERCONNECTED Glorietta and Greenbelt malls in Makati City, five kilometres east of Manila, and you'll understand why consumer demand accounts for 70 percent of the GDP in the Philippines. Shopping is more than a business or a necessity in Asia's booming economies; it has evolved into an art form, a way of life. Come 5 p.m., thousands of shoppers and window browsers descend on malls in Hong Kong, Taipei, Bangkok or Singapore and hang out there until closing time at 9 or 10 p.m. Sometimes they're shopping for a new item of clothing or yet another smartphone (most of my Asian friends own at least two phones, one for work and the other for personal calls or dating apps). Other times a mall becomes a place to spend time with friends and family. Unlike malls in North America, which tend to be associated with urban sprawl, rowdy teenagers and the less discerning end of consumerism, the Asian equivalents serve as destinations, the perfect spot for an evening or day out. At the very least, Asian malls offer a break from the blazing sun or the humidity of the afternoon.

The malls in Makati City serve all these purposes, and more. My visit to the Philippines in early 2015 coincided with Pope Francis's, and the main court of Glorietta 3 had been cleared to provide continuous coverage of his trip on a jumbo screen. About two hundred Manileños interrupted their shopping to watch his arrival in the city on a Thursday afternoon. It was a moment in the life of modern-day Philippines where Catholicism and consumerism seemed inseparable. Shortly after the telecast ended, shoppers wiped away their tears, said their final prayers and continued their search for a bargain or a place to eat before heading home, preferably before closing time to avoid the traffic that accompanies this nightly exodus.

Makati, a former swampland that has been developed into a business and commercial centre, is what the Philippines wants visitors to see when they come to the capital city. With its concentration of corporate headquarters, five-star hotels and high-rise luxury condominiums, Makati looks indistinguishable from Hong Kong or Singapore. It remains one of the safest districts in Metro Manila—the only one whose streets I felt comfortable walking alone in at night. The fact that security guards with machine guns stand outside hotels, businesses and malls to protect visitors and locals both confirms that sense of safety and draws attention to the potential of crime. Makati offers an aspirational fantasy for middle-class Manileños, who escape the poverty and crime of Manila proper by hanging out in its malls and parks. It also serves as a reminder of the disparity in incomes and quality of life here. Look at the lineups for the Jeepneys—those distinctly Filipino communal buses made of refurbished military Jeeps or Japanese vehicles—and you'll get a sense of how those working in downtown Makati struggle to get to and from their jobs. Waiting in the glare of a Gucci or a Guess store sharpens the contrast even more.

In his short story "Aviary," included in the anthology *Manila Noir,* San Francisco–based writer Lysley Tenorio taps into the contradictions (and menace) of mall life in Makati. The first-person narrator captures the experiences of a group of young men from the shanties who descend on Makati after hearing of a sign outside the Greenbelt mall that reads "Poor People & Other Disturbing Realities Strictly Prohibited." After an afternoon of thugging their way in and out of stores the narrator can't help mocking for having "nonsensical" names (Bvlgari) or others that "sound like a sneeze" (Jimmy Choo), the men place a fake bomb in the mall's chapel to inflict damage on the management. "We will have created unease here, severe emotional distress," concludes the narrator in the tale's final paragraph. Even the revenge fantasy of the powerless takes place against a backdrop of commercialism, and on one level revels in it.

The narrator captures something else I noticed in my evening mall walks: as he and his friends go up and down the escalators, he points out that "these are the whitest Filipinos we have ever seen." You only see darker-skinned Filipinos working in low-end chain stores or as waiters in cheap or moderately priced eateries. The fancier the store, the lighter the skin of the sales staff. Initially I thought my mind was playing tricks on me, forcing me to see light and dark skins where I wanted them to be. But after reading Tenorio's story, I went back to test his narrator's observation, and by and large, it checked out.

I also had another mission in mind: finding an authentic Filipino restaurant close to the malls. Two local men who'd worked in the service industry overseas for many years before returning to Manila had agreed to share their experiences with me over lunch. I found only two or three spots, however—locals flock to American and Japanese joints, leaving Filipino food for visitors like me who want to sample the "real" cuisine of the country. I made a mental note of a place called Dekada, in Glorietta 3, since it billed itself as serving "Historic Filipino Food." On Saturday afternoon, when I met up with Jonas and Oliver (and their friend Eric, who tagged along), we settled around a big table and started a conversation that would last almost until the dinner rush hit us.

My good friend Roberto, a Filipino-Canadian based in Toronto, introduced me to his two old school buddies from Marikina, another city that makes up Greater Manila. All three reconnected through social media twenty-five years or so after high school, and their stories illustrate, among other things, the differences between temporary Filipino migrant workers and those who manage to start new lives as permanent residents in a country like Canada. While Roberto's middle-class family relocated to

Edmonton in the 1980s, joining the ranks of well-to-do Canadians with all the privileges the First World bestows on its citizens, Oliver's and Jonas's parents were rocked by the political and economic turmoil in the Philippines. All three families started as middle class, but only Roberto's maintained its status or improved on it. By the time Oliver and Jonas started the search for overseas employment, they had no other choice.

Oliver's life began to change when his mother died unexpectedly in 1990 of cancer, sending his father into the grip of depression. "He started to lose interest in his job, in his life," says Oliver, an easy-going man in his mid-forties with curly greying hair tied into a man bun. With inconsistent and low income as the new norm, the father started selling the family furniture piece by piece to feed his children. A fifteen-year-old Oliver watched it all unfold—not as a teen but as an adult who now had to step in to provide for his siblings and father. He quit school.

That must have been a difficult decision, I remark as I begin to realize that his story is very different from that of the middle-class high school dropouts I've come across in Toronto. Still (and stupidly), I wonder if Oliver had other options and ask him if he considered staying in school and working part time. "We had nothing to eat. I wasn't able to focus on study. . . . We were penniless."

For about two years, Oliver earned a living as an assistant in a beauty parlour, sweeping hair off the floor and eventually learning the basics of cosmetic care: makeup, manicure and pedicure. While he didn't bring home a huge income, he at least earned enough to keep the family from starvation or homelessness. Still, the precariousness of the beauty business—a luxury for even middle-class Filipinas struggling to survive month to month—forced Oliver to follow in the path of millions before him and look for work abroad. With no formal training in the service industry and no high school certificate, he had to explore what was then an in-demand but shady aspect of migration in the Philippines: working as an entertainer in Japan.

Japan had been drawing on Filipino artists to provide musical entertainment for almost a century at that point, with records showing their presence dating back to the late 1880s. The US occupation of the Philippines introduced jazz and swing music to Filipinos, who developed a taste for it. American promoters and music managers began booking Filipino acts in Japan before the Second World War, and the American influence on the Philippines-to-Japan traffic in entertainers continued well into the 1960s.

Perhaps what has changed since then is the definition of the word "entertainer," an overhaul that hewed the job closer to sex work and away from the performing arts (although a performance of a sort does take place when Filipinas—and like domestic service, this is a line of work where women dominate—and Japanese men meet face to face). Once a Filipina receives an entertainment visa for cultural performance, she's eligible to work in hostess bars in the rural areas of Japan. In addition to performing cover versions of the latest Western pop music or putting together a burlesque act, she'll chat up Japanese men, convincing them to order drinks and food with marked-up prices.

It's a role once played by Japanese women. However, as post-war Japan transformed into an industrial powerhouse (the Japanese Miracle), local women sought other kinds of work, leaving this lowly line of entertainment to migrant women from other countries. Filipino commentators have suggested that Japanese men are acting out a cultural fantasy of über-masculinity by casting the entertainer in the submissive role that traditional Japanese women once filled. The exchange between entertainer and client unfolds as part sexually charged relationship, part historical re-enactment.

That Oliver was a man did not stand in the way of his career as a hostess. Not all female entertainers in Japan are born with the corresponding body parts. In fact, in the 1980s and early 1990s, a subculture of cross-dressing and transvestism thrived within the main entertainment industry. Oliver saw an opportunity and went for it. He applied for a licence to work as an entertainer in Japan after hearing about the high pay and giving up on the dream of making a decent living at home. He says he was about eighteen when he made that decision. To get a licence, Filipino wannabe entertainers have to audition in front of a committee of representatives from the government. Putting the skills learned in Manila's beauty salons to good use, Oliver performed an amateur drag show that met the committee's proof of talent. He was issued a visa and assigned to a club in northern Japan. For the first time, he moved away from his family and his country.

Oliver's early days in Japan were exciting and financially rewarding. Japanese bosses paid the equivalent of US$300 a month (in today's dollars), a fortune for the eighteen-year-old—even after the recruitment agency took its cut and expenses were subtracted. With this kind of regular income, Oliver was able to send his family nearly half of his take-home pay through remittances. It added up to more than three or four times his best-paid and busiest weeks at the hair salon. Performing hits by Paula Abdul, Whitney Houston and Madonna, the very young Oliver became a favourite in his local hostess bar. Still, his drag act lacked something. Many of his Japanese clients liked women's body parts on their male-born hostesses. To oblige, Oliver started a course of hormone therapy and underwent breast-implant surgery to give his chest a more authentically female shape. It extended his career as an entertainer and fulfilled the fetishes of the men.

However, the short nature of the government-issued contracts (they were granted for only six months to a year at a time) meant that entertainers had to return regularly to the Philippines and reapply for a new licence. After two extensions, Oliver decided to jettison the formal process and go underground, living in northern Japan for almost six years without an entertainer's licence or any kind of residence permit. Filipino overseas workers, particularly in Asia, routinely overstay their visas or work illegally, making them vulnerable to unregulated and exploitative employment conditions. Add in what Oliver and others describe as a distinctly Japanese form of xenophobia and you understand why entertainment jobs in Japan overlap with sex trafficking.

"The Japanese treat you like a Third World, third-class country, even though they too are Asians," says a now teary Oliver. "When Japanese employers know you've overstayed, they reduce your salary." Around 1998, after almost eight years in Japan, Oliver was arrested and deported to the Philippines. He says the prison where he stayed for two months before his deportation felt more like a hostel, with three meals a day, hot showers and recreational facilities. He has never set foot in Japan again but has found work with a recruitment agency that specializes in what's now the back door to entertainment (or any other) work in Japan for Filipinas: invitational matrimony. Filipinas enter into a marriage arrangement with Japanese men that allows them to work and live in Japan legally.

*

COMPARED TO OLIVER, JONAS had a less dramatic overseas experience, but he too was forced into it. His father lost everything in the early 1990s when he took out a business loan and failed to repay it. The bank foreclosed on the family's catering business and threatened to seize their home as well. At seventeen, Jonas faced two options: he could become an entertainer like Oliver or learn the culinary secrets of the old family business. Too rugged (and macho) and lacking the vocal talent to pass the audition for an entertainer, Jonas chose the second option, completing a culinary arts course and maritime training similar to the programs offered by the Magsaysay Center. He combined both to find work as a chef aboard container ships and eventually cruise liners.

For nearly a decade, Jonas worked routes in Asia, with Manila to Singapore as the major one. But in 2003, his life changed when he secured a job on a German cruise ship that sailed from Rotterdam in the Netherlands to Dublin and Cork in Ireland. Jonas abandoned ship once he'd sampled the good life in Dublin while on shore leave. (He managed to "steal" his own passport. It's common for the ship's bursar to hold the passports of Filipino mariners to avoid this very scenario.) After months of working under the table in gastro-pubs and pizza parlours in Dublin, he was approached by a man who ran a small hotel and offered him a job cleaning around the establishment. It was work that the middle-class Jonas found "demeaning," but at ten euros an hour and with restaurant work drying up, he accepted. He recounted in great detail the horror of cleaning other people's toilets for the first time. At that point, Jonas came to the realization that his middle-class days were behind him for good.

Word of mouth and that trademark Filipino work ethic helped him land various other under-the-table cleaning gigs. He made six hundred euros a week on average and managed to stay off the radar of the Irish authorities for six years. Only in 2010, when his eighty-four-year-old father's health began to deteriorate, did Jonas return to Manila. He used his savings from many years of cleaning homes and guesthouses to restart the family catering business with one of his brothers.

I ask Oliver and Jonas how they feel about seeing young workers go into potentially harmful or exploitative scenarios. As

Oliver pauses to reflect, Jonas steps in, saying: "It's better than settling for noodles for lunch every day." A cup of noodles from the local convenience store costs about twenty-five pesos and is still the main meal for millions of impoverished Filipinos. It's high on sodium and artificial ingredients, causing numerous health problems in the long run.

Oliver agrees with his friend, adding that as long as young people are briefed on the risks, they should be allowed to seek opportunities in Japan or elsewhere. But the two men place as much blame for the exploitation of Filipino migrant workers on their government as they do on unscrupulous bosses in host countries. Jonas compares his government's relentless promotion of overseas work to the British empire a century or more earlier, shipping thousands of its subjects from one colony to another to undertake major agricultural or infrastructure projects. Oliver sees Filipinos as both the slaves of the twentieth and twenty-first centuries and the ones enslaving others. He cites greedy and unprofessional recruitment agencies that take larger-than-standard cuts from their employees' salaries or knowingly send them to work in unsafe conditions.

Yet despite what is effectively a four-decade national debate—are oversees workers slaves or ambassadors for the Philippines?—the number of migrants increases every year. What is it about Filipinos that makes them so at ease in the world? Even Eric, the only one of the three friends who didn't have to travel (his family held on to its middle-class status), acknowledged that migrants "put their hearts" into their work—something, he says, all Filipinos are raised to do. "Filipino people adapt to a lot of things," he says. "It starts in the basic unit of the family. The way we were bred is to be closely knit with your family and friends. You serve your family."

In an exchange of messages a few days earlier, my Toronto friend Roberto had mentioned the role of Catholicism in fostering a culture of self-denial and service to others. I ask the three if this is part of the equation, but Oliver is not convinced. He offers a more secular and commercial interpretation: "When you need money, you have to work. And when you work, you have to please the people you serve." I suggest that the livelihoods of many Filipinos then depend on that fine line between service and servitude. Jonas agrees but adds that someone attractive and young has a better chance of succeeding abroad; Filipinos directly and indirectly sell more than just their labour. All three believe that a light skin forms an essential part of the attraction. Those with darker skin have to work twice as hard to get ahead in the service industry. Jonas in particular believes customer service workers, whose job involves dealing with people face to face, tend to be selected for their fairer skin. Just like that short story, I note.

But Jonas and Oliver are men—Oliver now identifies as an effeminate gay man, the opposite of "straight acting"—in an enterprise that has long been a "feminized sphere." The first overseas Filipino workers may have been male seafarers, but the new face of the country's globetrotting reality is the young female domestic worker, nurse, caregiver or nanny. So much so that I found it jarring to see a Filipina pushing a stroller holding an actual Filipino child or tending to an elderly person who bears a family resemblance. Like many North Americans, I associate Filipinas with serving middle-class and well-to-do families of different ethnicities.

But while women from the Philippines and other Southeast Asian countries, notably Sri Lanka and Indonesia, reap the same rewards and experience the same hardships as male workers, the jobs they do put them in a more vulnerable position. Domestic work, the area in which 83 percent of migrant women around the world toil, doesn't figure in the labour laws of about 40 percent of destination countries, according to a recent report from UN Women. Unlike construction workers or professionals, domestic workers tend to move from job to job informally and without legally binding contracts. This increases their chances of exploitation, abuse or deportation.

The same report estimates that domestic workers account for 7.5 percent of the total number of women in the workforce globally. The number of domestics continues to increase (at least fifty-three million women work in that field, with most coming from Asia) despite the slowdown in the world economy since 2008. Currently and for the first time, women far outnumber men among migrant workers in the Persian Gulf: twelve men for every one hundred women. While domestic work pays less than male-dominated professions, and comes with certain class-based prejudices, studies show that its social impact in countries of origin is greater. Women workers tend to invest more in their communities by supporting not just their immediate family but also initiatives to improve the health and education of children generally or to provide clean water or job training.

Stories of abuse or family estrangement usually drown out the positive side—the empowerment effect—of brown labour. I wanted to find out for myself what happens to the Filipina domestic worker once she leaves her home and accepts employment in another country. Is she a modern-day slave or an emancipated woman earning her keep? How do host societies, particularly in Asia, perceive her as both a woman and a brown-skinned economic migrant? I had to see for myself how her life unfolds inside the homes she cleans and alongside the families for whom she prepares three meals a day. Some answers (and more questions) came to me in Hong Kong, where I closely observed the world of Filipina (and some Indonesian) domestic workers and their daily battles with the colour lines of global labour.

CHAPTER 5

Hong Kong: Workers, Women, Mothers

On weekdays, the Hong Kong Bayanihan Kennedy Town Centre looks like the abandoned secondary school it actually is. Its only paid employee, Tess Ubamos, an administrator, spends her days there doing paperwork or arranging for plumbers to deal with drainage issues in the bathrooms or contractors to give the classrooms a fresh coat of paint.

But come the weekend, and especially Sundays, the Bayanihan turns into a social hub for domestic workers in the city. A charitable organization founded in 1993, the centre takes its name from the Filipino word for community spirit. While it opens its doors to domestics of all nationalities, the Bayanihan targets workers from the Philippines and is run by a large volunteer team of them. The Hong Kong government rents the building to a trust at a "cheap, cheap, cheap" rate, says Ubamos, as part of an initiative to offer recreational services for domestic workers.

The centre provides a safe space (some may say an escape) for Hong Kong's domestic workers to learn, express their feelings or simply hang out and do as little as possible. Women who prefer not to spend their one day off picnicking in the Central District's Victoria Park or exploring the many pedestrian bridges nearby come here for a mix of body-mind-soul tinkering.

The sports-oriented among them take part in weekly volleyball coaching. Judging from the grunts and groans coming from both sides of the net, it'll be a close call at the spring tournament. The martial arts club provides the release of a contact sport while teaching women basic self-defence. The coach tells me that warding off unwanted sexual advances in Hong Kong is one of the reasons for the high enrolment numbers, but most women are preparing themselves for the rough streets that await them when they return to the Philippines.

I'm at the centre on a Sunday in early April to take part in an art class organized by the Hong Kong University–based social inclusion group We Care HK, a registered NGO that aims to bridge gaps among different ethnicities in the city. Vicky Kung, a graduate student in social work, and Melissa Leung, a journalism major, have invited me to see how they use art practice to connect local Hong Kongers and domestic helpers in a context other than employer-employee, local-foreign.

I was a skeptic going in. Two weeks earlier, the two women had hosted a screening of the 2013 Singaporean film *Ilo, Ilo*, a story of the bond between a boy and his Filipina nanny set against the Asian financial crisis of 1997. Only a handful of students from Hong Kong University's residential college Chi Sun (where the screening took place) showed up, and neither Vicky nor Melissa touched on the film's themes in the post-screening discussion. This Sunday, I made my way to the Bayanihan Centre expecting a similarly dismal turnout and rehearsing excuses to leave early so I could catch up with the Sunday picnics in Central, my best shot at meeting with and talking to a cross-section of helpers in the city.

But the fifth-floor classroom—painted in a kind of bright green you see only in re-creations of the psychedelic sixties in *The Simpsons*—quickly fills with fourteen Filipina domestic workers and about eight locals (all but one of them female). Ana, an art teacher and therapist of Chinese-Canadian background, starts by explaining the afternoon's project to a very excitable audience. The first step, she says, involves pairing each worker with a Hong Konger. Since not enough locals have shown up, Ana asks some domestic workers to pair up. The women will begin by taking photos of their partners on a smartphone and emailing them to Melissa, who will print them out. To make the pictures consistent in size, Ana tells the women to think of ID photos. Smart move. It's a reference that the women should be familiar with, given how many such photos they had to attach to their immigration and employment forms in the Philippines and in Hong Kong.

While the printing takes place, Ana tells the women to get to know their partners by asking questions about their likes and dislikes, taste in music or hidden talents. "Can you sing?" Ana throws that out as an example of a good getting-to-know-you question, probably not realizing Filipinos' well-documented obsession with karaoke. At home or in one of the country's thousands of bars and lounges, Filipinos have turned this party favourite into a national pastime. Drawing on her background working with refugees and mentally challenged youth, Ana turns this part of the art class into an empowerment moment, borrowing from the all-women-are-beautiful sentiment of a Dove commercial. She tells her students that most children aged three to five will answer the question about singing in the affirmative. But a teenage girl of thirteen or fifteen will most likely say no. Somehow, women lose their sense of confidence and freedom as they get older, she explains. Heads nod in collective agreement and, I sense, wistfulness. The working lives of these women are so regimented that moments of spontaneity and joy become all too rare.

Once the photos are printed, Ana instructs the women to cut each in half to create a single face made of two different prints. Every pair is then asked to recreate the composite picture on a small canvas, using pencils and, once the outline of the face is clear, watercolours. Nothing that the women paint can possibly be wrong, Ana says, encouraging them to trust their feelings and inner creativity. This explains why her pencils have no erasers. The first stroke of the pencil is the truest—much like English romantic poets of the late eighteenth century believed that the first utterance of a poetic line is its purest rendition. The ultimate goal of this painting session quickly becomes clear: despite some physical differences, Filipinas and local Hong Kongers are one and the same. The illustration on the class's promotional poster on the We Care Facebook page emphasizes this point, literally—one half of it is painted in yellow hues and the other in brown. Sometimes, it does pay not to be subtle.

The simplicity of the message, however, should not distract from the complexity of life for most of the nearly 330,000 foreign domestic helpers in Hong Kong (about 5 percent of its population). According to Helpers for Domestic Helpers, an outreach program of St. John's Cathedral, in 2014 there were 171,145 Filipinos, 150,053 Indonesians and 7,843 in the other column, which includes Sri Lankans, Pakistanis and Indians ("other" not least because they're ethnically different from both local residents and the women who have held similar jobs for decades).

The segregation begins as soon as the women land at Hong Kong International Airport, where they are asked to join a separate immigration line for domestics. (When they leave

Hong Kong, they are also required to go through a different line, this time alongside foreign students.) Once they start working, they face monetary and social inequities. The current minimum monthly wage for a domestic worker is HK$4,110 (US$530). According to the advocacy group HK Helpers Campaign, when pro-rated to a forty-hour week, the pay falls short of Hong Kong's minimum wage by five dollars in local currency. And most helpers work seventy or eighty hours a week, on average. (The minimum wage increased to HK$32.50, or just over US$4, on May 1, 2015, in effect widening the income gap between foreign domestics and local workers.)

We Care differs from most NGOs and legal advocacy groups in its emphasis on the social lives of the women. The organization spends its energy and activist capital on making the workers feel less invisible and more accepted as women with rich, rewarding and creative inner lives. It leaves the legal and economic heavy lifting to others. Judging by the rapport between the women in the class this afternoon, Vicky and Melissa are on to something. The final paintings may not end up in one of the pricey galleries on the gentrified western edge of Hollywood Road—although some of them are vibrant and show talent—but the room is bursting with energy and laughter. That doesn't happen frequently enough, at least not from Monday to Saturday.

Mary Grace and Jacquisa, two helpers who've been paired up, speak fondly of We Care's role in their lives, saying the organization treats them as "normal people." The two women, both from the island province of Cebu, are cheating by painting each other, since they met three years earlier at a training centre in the Philippines before joining their separate employers in Hong Kong. They see each other on Sundays only. They both talk of getting "attitude" from their Chinese employers, but they rationalize their treatment with language that I've heard from many of their peers before: "We don't have the same beliefs or religion," says Jacquisa. "We don't know each other."

Margaret, by comparison, believes that her Hong Kong working conditions are a huge improvement on her previous job in Singapore, where 40 percent of domestic workers still don't get a full day off a week, despite a change in law that has made it mandatory. "I'm free here," she says. "Free to study and learn." She's taking computer lessons in her spare time. Her sister joined her recently to look after her employer's three-month-old baby. They share the same room and take different days off: the sister takes Saturdays, while Margaret, now in her third year in Hong Kong, prefers Sundays in order to take part in activities at the Bayanihan Centre, where she's a member of the bookworm club and the library team.

As I talk to the women in the class, admittedly interrupting their creative flow, I'm reminded of an observation attributed to postwar Swiss playwright and novelist Max Frisch. Commenting on Turkish migration to Germany in the 1950s, he's reported to have said, "We asked for workers; we got people." Nowhere does this intersection between workers and people—employees and human beings with feelings and desires and dreams—show more prominently in discussions of international labour migration than in the lives of female domestic workers. They must negotiate the boundaries between being dutiful, pliant workers and being (predominately young) women with more on their minds than cleaning their masters' toilets or picking up groceries from the supermarket. They play mother to children to whom they have no blood ties while their own biological sons and daughters grow up in the care of extended families at home. They take on roles normally associated with the wife in the gendered domestic economy: cooking, cleaning, picking up the kids from school. Go to any public or private school in the late afternoon and you'll see lines of Filipina and Indonesian workers waiting to walk their employers' children home. Sure, there's the odd Hong Kong native or Western expat picking up her own children, but you can count them on one hand.

And it's not just people that domestic workers serve. In the morning or late at night, you'll see them walking the family's dog, scooping poop or sprinkling water every time it pees. On Saturdays you can spot groups of them standing outside restaurants, minding the dogs while their employers grab brunch or afternoon drinks. It's hard not to witness that sight and wonder who's really being chained to the fence while the masters enjoy their meals. And through it all, they are expected to underplay or completely hide their identities as women, as mothers and as sexual beings. The Madonna-whore, saint-or-prostitute dichotomies cut deep into the lives of Filipinas in Hong Kong in particular, and much of that comes with racially charged and historically complicated undercurrents.

*

IMMIGRATION EXPERTS VIEW THE arrival of Filipina domestic workers in Hong Kong in the 1970s as the latest phase in the city's long history as a "destination of human circulation." In the late nineteenth century and throughout the twentieth, British, Japanese and mainland Chinese nationals have placed different political claims on Hong Kong. As a centre of international trade, with its location at the Pearl River Delta and the South China Sea, Hong Kong has attracted merchants from the West and the East, including Muslim and Jewish traders who arrived at its shores independently or as sub-agents of the British empire. This former British colony remains a global city and a tourist mecca to this day, almost two decades after the handover to

China and despite tensions between its youth and the mainland regime. Filipinos form the largest non-Chinese ethnic group in Hong Kong; in addition to the estimated 171,000 female domestics, there are men in various semi-skilled and skilled positions (gardening, catering and hotel services, for example).

In some ways, Filipinos have benefited from and been subjected to a particular brand of xenophobia that remains prevalent in Hong Kong, despite its global population. In the 1970s, Hong Kong opened its doors to Filipino workers just as it closed them to mainland migrants trying to escape Mao Zedong's Cultural Revolution. The same decade saw Hong Kong's economy transform from one based on male-dominated manufacturing industries to one based on services such as finance, design, technology—industries in which women participated and thrived.

This new development in the gender distribution of work, solidified in the 1980s and 1990s, created the two-income family, in which both parents worked full time while outsourcing household duties to imported labour. The pace of this outsourcing continues in today's Hong Kong, dubbed a society of working women by (conservative male) commentators. Statistics back them up. Women account for 53.5 percent of the current workforce, with that figure projected to reach 55.4 percent in 2026. In professional and managerial sectors, where staff members are more likely to work longer hours or have stressful jobs, the number of women has reached 40 percent, according to a 2013 study. When I mentioned my interest in domestic workers to a native Hong Kong financial adviser and mother of two, she told me that she took her annual holidays to coincide with her maid's—thus, in her own words, turning her responsibilities as a mother from a "vocation to a vacation." When her Filipina maid of more than a decade comes back from holiday, the mother returns to her office in an imposing tower near Admiralty in the central business district. Like many middle-class and English-speaking Chinese locals, this banker, who asked me not to reveal her name, has a preference for Filipinas over Indonesian or other South Asian women.

Proficiency with the English language, cleanliness, industriousness and pliability are among the usual reasons Hong Kong matriarchs cite for this ethnic preference. Historically speaking, however, Hong Kongers opted for Filipinas (particularly the Malay brown ones, as opposed to those of Chinese descent) because, write Vivienne Wee and Amy Sim, it was "easier to tell them apart." Workers from mainland China could easily disappear into the local population, where they could threaten stability and capitalist dominance by extolling the virtues of Communism. As I mentioned earlier, the Gulf countries used a similar strategy, giving priority to South and Southeast Asian workers over Arab nationals in order to segregate the ethnically different group more efficiently. In the case of Hong Kong, it was advantage brown. At least initially. Racial and skin-colour discrimination goes to the heart of negative attitudes toward Filipinos in Hong Kong.

Holly Allan, executive director of Helpers for Domestic Helpers (HDH), thinks that belief in the inferiority of darker-skinned workers and an ingrained sense of superiority among Hong Kongers underpin the dynamics she sees every day in her job. Allan tells me that many locals refer to Filipino workers as "locusts" because of their sheer numbers. She's worked on several cases involving domestics whose contracts were terminated because an employer believed that the woman looked darker than she seemed in her application photos. A dark-skinned domestic worker has the air of a cheap find or damaged goods sold at a discount—impressions that class-conscious employers do not wish to convey. To boss around a dark-skinned Indian or Sri Lankan woman makes for a hollow social victory.

Just before my meeting with Allan in the cramped church basement office of HDH—where one of the volunteers, a white American law student, at first assumed I was a worker with a problem (suggesting that, to some, all brown people look the same)—I witnessed one of her staff members helping a young Filipina with a complaint. She told the staffer that her employer, a night owl, often woke her up at two or three in the morning to do household tasks that could easily wait until the next day. The worker came to HDH to seek clarification on how many hours a day she's allowed to sleep. It all depends, she's told, on when she normally goes to bed. What followed was a comic but heartbreaking exchange where the staffer tried to determine what constituted a good night's sleep. If the worker went to bed early, around 8 or 9 p.m., and was woken up at 3 a.m., that would give her six to seven hours of sleep. Sounds reasonable on paper but wrongheaded by any other measure.

There's more to these cases than racism, Allan believes. "It's the materialistic culture of Hong Kong. The value people put on social standing. You're less of a person because you're poor." Allan, a Filipina with an MA in marketing who has lived in Hong Kong since 2000, when she joined her Australian husband, is more middle class than working poor, but her fourteen years with HDH has placed her in the centre of a struggle with pronounced class and ethnic dimensions. While HDH holds regular information and training sessions to make workers aware of their rights, the greater challenge lies in educating the general Hong Kong public about their responsibilities. The NGO relies heavily on volunteers and a large number of Chinese and expat corporate lawyers who provide pro bono services either out of a sense of religious or moral duty or as part of their firms' social responsibility mandate. International law firms and other corporations take the latter very seriously, and sometimes it's part of their licensing agreement with the Hong Kong government. Goldman Sachs, for example, sponsors a regular program where female workers take assertiveness training.

Allan is optimistic that, in time, attitudes among the Chinese population will change. She cites an increase in the number of local high school and university students who are currently completing academic projects on the subject. Like me, many of them ask to interview her. Shortly after our chat, she gave a presentation to sixteen students—most of them from the law school of Hong Kong University (a class on business law)—on the problems faced by domestic workers in the community and the many ways HDH helps. When I asked, only three students said their families had employed domestic workers while they were growing up. Almost all of them seemed genuinely surprised that discrimination on such a wide level took place, probably in their neighbours' or relatives' homes.

While racial and class prejudices apply to migrant labourers of various nationalities and both sexes, female domestic workers from the Philippines must also contend with their gender, which provokes ambiguous and sometimes hostile reactions from both men and women in Hong Kong. As their numbers swelled, debates about their moral character got louder.

To middle- and upper-class Hong Kongers, Filipina women conjure images of prostitution, a legacy of the country's history as an American military base. To this day, the red light district of Wan Chai parades sex workers from various European, Asian and African nations, including a large number of Filipinas (referred to as "little brown Eskimos" in George Adams's comedy *The Great Hong Kong Sex Novel*). Then and now, this association of Filipinas with the sex trade has cast them as a "moral threat" to the purity of the family. As evidence of a lapse in their ethical code and a sign of weak familial bonds, the Hong Kong media occasionally cite the fact that Filipinas leave behind their own children and families, especially their husbands, to look after their employers'.

Complicating the picture of domestic workers as providers of home service are comparisons between them and older (and now largely extinct) forms of family-based childcare in Hong Kong. The grandparents of current working families still recall being raised by *sohei* (sworn spinsters) or *mui tsai* (little sisters). The latter refers to young women sold by their poor parents to wealthy Chinese families as domestics, in arrangements that suggest both sex trafficking and child labour. These virginal and highly idealized examples of womanhood have cast a shadow on their successors, the caregiver and nanny from a more impoverished country and with a darker skin. The nature of domestic service invites workers to enter the private, intimate lives of the family, for which they get paid and are resented. They enter spaces generally considered off limits to strangers, such as the bedroom and bathroom. Even the simple act of washing clothes brings them in close contact with the lives (and private parts) of their employers. One domestic worker at Central's pedestrian bridge told me that she was often asked to hand-wash underwear smeared with menstrual blood or traces of the husband's semen. Another dreaded bathing her employer's aging father, who liked to stroke his penis, pretending to clean it, while she washed his hair. (To be fair, she cited that case more as an example of a funny occupational hazard than sexual harassment. Grandpa is almost ninety, and the worker is not sure he's aware she's a woman.)

As Kimberly A. Chang and Julian McAllister Groves suggest in their study of sex among domestic workers in Hong Kong, some workers distance themselves from the image of the Filipina as a sexual and morally ambiguous character by "embracing their identities as wives, mothers and daughters of migrant families." Filipino workers deny themselves any activities or accoutrements that may signal their material or sexual sides. They dress so conservatively they can be mistaken for Muslim women from Indonesia or Pakistan. They decorate their private spaces—they're not always separate rooms—at their employers' homes with mementos of their families in an attempt to reclaim their identities as devoted mothers, wives or daughters. Others build new attachments with their employers' families, unwittingly creating tensions and turf wars over children's (and sometimes husbands' or even wives') affections.

A recent study by a researcher in Singapore measuring the correlation between hiring domestic help and the well-being of Chinese couples in Hong Kong suggests that the effects are far from substantial. The rationale for hiring foreign workers includes improving family well-being and increasing leisure time between couples and among the family as a whole, but the study found that a full-time worker may actually "bring new conflict to families because sexual tensions or suspicions may arise."

While the above study focused on the employers, a substantial body of research—and advocacy work on the level of NGOs and international labour organizations—has put the spotlight on the psychological lives of female migrants as they juggle their identities as workers on one the hand and mothers, lovers or wives on the other. It's generally accepted that domestic workers must leave their own children at home, but their status as mothers becomes complicated when they get pregnant, by choice or accident, while working in Hong Kong. Most face contract termination, even though it is illegal. Some get desperate, choosing to abort the child or run away from their employers, becoming even more vulnerable to abuse and exploitation.

PathFinders, a Hong Kong NGO devoted to protecting migrant mothers and their children, estimates that there are about six thousand women in this subgroup. In its 2014 annual report, it says that 621 mothers and their children benefited from its support. Sixty-eight percent of those women were from Indonesia, 28 percent the Philippines and 4 percent other nations. The breakdown is very telling. Filipinas tend to be better educated about sexual and reproductive matters than their largely Muslim Indonesian counterparts. PathFinders CEO Kay McArdle—a former labour barrister who joined the organization in 2013, after almost sixteen years in high-profile legal firms in Hong Kong—believes that the large number of Indonesians served by her organization reflects their more recent migration history. They have fewer support systems and tend to be less educated than their Filipina counterparts. Despite the different religions, Kay says both groups have something in common: the concept of shame, which is not always defined by faith. "It's a common thread that repeats itself," she tells me in one of several conversations I had with her. "It has more to do with the patriarchal nature of their societies. They know they've done something wrong but don't articulate it in religious terms."

Less than a quarter of the mothers helped by PathFinders choose to go home, taking their children with them. In 2014, about 41 percent were in the process of getting their Hong Kong immigration status, while the remaining 36 percent already had a valid visa. Put together, the women's stories represent the clearest articulation of the workers-versus-people dichotomy in the global migration movement. With its focus on mothers and children, PathFinders stands out in the crowded field of NGOs trying to provide support for the domestic worker community. I wanted to find out more about how the largely volunteer, multinational staff works to ensure the safety and survival of the most vulnerable subgroup of workers in Hong Kong. It was both an eye-opener and a heartbreaker to follow this NGO closely over the course of a few weeks in the spring of 2015.

*

FRIDA IS A LUCKY baby. All of one month and eighteen days, she is about to get something that children born in Hong Kong to domestic workers long for: a birth certificate. It may take a few more weeks to secure, but it will give her access to all the health, educational and social services the government provides. When Frida gets sick, as all children do, her mother, Aesha, can take her to see a pediatrician without worrying about the cost of the consultation or the prescription. (I've changed the name of mother and child, at the request of PathFinders.)

You'll forgive Aesha for putting the price of a doctor's visit on top of her long list of things to worry about; she owes the Hong Kong public health system about HK$100,000 (US$13,000) for the delivery and postnatal services. For an Indonesian domestic worker who at best earns the equivalent of US$530 a month, that bill is about as large as the debt Spain owes the eurozone. Now that she's unemployed and nursing—a maternity leave without benefits or the prospect of a job to return to—the debt comes closer to that of Greece. But thirty-six-year-old Aesha does have a supportive Chinese husband, which puts her in a much better position than the many domestic workers who become pregnant or give birth out of wedlock. Although the two were already legally married when Frida was born, Aesha's residence status was (and remains) in limbo because she had left her job when her delivery date approached. The Hong Kong government rejected the husband's application to have Aesha declared his dependent because he didn't earn enough from his new job at a marine-themed tourist attraction. The verdict revoked Aesha's right of abode in Hong Kong, denying her access to the public health care system, ailing and inadequate as it is.

For now, both mother and child rely on the support and home visits of a PathFinders social worker and a volunteer nurse,

Christine and Cindy, respectively. Christine, a native speaker of Indonesia's Bahasa language, translates everything Aesha says for me and Cindy, an American who relocated to Hong Kong a year earlier when her husband accepted a job in the aviation sector. In just over a year of volunteering for PathFinders, Cindy has seen first-hand how the medical establishment discriminates against migrant mothers. "They are not afforded much respect," she told me before we met for this visit. I recalled an earlier conversation with Kay, who hinted at a certain resentment among women in Hong Kong—where fertility rates have declined for the past thirty years or so—toward domestic workers who seem too fecund, bringing more and more dark-skinned babies into their homeland.

Christine, Cindy and I are sitting in Aesha's room in one of those small Hong Kong apartments (this one is about four hundred square feet at best) that has been sliced into even smaller units or converted into shelters for migrant workers, refugee claimants and the city's most vulnerable. After a brief examination, Cindy expresses some minor concerns about Frida's neck, which tilts back involuntarily instead of staying flat. If this continues to be the case at next month's home visit, Cindy will take Frida to a doctor who has agreed to see PathFinders clients free of charge. (Cindy had just secured a pro bono arrangement with a family doctor to see up to five women or children a week.) Meanwhile, Christine talks to Aesha about the next steps in her legal battle with the government. If she can get her residency papers in order, then PathFinders will go to court on her behalf to ask for a retroactive waiving of her hospital bill. The fact that Aesha was married to a Hong Kong man at the time of birth makes her case reasonably strong.

While Cindy and Christine carry on with health and legal updates, I try to figure out something about Aesha's friend, who has sat through the home visit. How odd it seems to have a man in what is in essence temporary lodging for female domestic workers. At first I'd assumed he was the husband. But when I asked, his response came with a grin and a hint of frustration. "Husband? No, I'm not." Silence. Awkwardness. It takes me while to realize that the friend is another Indonesian woman from the small but fast-growing subculture of domestic tomboys—women who have adopted the butch lesbian look and have cast themselves as friends, protectors and sometimes sexual partners of other workers. Like everything in the culture of migrant domestic workers in Hong Kong, the tomboy tradition started within the Filipino community. Its Indonesian variation is a more recent phenomenon, and this tomboy, who asked not to be identified, fit the classic profile.

She (and I got the sense that "she" was her preferred pronoun) regards herself as the "landlady" of this three-bedroom apartment, which is home to ten other women, all of whom are in one form of trouble or another with Hong Kong immigration. Six sleep in one room—two per bunk bed and two on a floor mattress. Four share the other room, all on floor mattresses. No one was home when we arrived at four thirty in the afternoon, but two have finished working illegally in restaurants or cleaning services and are resting by the time Cindy and I leave shortly after six. (Christine stays behind to help Aesha with some paperwork.)

Aesha's room comes with its own private bathroom and an adjacent kitchenette that consists of a two-burner gas cooker. As Aesha and her friend note, this makes it the premium suite in the apartment. Its one window opens onto a smelly indoor courtyard, so it's kept shut at all times. Baby Frida doesn't get her own crib, as there is simply no room for one. She shares the bed with her parents—a practice Cindy doesn't recommend but accepts, since it's the cultural norm among the Indonesian community.

What I remember most clearly about this visit, even many months later, is Aesha's face. Despite all her problems, she maintained a big smile for her guests and kept looking so adoringly and proudly at her baby daughter. Though she's lived in Hong Kong since 1998, Aesha believes her current situation to be the first time she has felt loved, needed and looked after by so many people. If and when her residency papers are sorted and her hospital bill waived, she'll fulfill a lifelong dream: opening a small business to sell traditional Indonesian remedies to compatriots and local customers. Her husband can keep or quit his theme-park job, and all three will move out of the boarding house and into an apartment of their own (or at least with the in-laws). Lots of ifs and dreams here, but despite all that, Christine believes that Aesha's is one of the happier of the six hundred active or dormant-for-now cases in the PathFinders files. After talking to the organization's team of case managers and volunteers, I tend to agree.

In fact, Aesha has it easy. She doesn't have to give up her child for closed adoption, the standard in Hong Kong. In that arrangement, mothers exit the picture completely, never knowing where their sons or daughters are placed. On the morning I talk to Kristina, a PathFinders case manager, she tells me about an Indonesian woman who has until 1:15 that afternoon to sign papers that will take her son away from her for good. "She can change her mind up until 1:14 p.m.," Kristina tells me as she prepares to leave the office and accompany the mother to the adoption agency where the exchange will take place. Sign here. Take baby away there. At least until the child turns eighteen and actively seeks his biological mother. Unlike mothers who struggle with this decision and often change their minds, this one, I'm told, has been consistently clear about her child. She believes others can give him a better life than anything she can offer him now or in the future.

And at least baby Frida was born in a hospital. Stephanie, a Swiss national working for PathFinders, tells me the story of another Indonesian domestic worker who kept her pregnancy secret from her employers for almost nine months because "she didn't want to bother them." She had hoped to fly back to Indonesia and give birth there, but the baby decided to enter the world one day before her mother's flight home. When the contractions began, the mother retreated to her room, where she had sterilized scissors to cut off the umbilical cord and covered the bed with plastic to avoid staining the sheets with blood. The woman, who had worked as an assistant midwife in her village in Indonesia, then gave birth to her first child as quietly as was humanly possible. The only noise her employers may have heard was the sound of their two dogs barking outside the new mother's room. Perhaps the pets sensed that something or someone had entered the house.

The next day, the mother took the subway to the airport with the day-old daughter tucked in a sling and hidden behind a loose wool sweater. For some reason, she made it all the way to the departure gate without getting caught at airport security. She was found out only when the baby began to move and cry just as she and other passengers were about to board the flight. A member of the ground crew called the police, who arrested the mother on suspicion of child smuggling. Once DNA tests confirmed her maternity and the charges were dropped, the woman returned to her old job, her new child in tow. The employers, who had thought the worker was just gaining weight, turned out to be understanding and accommodating. A happy ending of sorts.

The workers and volunteers at PathFinders deal with such extreme cases on a daily basis. The NGO, which opened its doors in 2007, tries to provide medical, legal and social support for pregnant women, mothers and their children. When an employment contract is terminated or has expired, a domestic worker is given two weeks to find a new job or leave Hong Kong. While many non-pregnant women manage to switch employers within that short window, those with children (or visibly pregnant) find it harder to get work. Some overstay their visas and join a network of underground, off-the-books workers. The move traps them further in a cycle of abuse and financial despair. The labour system in Hong Kong is designed to run them out of town when they stop being workers and start living as women. Like other NGOs, PathFinders tries to assist its clients in practical ways while also advocating on their behalf with Hong Kong's legal and political leaders.

Kay, the organization's CEO, has a handy metaphor: the women and children helped by PathFinders are the bus, she tells me as she holds her iPhone in midair. But you can't expect the bus to stay safe or reach its destination if the road it travels on is full of potholes and roadblocks. Kay believes advocacy work (clearing the road) helps her better serve the needs of the mothers. The Hong Kong inland revenue department doesn't quite see it this way, however, and has been targeting PathFinders, along with a number of other NGOs, with audits or threats to withdraw its charitable status, making fundraising extremely difficult. This is all part of a larger crackdown on socially progressive organizations that the Protest Central movement has highlighted to the outside world. While the road has many bumps, one in particular enrages Kay, a mother of three boys: employers who terminate their workers' contracts and get away with it. "I wasn't fired when I got pregnant. Nor should these women [be]."

I've joined Kay, Yasmin and Jenny (the office manager and a volunteer law expert, respectively) in a morning "legal clinic." Once every two weeks, Jenny and several pro bono lawyers update Kay on the progress made (or hurdles faced) in various active PathFinders cases. The more complicated ones involve asking the state to become the legal guardian of children whose mothers have abandoned or neglected them. The general rule at PathFinders is to do what's in the best interests of the child, even if that sometimes conflicts with the mother's interests.

About forty-five minutes into the clinic, two women storm into the office, asking for a place to stay until 3 p.m., when they can relocate to a new shelter. One of them looks high and is acting erratically. Bruises on her face and a black eye suggest that she was either hit or involved in a fight with another domestic worker or a partner. A case manager for one of the women tells them where they can go until the new shelter admits them. Kay uses the incident as a teaching moment for Yasmin, on day four of the job. One of her tasks will be to ask women to wait before they can be connected with their case manager.

But to wait where? There's no reception area. Our meeting takes place in the front of the office, where staff members manoeuvre their way among boxes of donated baby clothes and toys, old newspapers from the Filipino and Indonesian communities in Hong Kong, and bundles of PathFinders fliers and booklets, including several on birth control methods. This makeshift reception area will get even more crowded later in the afternoon, when eight or nine mothers and their children are expected to drop by for one of the regular training workshops hosted by Carmin, the education program manager, on alternate Mondays and Thursdays.

In fact, Kay wraps up the legal clinic earlier than normal to allow the staff to prepare for today's workshop on the theme of positive and effective discipline. Carmin has given me permission to attend and to talk to the women present. An American social worker based in Hong Kong begins by asking each woman to list where, why and how she last disciplined her child. The women respond with standard answers. The wheres: the playground, home, the supermarket. The whys: hitting other kids or refusing to share toys with a sibling. The hows: a little smack on the back, a threat to take away the toys or a shout for the child to stop. Some may wish to add the PathFinders front room to the list of wheres. Despite the instructor's and the students' best attempts to stay focused, a small room crammed with ten children aged two months to five years is the ultimate test of effective discipline (or even anger management, the topic of a previous workshop).

Other staffers continue working within earshot of the screaming and crying children, seemingly unfazed by it all. For most of the children, this is their major outing of the week. Many of the women gathered here survive on social security, which consists of grocery delivery and an allowance of HK$50 (US$6) a week for incidentals, including transportation. Candy and toys for the children are luxuries. When I ask one of the mothers if her crying boy would like some chocolate, she looks at me as if I have just asked the dumbest question she has ever heard in her life. Of course he loves chocolate, but it's a rare occasion when he gets to eat a whole bar. She'll give him one half today and the other half tomorrow.

But the material disadvantages pale in comparison to the social isolation and stigma these women face from their own community. As Carmin tells me, Indonesians in Hong Kong and at home use the term "sin child" to describe anyone born out of wedlock. Some extended families in Asia's largest Muslim country refuse to look after sin children for religious reasons. The real reason, however, may well be that these boys and girls often have African or dark-skinned Indian or Pakistani fathers. You can see the variations in skin colour in the room: six of the ten children look more African than Indonesian. One has dark brown skin, inherited from his Indian father. Another is very light-skinned, suggesting a Syrian or Afghan father, and two look Chinese. Carmin says the darker the skin of the baby, the more ostracized the mother will become.

The ethnic mix doesn't come as a surprise to case managers, who know that their clients usually fall prey to and find comfort in a parallel community of male black and brown migrants and asylum seekers. They meet in the infamous Chungking Mansions in Kowloon, an international hostel and mini-mall, the nerve centre of African and Asian migrant life in Hong Kong. On Sundays, the men descend on Central to chat up women. Thousands of single women—or married ones with husbands they haven't seen in years—in one place and in a good, social mood. The only time I was ever hustled in Hong Kong was on a Sunday when two Pakistani men followed me as I tried to talk to the women. The men wanted to know if I would be interested in meeting some Filipino women for "private time."

It's no wonder that many domestic workers turn to religion for shelter from the cruelty of their employers and the opportunism of other brown and black migrants. St. John's Cathedral, with its large and largely Filipino congregation, is the more mainstream outlet for this religious need, but smaller prayer groups provide a more intimate space for faith and friendship. There's a battle for the bodies and souls of Filipina workers in Hong Kong.

*

ROSE, A DOMESTIC WORKER in her early forties, stands up in front of thirty of her peers and, in the parlance of the weekly spiritual gathering that is the Feast Hong Kong, takes part in the sharing moment. Brother Cruz has called on her to share her story with newcomers—and there are four, myself included, in the library room of the Bayanihan Centre this Sunday—and update regulars. For a year now, this Christian prayer group has been meeting at the centre on Sundays for a few hours of exchanging stories and affirmations. Last year, Rose was diagnosed with breast cancer—an illness she attributes in part to all the negativity in her past life as a domestic worker. Her doctors had given up on her and told her to prepare a will. But, Rose insists, her faith healed her. "Every morning when I wake up and start breathing, it's a blessing. I'm alive today," she tells the room, earning a round of applause and numerous amens. A fellow member of the group later tells me that Rose was "prayed over" by the sisters in the Feast, who in effect cured her.

A reluctant Amelia takes to the stand next, clutching the wireless microphone as if her life depends on it—and it may well be the case. Where Rose's story took on an inspirational, healing-by-faith feel (in line with the Feast's mantra of See Big, Feel Big, Speak Big), Amelia's elicits a sombre, tear-filled response. At first I can't follow her. She keeps complaining about a sister-in-law in Hong Kong who constantly puts her down. She says she was hospitalized and "almost died" three times. She doesn't go into causes, but I, like others in the room, immediately think a nervous breakdown at best and failed suicide attempts at worst. "Lord, what's your purpose in my life?" Amelia asks. "I want to sleep forever. Why do you want me to live?" Rhetorical questions all, since she has already figured out the answer: "He wants me to serve for him."

Amelia told me in a one-on-one chat after her sharing that she had lost most of her money to a philandering husband back in the Philippines who had taken on a new girlfriend and neglected their three daughters. The sister-in-law, a former domestic worker in Hong Kong who married a Chinese man and quit the business, called all the shots in Amelia's life, controlling even her relationship with her husband and children. Though Amelia and the husband had separated, he still looked after the children, and all four relied on Amelia's remittances to survive. The eldest daughter, seventeen, planned to go to university next year in Manila, and her tuition and living expenses were keeping Amelia working in Hong Kong, fighting for her physical and mental health.

Stories like Rose's and Amelia's don't make headlines in Chinese or Filipino newspapers. They don't have the requisite ingredients for an exposé on the abuse of workers by local employers or their exploitation by recruitment agencies. Neither complained about her current boss—Amelia described her Chinese employers as kind and gentle people—but both had experienced the physical and emotional setbacks that are common to women who leave their homes in search of a better life for their families (and to a lesser extent, themselves). Cancer recognizes no international borders. Neither does depression. There's no mechanism through which Amelia can seek therapy or even counselling. Most of the NGOs helping domestic workers in Hong Kong take on legal battles—contract violation, visa extensions, deportations, criminal charges—leaving the emotional and psychological needs to be addressed on an ad hoc basis, if at all.

This gap in the system explains why the Feast Hong Kong draws such a large number of Filipina workers to its weekly prayer meetings and sharing moments. At the heart of this Catholic fellowship and worship meeting group (founded by Filipino author, preacher and entrepreneur Bo Sanchez) is a one-to-one spiritual mentorship that allows each member to "make disciples of Jesus by loving one person at a time." The group's message follows an equally simple pattern: Love Someone Today, or LST.

To my secular mind, it's hard not to see something cult-like about the male-dominated group's targeting of domestic workers. Yit Barreda, a coordinator who invited me to the prayer meeting, insists that the Feast Hong Kong is open to everyone. Perhaps anticipating any suggestion of female exploitation, Yit reminds the group that all discipleship pairs must be of the same gender.

Men in need of a disciple can only be connected to pairs of other women, thereby eliminating any one-on-one sexual tension.

For the rest of this Sunday afternoon, I decide to put my doubts aside and take part in the prayer meeting. I'm encouraged by the positive messages Brother Cruz is showing in his PowerPoint presentation. Our God is a happy God and not a close-minded one, he tells his rapt audience at the beginning of the talk. (No one here calls it a sermon. Think more along the lines of those airport hotel self-improvement seminars that you see advertised in the back pages of free commuter papers.) The takeaway messages appear on screen in quick succession: "Dare to dream. It's free to dream." "If you want to be happy, don't follow your feelings. Let your feelings follow you." "You gotta faith it till you make it."

But one message stands out for me and also, I suspect, for many of the women in the room: "Tell a different story." Brother Cruz encourages the women to change their narrative of exploitation into one of empowerment through faith and community. Nobody denies or suppresses stories of eighteen-hour days, racial discrimination or verbal abuse, but the goal is to provide the women with one afternoon a week when they can rejoice in their faith and gain strength from one another. But as I find out when I speak to some of the women after the meeting, changing the narrative will require a lot more than a collective prayer. Singing along to R. Kelly's "I Believe I Can Fly" or Diana Ross's "If We Hold On Together" might bring temporary comfort, but what these women really need is a long-term resolution to their modern-day slavery.

Of the many women who shared their stories, Flor and Vilma left the biggest impact on me. They live their lives with a dignity that belies the constant emotional hurdles they face on and off the job. I promised to include their stories in this book because, I told them, their bravery and resilience need to be known outside Hong Kong and the Philippines.

*

IN 2012, FLOR'S nine-year-old daughter, the only girl in a family of five children, asked her mother for four hundred pesos (just under US$10) to pay for a school trip. To Flor, four hundred pesos was a lot of money. It was the cost of one large sack of rice for her business, a food stall in a working-class neighbourhood of Quiapo, part of the Metro Manila area. Not wanting to choose between pleasing her daughter and spending on the business, Flor made a third decision: "That was the time I told myself I need to get out." She decided to seek work as a domestic in Hong Kong. Although she entered the city on a tourist visa without any firm prospects, Flor lucked out and landed a job within a few weeks with a German family with three children. Her own five children she left with their father and her partner. (Flor, thirty-eight, is not married but has lived with her partner for more than fifteen years.) She describes him as a good man who has taken over the food stall, contributing to the household budget. Like many of her peers in Hong Kong, Flor is now the real breadwinner in her family.

For the self-described Tiger Mom, raising a family in absentia involves regular lessons in gender politics. She trained the four boys, who range in age from fourteen to seven, to do household chores, including cooking and cleaning. "I was afraid my daughter would end up as the boys' maid." The stocky, short-haired Flor, who struck me as butch but not enough to be a tomboy, has a soft spot for her one girl, with whom she Skypes daily on her mobile phone. Those video calls, however, do not replace the intimacy of family time or lessen the loneliness of the domestic worker. When it gets dark, Flor retires to her room, and the longing begins. "During the morning, you don't feel the loneliness. You're busy with the chores. But at night. . ." she trails off, but I get what she means.

Although she's been in Hong Kong for only three years, Flor has flown home every Christmas to be with her children. But living so far apart means missing out on all the other milestone moments in her children's lives. "Birthdays are big days for me. I always call and ask what they want for a present." As they get older, the children ask for gadgets that cost more than the clothes or shoes they once craved. It means saving even more of her disposable income and denying herself any small pleasure.

I ask how she feels about struggling to meet her children's needs while her employers' kids get anything they want and much more. "We don't have their toys and we can't afford to eat out like they do, but I'm paid to look after them and that's what I do," Flor responds, preferring not to compare her life with her boss's. Truth be told, the two women share the mothering of one set of kids. (Flor refers to her own as "children" and her boss's as "kids.") When the youngest of the German kids returned to Hong Kong after a Christmas break, she surprised everyone by running into Flor's arms and calling her "Mama." Flor insists that she has never sensed any resentment from her boss, who has given her permission to "discipline the kids as if they are mine." In fact, the employer is entrusting the life of her youngest child, born with severe thyroid problems, to Flor, who has to administer her daily thyroid supplements. Household harmony in this Hong Kong apartment hinges on Flor getting out of the picture when her bosses return from work. As she retreats to her room, around 8 p.m., the kids become someone else's children and responsibility.

On Sundays, Flor gets a whole day to be not a worker but a woman who hangs out with a group of friends and prays at the Feast. Ever since a friend first invited her to one of the meetings two years ago, Flor has been attending regularly. "They sustain me," she explains. "I feel lifted when I'm here." Flor says the group is nurturing her "longing for hope." One of these hopes is to go home and open a small computer shop, but that won't happen for a few more years. She needs to save more money. She'd also like to add to her skill set in order to increase her earning potential—perhaps study cooking or learn to drive and seek a more semi-skilled position, away from the world of domestic work. Until then, she has to deal with being separated from her children and living in a society that can be quite judgmental about Filipinas in general. "They look down at us. When you bump into a Chinese woman in the street by accident, she looks at you as if you threw acid on her." But perhaps nothing better illustrates the double standard in Hong Kong society than attitudes that equate the clothes or makeup that some Filipinas wear with a sexual invitation. "Hong Kong women wear short shorts and sleeveless dresses, but [Hong Kong men] don't judge them. Filipinas dress up and put on makeup one day a week. Why can't you let us have it?"

If Flor ever fulfills her dream of opening a computer shop in Manila, she should consider hiring Vilma, a college graduate in computer programming who started work as a domestic in 1995, not long after finishing her studies. Her first stint, looking after the elderly grandparents in an extended family, lasted five long and unhappy years. She was twenty and "didn't know much about life." While her employer, a brown Indian family with deep roots in Hong Kong, treated her with respect, her aunt, a domestic worker for a different branch of the same family, interfered in every aspect of Vilma's life. She criticized her decisions and called her names for dressing up or talking to other workers. "It was painful. I kept praying that one day my aunt will change." When her prayers weren't answered, Vilma packed her bags and returned to Manila in 2000.

The trip home was a gamble for twenty-six-year-old Vilma. Even if she found a job, she would earn half of her Hong Kong salary. As it happened (probably one of her prayers was finally answered), she landed a job in a Korean restaurant in a part of the city popular with tourists. Within a few months, she had taken over as floor manager and was trusted to close the restaurant at night and deposit any cash in the bank the next morning. Still, her salary and tips barely covered household expenses. Despite being the youngest of seven children, Vilma was the main breadwinner in her family.

The family's financial situation deteriorated in 2005, when the owner closed the restaurant and returned to Korea to retire. Unemployed again, Vilma tried to find work in retail or catering, but nothing came up. Her romantic prospects improved when she met a "lovely" factory worker and had two daughters with him in 2006 and 2007. To be single and struggling to feed and clothe older siblings is one thing, but to be the mother of two babies who rely on you for everything is something else entirely. Vilma knew the time had come to change course again. She decided to swallow her pride and return to the life of a domestic worker in order to give her daughters, Chynnie and Hannah, a better life. "I tried. I couldn't find a job [in Manila]. I want to raise them well. They are my life. My love is for them. My heart is for them. But how can you help your children when they are hungry?"

In 2008, before Chynnie's second birthday, Vilma returned to Hong Kong to work for the son of her first employer, the Indian family. Unfortunately, that didn't last long, as her boss relocated to the United Kingdom, leaving Vilma to take up her first job with a Chinese family. "It was different," she says with a mischievous smile, her first during our hour-long chat. The grandmother in the multi-generational household where she's still working can be very demanding. She often accuses Vilma of being "stupid" or "lazy," and humiliates her in front of other members of the household because her skin is darker than theirs. Yet Vilma is surprisingly understanding, blaming the grandmother's actions on old age. "It's a power thing. I can tolerate anything."

Vilma's day starts at six thirty in the morning and ends, at the earliest, around eight in the evening. She looks after three children, two boys and a girl. The eldest boy is nine and has taken to punching her in the arms, mostly in jest but at times in anger. While the parents seem supportive of her, they don't spend enough time at home to notice their son's actions or detect his abusive tone of voice when he orders Vilma to bring him water or a snack.

Like Flor, Vilma only has time to herself when she retires to her room for a few hours before falling asleep. This is when she checks in on her daughters, now nine and eight years old. Like the proud mama she is, Vilma describes Chynnie as a very talented, smart kid who is always at the top of her class. She has sent her daughters to a relatively expensive private school to ensure that they get a good start in life. The school fees for both girls come to about two months' salary. When you factor in regular remittances and personal expenses, Vilma has only enough left to pay for her transportation on Sundays to and from the Bayanihan Centre, where most activities are free or heavily subsided. (She volunteers to help with many activities in order to get in for free.) Vilma makes this sacrifice gladly because she is adamant that family history will not repeat itself: "I don't want [my children] to follow in my footsteps. I don't want them to become domestic workers." If that means being unable to kiss them, to hug them or to celebrate their birthdays, she says, so be it. It's for their ultimate greater good.

Until she can be reunited with her daughters—in a "few more years"—Vilma, like Flor and the other mothers in the room, will have to rely on Skype and the community that the Feast Hong Kong has provided for them. "It's what keeps me going. God has a plan for me. I will follow that plan."

CHAPTER 6

Sri Lanka: In the Shadow of the Philippines

Like any mother whose daughter is about to travel abroad alone for the first time, Nirosha looks worried. Will twenty-one-year-old Atab be safe or will she fall victim to scammers? Can she defend herself in case of a physical attack? And what country is the city of Turkistan in again? Atab is getting her papers to qualify as a domestic worker in a place that neither mother nor daughter knows anything about.

I'm standing outside the Colombo headquarters of the Sri Lanka Bureau of Foreign Employment (SLBFE), a government-created clearinghouse for new and repeat local workers seeking job opportunities almost anywhere in the world. I decided to visit the SLBFE a day ahead of an official appointment with a civil-service representative to get a sense of the place from the outside in. A local researcher told me to keep an eye on the hordes of people standing outside the building's walls and at its security checkpoint. "They're supplicants, not applicants." She meant it partly in jest, but it betrayed her frustration at her government's level of bureaucracy.

While seasoned cab drivers struggled to find some of the research centres I visited in Colombo, the two who drove me to the SLBFE in the Battaramulla district could have done it blindfolded. Everyone in Colombo knows how to get there if they want to get out. Sometimes they head there to complete their own paperwork; other times they're helping a relative—usually a son or daughter who can't afford to skip a day or two of work—with their overseas employment adventure.

Nirosha is no stranger to the building or the long waits outside it, having completed a seven-year stint as a caregiver for an elderly woman in Tel Aviv. She picked up most of her English there and saved enough money to take up part-time work in Colombo when her Israeli contract and employer expired. I do the math in my head and realize that Atab would have spent her teens without her mother, a fact that becomes more startling when I remember she's the family's only child. The mother-daughter reunion must have been brief; it's time for Atab to pay her dues and keep this small family afloat. "She needs to earn money. . . . As a mother, I'm worried and I will miss her." Nirosha says Atab has to learn how to become independent, and this is something you pick up not from a mother's advice but on the job, in real time. I ask if she'll consider taking up a caregiver gig in Turkistan or somewhere nearby so that at least the two can see each other more often. Nirosha smiles and suggests that she's too old for that kind of work now. She's in her early forties—a senior citizen in terms of domestic work, which is dominated by women in their twenties and thirties.

Lasantha, a sturdy man in his mid-twenties who is also waiting outside the SLBFE building, cites the chance to reconnect with family as one reason among several for his imminent departure for Saudi Arabia. His older brother, a machine operator on construction sites, has lived in the capital, Riyadh, for five years and has secured a contract for Lasantha. The younger brother has heard stories of workers' abuse and knows that conditions on construction sites can be, to put it mildly, unforgiving. But the promise of a paycheque of US$1,500 a month helps him rationalize the negative. Even if he could find the same kind of work in Sri Lanka, he'd be lucky to make US$500 a month. He demonstrates the difference in pay by joining three fingers and waving them in my face repeatedly. It's his way of making sure I get the point: triple, triple, triple. (The driver I retained for the afternoon thought Lasantha was about to hit me, such was the force of the young man's body language.)

Other workers milling outside the building share similar stories with me, though they are less animated than Lasantha. No, they say, reports of workers suffering physical and mental abuse or not getting paid don't scare them off. Family separation is a genuine concern, but so is being unable to feed your children and other dependents. (Dependents often show up in brown societies, where extended families live off a single income.) Yes, they wish the government would do more to protect its workers abroad, but the monetary rewards outweigh the physical or emotional risks. If the answers seem consistent, it's because the applicants have been rehearsing them on their own and with their family members.

I've heard variations of this before, of course, from Filipino people in Manila and several other nationals during a short visit to Dubai the previous year. Brown labour migration is hardship migration. It's less about thoughts of self-improvement or return on investment and more about an instinct to escape economic degradation and political chaos. But perhaps it's the extent of the hardship in Sri Lanka and the instability of its political situation that make its migration stories more shattering to hear.

The country has been on the wrong side of history more than once since independence from the British in 1948. The thirty-year separatist armed conflict between the Tamil rebels and the Sinhalese government ended in 2009, just after the global recession dragged down world economies. Even with six years (and counting) of relative stability and the worst of the economic slump behind it, Sri Lanka continues to send out, on average, 247,000 workers a year. (The country has a population of about twenty-one million.) In 2013, the total rose to just over 293,000. In the same year, remittances from migrant workers reached US $6.4 billion, or 9.5 percent of Sri Lanka's GDP. Remittances took the top spot in an analysis of Sri Lanka's foreign exchange earnings during the five-year period ending in 2013 (the peace years), consistently outranking tourism and exports like garments, tea and rubber. Current estimates put the number of Sri Lankan nationals working abroad at one million. Experts suggest that the number is actually higher, given how many are off the books.

In the Philippines, exporting local workers (and ensuring their protection) has evolved over many years into a regulated, if far from perfect, industry. Sri Lanka, by comparison, is struggling to find a balance between the economic windfall of sending labour abroad and the reputation damage that comes from workers being abused by employers and recruiters. People in East Asia and the Gulf think of Sri Lankans as the poor, distant and darker-skinned relatives of Filipinos. Death, imprisonment and execution of workers in the Gulf provide fodder for Sri Lanka's thriving newspapers and talking points for its nationalist politicians, who believe the government can do more to protect its people.

Most Sri Lankans I've met sigh at the mention of Rizana Nafeek. Like Flor Contemplacion, the Filipina maid who was convicted of a double murder and executed in Singapore, Nafeek has become a symbol of the violence that working Sri Lankans face abroad—and the inability of their government to protect them. In 2013, Saudi Arabia beheaded Nafeek, a domestic worker, after she confessed to smothering an infant in her care following an argument with his mother. Documents suggest that at the time of the incident in 2005, Nafeek was only seventeen, and many human rights organizations complained that trying her as an adult contravened the UN Convention on the Rights of the Child. She insisted that her confession was made under duress, but all appeals to King Abdullah for clemency from Nafeek's parents, and diplomatic efforts from the Sri Lankan government, failed. According to a BBC report, Sri Lankan opposition MP Ranjan Ramanayake captured the racial overtones of the execution and the widespread discrimination against workers of brown and black skin when he described the rulers of Saudi Arabia as dictators who would execute only Africans and Asians, and never people of European and American descent.

While the death of this domestic worker does reveal something about the brutal and colour-based justice system in Saudi Arabia, it also highlights the dilemmas that the Sri Lankan government faces every day as its people sign up for foreign employment—often without much training or thought given to what they might do at the end of their contract. So many people want a way out, and it's in the government's interest to keep shipping them out. But at what cost? When does the dignity of the brown domestic servant trump the dollar signs her government sees in her? Call it a battle between the greenback and brown survival. Are brown Sri Lankan workers destined to lose this one? Or are there signs that they're at least pushing back?

*

HISTORICALLY SPEAKING, SRI LANKA was always a land of migration. For much of the nineteenth century, when the country was under British rule, Sri Lanka hosted thousands of migrant workers on its tea and rubber plantations. The majority came from the Tamil community in India and were brought over to what was then Ceylon by colonial administrators. Following the country's independence in 1948, the new government barred these workers from obtaining citizenship. About 330,000 Tamils were repatriated to India over two decades starting in 1964, when the two countries signed an accord. You can argue that the country was built on the foundation of migration *to* it.

Migration *from* Sri Lanka for contract or long-term work began in the late 1970s, with 1977 and 1978 as transitional years. Nisha Arunatilake, Priyanka Jayawardena and Dushni Weerakoon, authors of the Sri Lanka chapter in editor Saman Kelegama's book *Migration, Remittances and Development in South Asia,* argue that government economic reforms relaxed the rules on the flow of foreign currency out of the country and in general made travel easier. This liberalization of Sri Lanka's monetary laws coincided with an insatiable demand for unskilled or low-skilled workers in the oil-rich countries of the Gulf. To date, almost 95 percent of migrant Sri Lankan workers end up in one of the countries in the Gulf Cooperation Council (Saudi Arabia, Kuwait, Bahrain, Qatar, the United Arab Emirates and Oman). Israel, Lebanon and Jordan also host a steadily rising number of Sri Lankan domestic workers.

From its earliest phases, Sri Lankan migration revolved around domestic workers, women with virtually no education and little training. For almost two decades (from 1988 to 2007), women consistently outnumbered men in the total number of migrants.

In 1995, women accounted for 73 percent of all Sri Lankan migrants. The number has trended down since 2007, with 2012 being the first year in the country's recent migration history when women's share fell below the halfway mark, to 49 percent. Broadly speaking, this reflects the increasing global demand for skilled (mostly male) workers in the construction, manufacturing and service industries. It also shows the effects of Nepalese, Thai and Indonesian domestic workers entering an already crowded marketplace, edging out the less educated Sri Lankan women.

Gender plays another part in the migration story of Sri Lanka. Spouses who are violent, have alcohol issues or have abdicated their financial responsibilities can be the impetus for women to leave their own families behind. Others travel to escape unhappy marriages, even if temporarily. About 90 percent of Sri Lankan migrant women find employment as domestic workers, increasing their chances of ill treatment. Labour laws that protect workers on, say, a construction site or in a factory don't apply to the home sphere, where women face challenges ranging from overwork and verbal abuse all the way to physical violence. The United Arab Emirates does not consider a household a workplace, and the people who hire domestic workers can't by law be called employers. The very idea of assigning home inspectors to check on the domestic workers' physical and mental well-being sounds preposterous to many Arab families.

Early Sri Lankan migrants struggled with the additional disadvantage of not speaking Arabic or English, making daily communication with the families for whom they worked difficult and frustrating for everyone. Only in the last decade or so did basic language training for would-be migrants become mandatory—at least for those using official channels of employment (as opposed to informal or unregulated recruitment agencies). Proficiency in English has given Filipina domestic workers a competitive edge over Sri Lankan women, and that in turn has led to a discrepancy in pay between the two, even when they're performing identical work. On average, a Sri Lankan domestic can expect to be paid about one-third less than her Filipina counterpart.

As economist Bilesha Weeraratne points out in her study of Sri Lankan domestic workers in the Middle East, many women fall victim to what is referred to as the "double contract" system—they sign one contract in Sri Lanka before departure but find another one waiting for them in their destination countries. The second contract often differs from the first, especially when it comes to benefits and working conditions. The low level of literacy among these women leaves them ill prepared to negotiate contracts written in legalese, and sometimes in Arabic. Weeraratne's study suggests that whether women find foreign employment on their own, through referrals or family connections, or through agents or sub-agents, they face the same chance of exposure to "violence, violent threats or having to work where there are potential health risks." The system fails Sri Lankan women almost by design, since expectations from official recruitment channels are set so low.

On average, 771 to 800 people leave the country daily, and the numbers are projected to rise in what some call a vicious circle: the more people migrate, the more follow in their footsteps. When would-be migrants learn of the salaries that can be earned abroad, they tune out the horror stories (or at least assume that their experience will be different).

"You can't stop migration," declares Myrtle Perera, vice chairperson of the Marga Institute Centre for Development Studies, when we meet in her Colombo office. "Dead bodies are being brought home daily." Located in a charming but hard-to-find corner of this busy city, the Marga Institute strikes me as more of a retreat than a think-tank that engages in Sri Lankan labour policies. The gentle facade of the soft-spoken, white-haired, guru-like Perera conceals her frustration and anger at the mistreatment of Sri Lankan workers abroad.

The best course of action that the Sri Lankan government can take through its various labour agencies is to reduce the harm and suffering of its workforce abroad, she says. It starts with better regulation of recruitment agencies and stronger oversight of sub-agents who draw from the rural areas, where education levels are low and desperation levels high. Sri Lankan women have to change their mindsets as well. Over the years, Perera has met many domestic workers about to board flights to the Gulf, and she says their appearance factors into their eventual mistreatment. I'm not sure I understand what she means by this. Is it their darker skin? The exposed parts of their bodies, which some Muslims may find offensive? No. "They go like slaves and beggars," Perera says, describing how rural women in particular dress for their flights. I suggest they don't have a huge wardrobe to choose from, but Perera believes many of them exaggerate the impoverished look to gain sympathy from future employers. Filipinas, she says, dress up for their flights so they will be taken seriously; Sri Lankans dress down, way down. "[Filipinas] are very well groomed. . . . Grooming has very strong connotations. They go to rich people houses. They are maids and not domestic workers."

Many Sri Lankan migrants end up living in a big city for the first time in their lives. Challenges begin on their first day on the job. Most of them, for example, have never seen or used an electric stove, a vacuum cleaner or a dishwasher. In the early years of Sri Lanka's labour migration, some women were transported from their mud homes in the countryside to high-rises in Jeddah or Kuwait City without any training in how to use modern appliances or basic lessons in food safety and fire protection. Many Sri Lankans remember hearing stories about domestic workers in the

Gulf who nearly burned down or flooded their employers' homes when using stoves or washing machines for the first time.

Even though migration transforms these women from economic pariahs into breadwinners, the centuries-old culture of the submissive female still travels with them. These gender norms and the country's class-based hierarchies also explain why many Sri Lankan women remain silent about verbal and physical abuse. Defending your rights can be a tall order for women who have been told all their lives that their role in society is to churn out children and obey their parents, husbands or social superiors. Employers in some Gulf countries routinely "lend" their domestics to other family members for cleaning or cooking duties, creating fifteen- or even eighteen-hour days, seven days a week. By the time someone blows the whistle, it can be too late. What Perera calls "jumping the wire" happens only when a woman begins to fear for her life. Then she will leave her employer's home to seek shelter in an agent's house or at the Sri Lankan embassy or consulate.

Only the better informed make it that far, however. Many domestic workers don't have a notion of the diplomatic service or grasp its role in protecting Sri Lankan citizens abroad. And once a woman gets to a safe house, her chances of satisfactorily resolving the conflict dwindle significantly. The best-case scenario is a new contract in another household; the worst is that the employer withholds the domestic worker's documents or files fake theft charges against her. According to Perera, some domestics even end up in prostitution rings run by criminal elements connected to the recruitment and employment agencies. Many are deported from their host country with nothing but the clothes on their backs and whatever cash they have hidden in their bosoms.

What happens to them when they return to Sri Lanka remains under-researched and under-reported. Local journalists have a morbid fascination with stories of hardships abroad, but they lose all interest in the workers once they come home. If I want to know more about this, Perera tells me, I should talk to Nisha Arunatilake, a fellow at the Institute of Policy Studies (IPS) of Sri Lanka. In 2014, she co-authored a seminal report titled *Returning Home: Experiences & Challenges*. With her PhD in economics from Duke University, Arunatilake represents the other extreme of Sri Lankan women in the workplace, but her academic research and personal interests lie in the area of migration and labour of vulnerable female and male workers. Within twenty-four hours, I found myself in her office at IPS's building in Colombo's Independence Square, but our conversation quickly went beyond the experiences of returnees. There can be no returnees without there first being outbound workers.

*

THE STORY OF THE returnees can be summed up as one with some good news and a lot of bad news. As Arunatilake and her co-authors argue, returnees bring home new skills and capital in the form of personal savings, which can be invested in their communities and add to local job growth. But there's a catch even to the good news. The perceived gains can take place only if the funds are "properly directed and integrated to the economy and the society of the home country." That's a big if. The report suggests that most returnees find social and economic reintegration into Sri Lankan society a challenge. On the economic front, many can't access or don't know how to make use of existing information on starting small businesses or investing life savings. On the social front, returnees face the hardships of weakened ties with family and community. Migrants who have left their hometowns for a decade or more find that social dynamics have shifted. Husbands have to adjust to the more independent wives who have emerged as the decision makers of the family in their absence. Similarly, female domestic workers whose employment has been free from abuse return home more independent and less beholden to gender norms that give men the run of the family home.

Although the report suggests that both skilled and unskilled workers experience reintegration problems, the latter group poses the greatest challenge to Sri Lanka's migration culture in general. "The least skilled get into the most problems," says Arunatilake. In part this reflects the very reasons they chose to work abroad in the first place—out of desperation and not in pursuit of career enhancement or a shot at social mobility. "They are trying to escape difficult situations, from unhappy marriages to abusive partners. Sometimes the job opportunities in rural areas are not that great." Commuting to and from work, especially for women in rural communities, can be both unsafe and time-consuming because the public transportation network, such as it is, doesn't cover all regions. Many women find it easier to go abroad and live in their employers' homes than to commute from villages to nearby towns. To escape, many poorly educated men and women fall victim to ruthless recruiters who charge them upfront, forcing the migrants to borrow money to cover costs. Many get into debt before they even leave home and must direct earnings from their first years of foreign employment toward paying it off.

If there's a silver lining to this narrative of desperation, it's been the shift over the past few years to a more demand-driven model, Arunatilake says. As the East Asian and Gulf economies have rebounded from the global recession, the need for migrant workers in the construction and domestic-service industries has returned to pre-2008 levels. The more competition for brown workers, the more employers are willing to pay agents to find them, thereby absolving migrants from recruiting fees.

It didn't take long for me to meet a returnee—and one who sounded like the model of reintegration and business savvy that researchers like Arunatilake would love to see more of. Arun, an independent car driver, worked for seven years as a supervisor in a textile factory in Amman, Jordan, before returning to Colombo to start his own small business. I don't normally chat up or rely on taxi drivers as sources in reporting—but it's impossible to avoid that scenario in Colombo. Almost every hotel or private car driver I met in the city was either a migrant at one point or in the process of becoming one. Upon seeing my brown face and Arabic features, some assumed that I was in Sri Lanka to recruit workers for the Gulf countries. Those who have spent time abroad are usually looking for their second opportunity, driving cars until such time as a job offer comes their way. Arun bucked that trend, however, and Colombo's gridlocked streets, even in the relatively early afternoon, gave me some time to hear his story.

A Colombo native, Arun left his family and friends behind in 2004 for his first real work experience. Unlike the majority of even skilled workers, he had completed his high school education by that point and showed a knack for the English language. Through a local employment agency recommended by the SLBFE, he landed a job in an Amman textile factory that already employed migrant workers from other parts of South Asia. It didn't take long for managers at the factory to pull him from the ranks of floor workers and promote him to supervisor. The outgoing Arun struck me as someone who would do and say the right things to set himself apart from the masses. Our conversation was interrupted by his regular criticism of almost every other driver we encountered. ("No one knows how to drive here" seemed to be his mantra.)

The promotion in Amman meant that Arun had to become more ruthless and demand a high level of productivity from an overworked labour force, but it also led to the kind of financial windfall that no young man without a post-secondary education—from a lower-middle-class family at least—could turn down.

Ultimately, his conscience won. After about six years in the taskmaster role and with a few thousand American dollars saved—Arun estimated his salary at about US$1,000 a month for most of his time in Amman—he decided to terminate his contract and return to Colombo. Early business schemes went nowhere, but his luck changed once he started running his own private car service. His Indian-made Tata Motors vehicle now doubles as his office and his major investment.

Arun tells me that he puts the time-management skills he learned in Amman to good use in his own business and entertains no thoughts of working abroad again, especially now that the country's civil conflict is over. What if he's offered a better-paid contract in the Gulf or Southeast Asia, where he can make double what he did in Jordan and probably four or five times his earnings in Colombo? His answer remains a firm no. Having seen and read how Sri Lankan workers are treated in many such places, he doesn't intend to join the ranks of the abused and helpless.

No doubt there are many Aruns—people who turn their migration experience into success back home. But reports suggest that he's in a small group of returnees. In her study, which draws on a purposeful sampling of 1,981 returnees, Arunatilake writes that only 47 percent find employment at home. Among skilled workers, only 28 percent report any kind of improvement in the family's economic situation after they return. Institutional programs to help returnees have reached only about 10 percent of the sample demographic in the study. Once again, experts look to the Philippines as a model of smart labour management, before, during and after migration. Reintegration education for Filipinos begins before a migrant even leaves his or her home, Arunatilake says. Workers and their families are encouraged to draw up a list of goals to be achieved during the migrant's absence. The returnees' economic needs do not overshadow their psychological ones; they're offered services such as family counselling and stress debriefing. Representatives from the Philippines Overseas Employment Administration regularly visit workplaces with a high concentration of Filipinos to advise them of business or investment opportunities back home.

Neither Perera nor Arunatilake will go as far as saying that the darker brown skin of Sri Lankan migrant workers and the lighter skin of Filipinos explain the harsher treatment meted out to the former and the relatively softer one to the latter. But both researchers suspect colour is an element in a more complex process, with training, education, government oversight (or lack of all three) and personal choices determining the path each country has followed in labour migration. The more Sri Lanka prepares its migrant workers for what awaits them in the world, the less likely they'll come home penniless or in body bags.

So it all comes down to the training, or what is commonly referred to as the National Vocational Qualification, a seven-level program that all migrants are required to take. The minimum level for a work licence abroad is three (housekeeping), while seven qualifies graduates to work in more skilled positions (hotel clerks, drivers, carpenters, factory supervisors, etc.). I wanted to know more about this program and others like it, so I arranged to talk to one of its architects at the SLBFE. This would give me a chance to get past the security check of this fabled building—fabled among Sri Lankan migrants, that is—which either facilitates or impedes a national dream to work abroad.

*

IF THERE'S A PUBLIC face to Sri Lanka's migrant policies, it's Mangala Randeniya. The deputy general manager for the Sri Lanka Bureau of Foreign Employment appears in almost every media story about migrant opportunities or strife abroad. Writing about the dangers of illegal migration by workers who enter host countries on a visitor's visa? Randeniya will offer some harsh words to his sneaky countrymen and -women. Need a response to the accidental deaths or murders of Sri Lankan workers in the Gulf, conservatively estimated at three hundred annually? Count on Randeniya to provide a breakdown in which death by natural causes accounts for 69 percent of fatalities, traffic accidents 27 percent and suicide a mere 6 percent. When reporters want to know why the number of female domestic workers has been going down year after year, Randeniya tells them it's all part of the SLBFE general plan to discourage women from this risky line of work. Randeniya has emerged as the go-to man for Sri Lankan migration, and I have one hour on a Friday morning to get into his head.

But first I have to get to his office. The interior of the SLBFE looks more like a maze than a standard government building. Work seekers have to navigate pathways and halls that divide the different departments within the bureau: training, legal, document certification, etc. Branches of the National Savings Bank and the Bank of Ceylon can be found on the ground floor, alongside Internet and photocopying services. Many workers in their twenties and early thirties will open their first bank accounts here to facilitate the repayment of loans or to send back remittances. The place echoes with the din of men and women arguing with bureaucrats behind glassed walls. No employees are in sight in the hallways.

I know that Randeniya's office is on the second floor, but which part of it? After I interrupt a young man's telephone conversation with a plea for help, he walks me to where I can find Randeniya. I'm already ten minutes late, but I'm told not to worry because he hasn't finished his morning meeting yet. There's nothing for me to do but wait and watch while four or five rows of public employees go through paperwork in a choreographed scene that looks straight out of a gritty Indian or Egyptian movie about the soul-crushing nature of bureaucracy (or a *Modern Times* set in an office instead of on an assembly line). It's a familiar scene in brown countries, where the public sector has to absorb the many graduates promised a job at the end of their university education.

At twenty minutes after eleven, the employee seated closest to Randeniya's office tells me to knock and walk in. I hesitate but take her advice. It works. As soon I remind him of our appointment, Randeniya dismisses his two co-workers and we start our conversation.

"What do you want to know?" he asks me, indicating that he can provide answers to *any* question I may have about migrant workers. A good place to start, I suggest, is with an overview of migration reforms. When did Sri Lanka begin to regulate its people's employment abroad, in particular in the Gulf, and what prompted the move? Randeniya says that if he has to pick a single turning point, it would be 1985, when Parliament passed the Sri Lanka Bureau of Foreign Employment Act. Between 1977, when large-scale labour migration began, and 1985, when the act came into effect, there was no government oversight, he says. After 1985, "you couldn't send a single person abroad without licence of the SLBFE." I pretend to know nothing about unofficial migration channels and just let him talk. With his encyclopedic knowledge of the country's migration history (and his six-foot-two body), I'm not exactly a match.

The first order of business, Randeniya explains, was to regulate the recruitment agencies, which, as the gateway to foreign employment, could make or break a migrant's job search. A shoddy agency meant trouble for workers and hassle for the government, which was expected to rescue them. The SLBFE stipulated that all agencies had to own or rent offices of at least five hundred square feet; they were also required to deposit up to a million Sri Lankan rupees (just under US$7,000 at current exchange rates) as a guarantee before they were issued a licence. For the first time, a criminal record check became mandatory, effectively sidelining a number of agencies that had served as fronts for money laundering or organized crime, especially human trafficking.

Although the SLBFE Act addressed some of the challenges of preparing migrants for work abroad, its provisions were largely ignored by recruiters and government officials alike. It wasn't until 1995 that Randeniya, then a newbie at the SLBFE, and some of his colleagues initiated a few training programs to address complaints from employers in the Gulf about the poor quality of domestic workers from Sri Lanka. In 1995, the first training program became mandatory for female domestic workers who wanted to work abroad. It was an intensive five-day session that introduced applicants to the basics of cleaning houses, washing clothes in a machine, and handling gas and electric cookers. In 2000, the training was extended to ten days, then thirteen, then fifteen. Today, would-be migrants must complete a required twenty-one-day housekeeping program (level three of the NVQ, as mentioned earlier).

"I want to modify the housekeeper role," says Randeniya, hinting at some shortcomings in the current program. His plan goes beyond the minutiae of which detergents and what temperature to use for white versus coloured clothing. "It should end with skilled, competent and empowered women." Once he mentions the word "empowered," the rest of our conversation revolves around its meaning to female domestic workers. Although Randeniya's media training leads him to underplay the stories of physical and emotional abuse suffered by Sri Lankan domestics in the Gulf (he can't criticize host countries too loudly or they'll look elsewhere for workers), he claims the real problem is that his own country sends out workers who simply don't know how to negotiate with their employers or how to ask for what's legally theirs. Get that part of the training right, he says, and watch the number of problems slide down. "If a person is very skilled and empowered, you can prevent what may happen to [her]."

But how exactly do you empower women in their mid-twenties—the new minimum age for domestic workers abroad in general is twenty-three, and for those travelling to Saudi Arabia it's twenty-five—who have been taught their whole lives to cede that power to men or other women in higher social positions? Randeniya acknowledges that a "certain maturing" has to take place before women are ready to face the challenges of work abroad. In his capacity as a supervisor of trainers, he knows that these women's very lives may depend on how well they absorb the lessons in the twenty-one-day training. For some women, this will be their first time in a classroom since elementary school (if they got even that far with their education). For others, even those with a higher level of education, the content can be too racy. Part of being empowered as a woman (and the rules apply to men, too, Randeniya insists) is confronting issues related to desire, sexual advances and rape, in that order.

First comes desire, or in more informal terms, feeling horny. "The worker has to satisfy sexual desire with or without his or her partner," says Randeniya. How does she satisfy her desire in societies where engaging in sex outside marriage is a crime? Randeniya tells the women that the answer is masturbation, or "self-satisfaction." If that doesn't address their sexual needs and intercourse becomes inevitable, women must be aware of the risks of STDs, including HIV. The class includes information on birth control methods, with an emphasis on condoms whenever the pill is not an option for cultural or medical reasons.

If and when men push domestic workers to have sex with them, women must change the dynamic so they don't find themselves in a vulnerable position. Again, Randeniya uses the word "empowerment." A woman who is the object of a man's advances needs to know she is in the driver's seat. I'm not sure I agree with this assertion, given that men (who can be recruiters, employers or other Sri Lankan workers) often hold the balance of power in a relationship. Randeniya believes my concerns apply only to the third stage of sexual interaction: harassment and rape.

Female workers, he asserts, "need to understand the rapist's mentality." If I understand him correctly, Randeniya is saying that the responsibility for avoiding rape falls largely on women's shoulders. Women should not allow themselves to be in situations where a rape might happen—for example, they should not be alone with a man (or men) in remote or unattended areas. To my feminism-tuned ears, this sounds very much like victim blaming. But I realize it has to be seen in the context of a nascent conversation between migration officials and domestic workers about self-protection and, yes, empowerment. While the SLBFE can try to exert some influence on male workers—teaching them not to rape or attack their countrywomen—it has no jurisdiction over Gulf or East Asian employers. Many host nations simply deny that such things happen within their borders and accuse Sri Lankan women of falsifying accounts. Placing the responsibility on women makes *some* sense in this context.

Once again, the Philippines pushes its way into the conversation as the model to which Sri Lankan officials aspire. If a Filipina was solicited for sex, Randeniya believes, she'd probably demand to be compensated for it. Those women know how to negotiate extra pay for any work above and beyond the specifics of their contract, he says. "Sri Lankan women are not at that stage yet." Filipinas also take advantage of their relatively light skin colour, which makes them both more desirable and more empowered.

Like Perera and Arunatilake, Randeniya believes skin tone is part of a larger package that influences how Sri Lankan workers in general are perceived outside the country. "Skin colour is first impression," he offers, suggesting that in some parts of the world, it places Sri Lankans at an instant disadvantage. But a person's body and face determine what happens next. Facial expressions that show disrespect or body language that signals a defiant or unprofessional attitude can be detrimental. It's not that Sri Lankan women are raised to be arrogant or inconsiderate, Randeniya explains; it's just that they don't understand how others read their body language. "Sri Lankans are socialized in a different manner," he says, adding that misunderstandings or even animosities arise from time to time among the country's different ethnic groups. That includes discrimination by lighter-skinned urban Sri Lankan women against workers from more rural areas, who tend to be darker from prolonged exposure to the sun. In his days as a trainer, Randeniya encountered several examples of women from different levels of society accusing each other of harassment and discrimination based on skin tone or geographic origin.

It's almost twelve thirty and my time is up. Given how generous Randeniya has been with me, I push to see if he'll let me sit in on one of the training sessions of the NQV program. As it happens, the centre near his home offers Saturday classes. He agrees to take me there to show me what his trainers do. Language will be a problem, since the trainers use Sinhalese—in Manila, all training was in English—but he'll show me where the instructors teach would-be migrants basic words in the host country's language (Arabic, Hebrew, English and even Greek and Italian). I wonder if Atab, Nirosha's daughter, received some training in Kazakh or Russian before leaving for Turkistan. I make a mental note to ask the next day. "Call me early in the morning and we'll make arrangements. Maybe you can come to my house, too," he offers. I'll be in touch around nine in the morning tomorrow, I assure him.

On the way out I notice that the large crowd waiting outside when I came in has thinned out. I recognize at least two faces from the day before, when I lurked outside the SLBFE. They're still supplicating, I guess. Lasantha, the Saudi Arabia–bound construction worker who likes big hand gestures, sees me coming out of the building and asks if I have any connections on the inside. He's been here almost every day this week. Because he has secured his contract privately, the SLBFE wants him to jump through more hoops than those using government-approved agencies. At least the bureaucracy is intended to protect him, I tell him, and I wish him good luck. He nods, telling me that he expects to wait outside the building for most of the following week as well. I wonder if he'll eventually become an Arun, a returnee success story, of if he'll be one of the three hundred Sri Lankans who come home in body bags every year.

*

ONE MINUTE AFTER NINE on Saturday morning, I try Randeniya's cellphone. He doesn't pick up and no voicemail kicks in. I wait fifteen minutes and try again. Same thing. I try every twenty minutes and send an email in case it's easier for him to respond with a quick note on his smartphone. Nothing. At around noon, I finally get through to his voicemail and leave him a message to call me back or email me. Still nothing. It's my last full day in Colombo and I suspect I probably won't get another chance to visit a training centre. I'm disappointed, but I know that my exploration of the lives of Sri Lankan migrant workers will resume in a few weeks, when I visit Doha, Qatar, home to an estimated 150,000 of them (in 2013). For now, I leave Sri Lanka knowing that despite a late start and an abundance of trouble-prone unskilled workers, the country is finally taking steps to rewrite its migration narrative of exploitation and abuse. There's still a long way to go. And it can always keep looking to the Philippines for policies to borrow or steal. Sri Lanka may not be able to compete in the skin-tone department—fair is fair, so to speak—but it can divert attention from that by focusing on what the rest of its workers' bodies and minds can do.

CHAPTER 7

Qatar: Between Men

In the spring of 2015, Qatar, one of the richest nations in the world, faced a public relations blunder that no wads of cash or teams of spin doctors could fix. It became fodder for human rights groups and international labour organizations that for years have been closely watching and criticizing the Gulf State for its treatment of migrant workers, particularly in the construction industry. The criticism had only intensified since December 2010, when the international soccer federation, FIFA, awarded Qatar the right to host the 2022 World Cup. Fittingly, the March 27 "incident" involved a sporting event that, according to its official website, had been designed to show the country as an "outward-looking state" that encouraged "the non-discrimination attitude among the nations." (The site has since been shut down.)

If achieving the exact opposite of what you set out to do were a sport, then the folks behind the Qatar Mega Marathon 2015 would get the gold medal. The event organizers planned to shatter the existing Guinness World Record for a marathon. With over 50,000 individuals taking part, the Qatar Mega Marathon (or half marathon, as it eventually turned out to be) would easily beat the current record of 50,173 participants (of which just under 37,000 actually finished), set in the United Kingdom in 2000.

But when it looked like the number of runners would fall well short of the target, organizers decided to bus in construction workers from Doha's Industrial Area, home to thousands of the country's estimated 1.2 million migrants. The half marathon started at two in the afternoon, when the desert sun was at its most punishing, and took place on a Friday, the men's only day off. Workers, who didn't receive any training or warning, were seen running in jeans and flip-flops, or even, according to *Doha News*, barefoot. The more digitally connected among them took to the event's Facebook page to complain about, among other things, safety issues: Doha traffic police reopened lanes to some vehicles while a number of runners were still trying to complete the race. The police also made it difficult for volunteers to hand out bottles of water to dehydrated runners.

Although representatives from the marathon issued an apology, declaring they were not "100 per cent pleased with how the event went," the damage had been done. International media swooped in. *The Daily Beast* headlined its coverage "Slaves Forced to Run Marathon Shoeless in Qatar." The UK's *Daily Telegraph* opted for a more muted assessment in its headline: "Asian Labourers 'Press-Ganged' into Joining Qatar Marathon Record Attempt." For human rights watchers, the marathon fiasco, typical of Qatar's penchant for attempting world records, simply confirmed the stinging opening comment in a 2014 report by the International Trade Union Confederation (ITUC): "Qatar is a country without conscience." If current patterns continue, the ITUC believes four thousand workers will die before the opening ceremony of the World Cup.

I couldn't help feeling sorry for Qatar. As a Canadian of Arab origin, I've always held some admiration for Qatar and the United Arab Emirates as both prepare their economies for a post–fossil fuel world and rebrand themselves as global centres of travel, finance and entertainment. In general terms, both countries have disrupted well-established models for aviation and hospitality, among other sectors. In Qatar, the oil-and-gas industry still accounts for 62 percent of revenues, but investments in the financial and construction sectors stand at just over 50 percent of nominal GDP. Both countries represent a departure from the narrative of sectarian and political violence that plagues many of their neighbours, including my birthplace of Yemen. As a journalist, I also respect Qatar's investment in the Al Jazeera news network, which, despite its biases, remains one of the more reliable sources of information in a region where you can draw a direct line between news media and the state. But the more I looked into reports of Qatar's treatment of migrant labour, particularly in the construction sector, the more that admiration waned.

It's hard to respect a country where, on average, one migrant worker a day dies building its office towers, stadiums, roads or transport hubs (subway or airport). Both Amnesty International and Human Rights Watch have been reporting on Qatar's failure to improve the lives of its labour force for so many years now that it's become standard to refer to the situation there as the new slavery. Since 2013, world trade organizations, the European Union and the UN have focused on the *kafala*, the sponsorship system that ties workers to their employers and prevents them from seeking other opportunities or even leaving the country without an exit permit. It robs workers of choice, dignity and freedom.

Because of the 2022 FIFA World Cup—already mired in allegations of bribery and corruption—the world media are looking more closely than ever before at this small Gulf State. Whatever building boom Qatar experienced in the decades before 2010 pales in comparison with what's to come. Analysts estimate that the country will spend about US$139 billion, or 10 percent of its GDP, on World Cup–related projects and infrastructure. The construction sector alone is set to increase twentyfold, from US$5 billion to US$100 billion, according to one report. All this is to take place within a culture that gives employers control over every aspect of their workers' lives—from how much they get paid to how many hours they work to where they live to when and if they can leave the country. And although Qatar's laws include several provisions to protect workers, implementation and oversight remain spotty at best. In April 2015, the ministry of labour doubled the number of state inspectors to three hundred—an apparent breakthrough until you realize that those three hundred have to inspect the building sites and living quarters of more than a million workers.

What's going on in Qatar? How can a country ranked third in the world in per capita wealth be so cavalier about the lives of guest workers and so oblivious to the damage to its reputation as a moderate, "outward-looking" state? Is this a case of unfettered capitalism relying on the exploitation of human capital to survive? Or is it a reflection of the country's ancient tribal roots, in which slavery was normalized?

How can a native brown population be so uncaring about the lives of so many fellow brown people? Are the reports of death and abuse exaggerated by a Western media uncomfortable with the idea of a dominant Arab state—or as the marathon organizers described it, "a campaign waged by the sector of envious haters"—or do they represent the reality on the ground?

I had no choice but to visit Doha, spend some time among its workers and experience for myself what it's like to be a brown worker in a brown country. I had questions that only these men could answer. Having seen Sri Lankan migrants wait and wait outside government offices for clearance to work in the Gulf, I was also curious to explore this end of the migration cycle. Now that they'd reached their destination, did these men view the journey as worth the planning, the expense, the separation from family and homeland? Did money really dull the pain of homesickness, as one worker in Colombo put it to me?

*

WALK DOWN AL-ATTIYAH Street in Doha and you will be forgiven for assuming you've entered a homoerotic dreamland. Thousands of swarthy, muscular and mostly young men are standing outside stores, restaurants, barbershops and banks. Everywhere you look, groups of four to six men horse around, being tactile, jovial and intimate with one another. The odd worker walks around shirtless, which is a natural response to the thirty-seven-degree heat on this Friday afternoon in April, but also reflects the gender balance in this area. There are no women anywhere to be seen. For miles and miles. (My mind goes to an episode of the sitcom *Will & Grace*, in which Jack, the sidekick character, develops a show for a gay TV network about a town where all the women have disappeared.) Al-Attiyah, which intersects with fifty-four other streets, forms part of a large men-only complex of factories, workshops and residences known as the Industrial Area.

Ground zero of Qatar's infrastructure and construction boom, the Industrial Area hosts tens of thousands of its 1.2 million migrant workers. Physically and metaphorically, it's so far removed from the Doha of West Bay, the city's commercial and luxury centre, that it might as well be another country. And in so many ways, it is. Several other countries. The only rarer sight than a woman is a Qatari national, virtually an endangered species at 6 percent. The

Industrial Area belongs to foreign workers from India, Sri Lanka, Nepal, Pakistan, Bangladesh, the Philippines, Egypt, Sudan, sub-Saharan Africa and mainland China.

The majority of the men here work in the construction sector, where exposure to sun and heat has been linked to fatal heart attacks and strokes. Not everyone identifies as a labourer, but almost everyone works in the construction industry, as carpenters, masons, plumbers, electricians, site supervisors, night guards, etc. Unlike the more middle-class parts of Qatar, the Industrial Area is full of unpaved roads, making for a rugged terrain in a land of predominately flat desert. And judging by the traffic jams and the chaos on Fridays, little thought has gone into its planning. The Industrial Area feels more like the less developed parts of a Third World country—the kind of world most of these migrants left behind—than the opulent Doha, home of the seven-star hotels and the national airline. In fact, the area reminded me of Yemen, the poorest country in the Arab world, and in particular its capital, Sana'a, home to my immediate family—the low-rise buildings, the overstuffed stores and the persistent merchants inviting you to buy something, anything. This may explain why I felt at ease walking up and down the streets of the Industrial Area. I did get the odd stare, which I put down to the fact that I was wearing sunglasses—another rare sight here, despite the blazing sun—or to my general effeteness, which contrasted with the muscular vibe giving me those initial homoerotic sensations. But by and large, I was just another brown face—a fact underscored when more than one South Asian worker expected me to be familiar with either Hindi or Urdu. (I expected them to speak Arabic, but they didn't.) On one level I felt at home here with my fellow brown people, but on another I couldn't be further away from it, and them.

The Qatari government may have designed the Industrial Area as a place to keep the workers out of sight and out of mind, but over the years a subculture of restaurants, retail outlets (lots of luggage shops—everyone here is transient, on the move) and private transportation networks of minibuses and communal taxis has grown. Many workers stay in their dormitory-style residences on Fridays and sleep off their sixty- or seventy-hour workweek. Some take on overtime weekend shifts, either because they have no choice or, as Mohamed, a twenty-five-year-old Bangladeshi electrician told me, because there's nothing else to do if you don't like shopping. Still, the Industrial Area comes to life on Fridays from about noon until eleven at night. As is always the case in countries with a critical mass of migrant groups, people from the same country congregate to socialize or play the same sport. You can tell the Pakistanis and Sri Lankans from other nationals because they are the ones playing cricket. The Nepalese love their volleyball. The Filipinos prefer a game of basketball. Restaurants work along equally segregated national lines.

While this separation can be seen as an expression of national pride, it hides the ethnic stereotypes and racial tensions within this community of male workers. A Bangladeshi car driver warned me about the Sri Lankan crowd, saying, "They're no good, lazy." An Egyptian who identified himself as *ibn nas*, or a man from a respectable family, described both Bangladeshis and Sri Lankans as *aghar*, the Arabic word for gypsies. He was using it derogatorily, in the sense of ill-mannered or dirty, and not to mean a nomadic people, which would have been the more apt descriptor for everyone here. Despite being segregated, workers in the Industrial Area have mobility and freedom of association. Compared with Dubai, where workers lead isolated lives in purpose-built camps that do not permit outside visitors, Qatar follows a more liberal model. The Industrial Area may sometimes feel like a prison, but it's one with unlimited in-and-out privileges.

On my first Friday in Doha, Prem, a Nepalese carpenter—speaking through an interpreter—invited me to his compound to see his "home." I agreed not to reveal the name of the company Prem works for, but it specializes in landscaping and general contracting work for commercial and residential low-rises. Located on a side street off Al-Attiyah, within a few minutes' walk of the commercial centre, the compound is home to a largely Nepalese community. The first thing I notice as I walk through the small courtyard is a stack of identical sand-beaten boots the workers must take off before they enter the building. I can't imagine how any of them can recognize which pair belongs to whom. Although it's late afternoon, the peak social and shopping hours, two dozen or so men are lounging about in the large kitchen and hallway on the ground floor. (There's no common area; designers of workers' dorms normally don't spare a thought for social time.)

Prem and five other Nepalese men share three bunk beds in a space of about one hundred square feet. As he takes a break from updating his Facebook page, one of Prem's roommates tells me this is one of the better complexes. It has running water and an A/C unit, and the kitchen is large enough for several workers to cook their meals at the same time. (In his previous compound, the kitchen was so small, men waited in line for hours to prepare dinner.) Even the bathroom, Prem says, features five squat-style toilets, showers and a handful of urinals. The morning rush can be brutal, however, as the same bathroom serves about sixty-four men getting ready for work at the same time.

But even within this relatively well-run compound, many workers vent to me about their working conditions and irregularities in their contracts. One of them complains about a technicality that means he cannot earn the salary specified unless he works overtime. If he doesn't, about QR400 (US$110) a month, or a quarter of what he's been promised, gets deducted from his pay. He has no choice but to work most weekends now.

With no exception, the men's reasons for coming to Doha boil down to money and the lack of jobs back in Nepal. Those who have worked in other Gulf countries—Saudi Arabia came up a few times in our conversations—prefer life in Qatar. When I ask how the Qataris compare to the Saudis, one thing becomes clear: throughout the countries of the Gulf Cooperation Council (GCC), migrant workers never come in contact with the local population unless they have been hired as private drivers or gardeners. If you are a labourer in Doha, you have probably not spoken to a Qatari and never will. The closest the two communities come into contact is when they share the roads.

A Qatari person walking down the streets of Doha during the day remains a rare sight. The local population drives (or is driven) from home to work and back again, travelling from one air-conditioned space to another. Judging from the proliferation of the Fair & Lovely skin-lightening creams in drugstores and at makeup counters, Qataris, like many brown people, worry about getting darker in the sun. After a few days in Doha, I also began to limit my exposure to the afternoon sun. The only people I saw walking down the streets before sunset were South Asian workers of different skill levels: labourers, accountants and technicians. At first, I thought I'd arrived at an egalitarian migrant society, where social standing is subsumed into the larger category of a brown worker. But as I talked to more and more migrants, particularly those from Sri Lanka, I came to the realization that social divisions still trump colour unity.

*

"WE'RE NOT LABOURERS."

Mohamed and Akbar demand that I take note of what they are not almost in the same breath as they reveal what they are: "We are professionals." Quantity surveyors, to be exact. They estimate and provide costs for building materials across multiple construction projects. They work in an office, sit in on company meetings and report to the site manager.

The two Sri Lankan men have just finished their biryani and dahl (lentil) Friday lunch at one of the two branches of Colombo Restaurant in the Industrial Area. This is the larger and less crowded one off Tenth Street. Getting a table in the more central Twenty-third Street venue can be difficult on Fridays, when Sri Lankan men descend on the commercial spots by the thousands. Colombo Restaurant, which doubles as a community meeting place, opens at 5 a.m. for the breakfast rush and takes last orders just before midnight to cater to different working schedules. On an evening visit, I found a crowd of professional men like Mohamed and Akbar, as well as many sand-soaked labourers (who are expected to clean up in the back bathroom before taking a table) from whom the professionals tried to distance themselves.

Their defensiveness is understandable. They may all come from the same country, but it's one where class and colour consciousness permeate everyday life. Mohamed and Akbar have light skin, the universal signifier of a middle-class life for brown communities. Even when they work on site (as opposed to at the company's headquarters), they do so in an air-conditioned office with other engineers and administrative staff. If I'm talking about the two men as if their experiences are identical, it's because, on the whole, they are.

They met at the engineering program at the University of Kalmunai in Sri Lanka's Eastern Province, and both graduated the same year with a major in quantity survey. Both had just turned twenty-eight and picked their field of study for the express purpose of working in the Gulf's construction business. "You study for that goal because in my country one cannot find a job," says Mohamed. "Jobs in Sri Lanka have low salaries and the cost of living is higher [than in Doha]." Qatar, United Arab Emirates, Saudi Arabia or Kuwait—it didn't matter where they ended up, as long as they got out of Sri Lanka. If doors were to open in, say, Malaysia or Singapore, they'd jump through them. "The world is big," says Mohamed, echoing what millions of migrant workers of different skill and education levels have said before and will go on saying. Where there's work, there's a chance of a new life for them and their families.

Akbar moved to Doha a year before Mohamed and spent his spare time helping his university friend land a contract with the same construction firm. It's the one time in their ten-year friendship that the two friends have been separated. Now they not only work together but also share a room in a house in Al-Saad district, a slightly more developed enclave than the Industrial Area. Although their relationship seems to suggest that they're gay—they may well be, but they point out that two other men share the same room—it's typical of the close bonds that migrant men form when they find themselves in a new country away from family, friends, wives or sexual partners. Despite the extreme conditions in which men in the construction sector work—conditions that you'd think would make their hearts as hard as the steel they use to reinforce concrete—I was struck by a kind of camaraderie I don't usually see in my bourgeois life, where professional jealousies too often define work relationships. The way some men at Colombo Restaurant shared plates to avoid spending more than they could spare on their meals struck me as the ultimate expression of lives intimately intertwined.

Akbar and Mohamed even share a dream: to start a construction company in Sri Lanka after a few more years of working and saving in Doha. It's a common dream among Sri Lankan migrant workers, one that transcends class and education levels. Owning a business gives the men some sense of control over their destiny and the future of their families, because almost everything else in their home country's economy and politics is out of their hands.

Amran (not his real name), a chef at another popular Sri Lankan hangout for workers, hopes to open his own restaurant in Colombo as soon as he returns home. Eventually. Amran, whose specialty is beef curry (although he dines on pizzas and pastas on his days off), has been working in Doha since 2003 and shows no signs of packing up and leaving. Even though he tells me he preferred his previous job at a four-star hotel in Kuwait, he admits that Doha feels like home. A relatively high monthly salary of QR2,500 (about US$700) keeps the fifty-year-old father of five children churning out Sri Lankan main courses and appetizers in twelve-hour shifts six days a week. When I ask him why all the men in his restaurant choose to come to Doha, he surveys the room, adjusting his hair net in the process, and deadpans: "We need money. That's why."

To Amran, the fact that I've asked this question raises his suspicions about my ability to do justice to his people. "Have you spoken to workers?" he asks. No one here works just for himself, he tells me. Every migrant has left behind an immediate or extended family. Even the very young—and I spoke to Nepalese and Bangladeshi men who looked too young to grow facial hair—probably support parents or siblings. Once your eighteenth birthday rolls around, you get a passport and a work permit, and you leave home. Amran himself was in his mid-twenties when he first left Sri Lanka for that job in Kuwait City. His children, three girls and two boys ranging in age from twenty-three to ten, have grown up seeing their father only on his annual vacations or during brief hiatuses between overseas contracts. Like the Filipina domestic workers who don't want their children to follow in their footsteps, Amran hopes his own kids will pursue professional paths. It's what migrant parents do: toil in semi-skilled or unskilled jobs so that their children don't have to. In fact, Amran's first son studied mechanical engineering and has recently joined his father in Doha. But father and son don't live together. Because the son works in a professional position, he's housed in a different (and much nicer, Amran says) compound. Amran couldn't be more proud of his son's superior residence and higher salary, even if that means the socio-economic gap between father and son will widen with time.

Migrant workers in Doha place so much emphasis on their accommodation for a very compelling reason: where you live is a test of the business and ethical standards of subcontractors who secure labour for the big construction firms. The compound for the Nepalese workers, while humble and crowded, is at the higher end of the market. Most workers live in more extreme conditions that violate the terms of their contracts and even the most modest standards of dignity and privacy. One place has come to stand for the worst in neglect and abuse of workers: Al-Sailiya, a camp about eight kilometres west of the Industrial Area. Like actors who won't say "Macbeth" in a theatre, workers believe Al-Sailiya carries a curse. If you say its name, bad things will happen—or worse, you may end up living there.

*

LOCATED IN THE MIDDLE of a large stretch of desert off the highway that connects Qatar and Saudi Arabia, Al-Sailiya, a taxi driver tells me, makes the Industrial Area look like "luxury accommodation." No electrical grid, only generators. No water pipes or sewage system either. Trucks drive up and down its street to fill stand-alone tanks with water; others collect sewage and waste from septic containers. This ritual of depositing clean and removing dirty water takes place early in the morning, as workers head out to their job sites, and late in the evening, as they get home for dinner. The narrow, unpaved roads of Seventeenth and Twentieth Streets, home to the two main residential camps, somehow manage the flow of sanitation trucks, company buses that pick up and drop off workers, and minivans that deliver food and supplies to a host of Sri Lankan, Indian, Afghan and Pakistani diners and hotels. (Restaurants here are often referred to as hotels, probably in the sense of places where workers stop to eat and relax on their way home.)

I marvel at how cheap everything is. A kebab sandwich is the equivalent of about two American dollars, and a biryani is roughly three, depending on which meat you order. The same dish at Colombo Restaurant costs about four to five. But my interpreter tells me that only semi-skilled workers—the carpenters and electricians—can afford these prices. The lowest-paid labourers will instead splurge on a plain curry, half of which they eat in the evening and half of which they save for the next day's lunch. A labourer will stretch the meal and satisfy his stomach by adding one or two slices of Arabic bread (a variation of pita).

When I walked down Seventeenth Street for the first time, thoughts of homoeroticism were replaced by memories of the movie *District 9*, which tells the story of a race of extra-terrestrials living in slum-like conditions in Johannesburg, where they are exploited and discriminated against. (That film was a not-so-subtle allegory for South African race politics.) Conditions in Al-Sailiya may not be as extreme as those depicted in *District 9*, but the place did strike me as a (real, not metaphorical) shantytown, a ghetto within the ghetto of the Industrial Area. Although I'd blended in with the crowd on Attiyah Street, I stood out like the one true alien I am on Seventeenth Street. On the former, the looks were curious; here they were suspicious. Workers who opened up to me in the Industrial Area put up resistance in Al-Sailiya. Or perhaps what they showed me was not resistance but indifference or skepticism. I got the feeling that I wasn't the first writer from a rich Western country to sneak into their community to check on their living conditions. In this context, our shared brown skin played little or no role in breaking down barriers.

After several failed attempts to engage anyone in a conversation, I finally got Bibian, a Sri Lankan assistant carpenter in his twenties, to respond to some of my questions. His contract ends in six months and he doesn't care to extend it—at least not with the same company—which may explain why he's willing to talk to me when so many of his friends have declined. It's not the long hours or the working conditions that have soured him on Doha but what he believes to be a bait-and-switch operation by his recruiters. He was promised a room with three others—Qatari law stipulates that no more than four workers can share a single room—but he found himself living with seven people. Eight people in a room that's already too small for four, Bibian reminds me. After eighteen months in Doha, and despite several complaints to his supervisor, his living arrangements have not changed. He offers to show me his room, but it's after eight thirty in the evening and some of his "roommates" have gone to sleep. Most get up at around 5 a.m. to work before the sun begins its daily assault.

I don't really need to be shown Bibian's room. The two-level military-style camps all around me have several open common areas that give me a glimpse of life on the inside. Hand-washed clothes are hung to dry overnight. Insomniacs—those who stay up past nine, that is—idle outside the kitchen area, probably waiting for their turn at the burner to prepare dinner or tomorrow's lunch.

I strike up a conversation with a group of Nepalese workers on Twentieth Street for a few minutes. It is days after the April 2015 earthquake in their home country, and they talk about their struggles getting in touch with their families. But our chat is interrupted by a large Indian man who asks me and my interpreter to leave and instructs the workers not to talk to outsiders. At first I assume he's acting on behalf of the Qatari government, which has been cracking down on Western reporters covering conditions in the Industrial Area in the lead-up to the 2022 World Cup. (A few weeks before my visit, a German television crew was arrested by intelligence services and detained for five days.) But my interpreter tells me that the Indian tout most likely works for one of the subcontracting firms that hire and house migrants. He knows that by putting more than four men in a room, his company is in violation of Qatari labour laws. To him, I could be an undercover Qatari inspector. After all, I am Arabic-looking. But I don't protest too much. I've seen enough of Al-Sailiya, and it is getting late anyway. Shops are closing, workers are making their way to their rooms, and now that the water and sewage trucks are done for the night, the noise level in general has gone down.

But I'm not done with Al-Sailiya yet. I need to come back on a Friday during the day. Two Sri Lankan construction workers who live there have agreed to talk about their experiences. Perhaps they will offer a different take on the area, or on life as brown workers in general. I'm still looking for that feel-good story that balances the tales of broken promises I've been hearing in Doha for over a week.

*

WHEN I REACH AL-SAILIYA on Friday afternoon, Sripala and Basnayaka ask if we can have our conversation outside their dorm room, which they say is not "clean enough" for me to visit. I don't want to add any more stress to them, so we settle on a local restaurant.

Sripala, the older of the two men, believes Doha will be his last "tour of duty." Since 1982, when he was twenty-three years old, the certified mechanic from Galle in Sri Lanka has been working in one Persian Gulf country or another. He took up his first "post"—he loves using military and diplomatic terms—as a diesel mechanic in Muscat, Oman, to resolve a financial problem, as well as a romantic one. When his parents objected to his choice of a wife, he knew he couldn't keep the tradition of the new spouses living with the groom's parents. "We rented a house, but it [the rent] was too much. We had a plan to buy land and build a home but didn't have the money to do so." The newly married couple had chosen to put off having children until their economic situation improved, so Sripala decided to work for what he believed would be a few short years in the Gulf. Sri Lanka's new government had developed policies that encouraged the migration of its citizens and welcomed their remittances. The timing was right for Sripala to leave Sri Lanka behind.

A pattern of sorts followed: three or four years in one country would be followed by a year or two back home to see his wife and, over the years, his three children, all now in their early to middle twenties. Usually the jobs would fall within his general line of expertise as a mechanic, but in one particularly unhappy stint in Saudi Arabia, he was forced to take up a position as a workshop cleaner, mopping floors and washing spare parts. "I had to do it. They told me if I didn't, I could stay in my room and not earn any money." He lucked out with his next contract in Dubai, where he worked as a taxi driver. To date, it remains the highlight of this migrant's tours of duty in the Gulf, except that the sedentary and stressful life of roaming Dubai's streets exacerbated his diabetes. He had to quit and return to Sri Lanka. Every return home carried the promise of finding a well-paying job in Galle. Every return home dashed this promise. After a few months of searching within Sri Lanka, Sripala would find himself turning to the section of the paper where recruitment agencies advertised foreign jobs. Those pages are the Sri Lankan migrant's version of a siren song—irresistible despite its notes of doom. In 2009, just as the civil war in Sri Lanka came to an end, Sripala was hired as a driver for an Indian construction company in Doha. It meant parting company with his wife and teenage children. Again.

I ask Sripala what it feels like to be an itinerant father. "Very, very bad," he responds. "To be away from my children, very bad feeling. But everything costs so much [in Sri Lanka]. My children needed after-school tutoring because the schools they went to weren't very good. I had to look after my children." The few jobs he found in Galle either paid too little or came with social stigma attached. He turned down offers to work as a security guard in local factories, for example, because his wife worried about their children's standing in school if their classmates found out how their father earned a living.

Sripala places the blame not on social customs but on the nepotism of the political establishment in the past twenty or thirty years, before and after the war. Government officials don't help the poor people, he says, but instead give jobs and award contracts to their relatives and close friends. This forces people like him to take their chances with Sri Lankan recruiters and Gulf-based businesses.

I could tell that Sripala didn't like it much in Doha. While older and educated Qatari people are at worst dismissive toward migrant workers from the subcontinent, younger Qataris are outwardly hostile. "The young are angry with expatriates," he says, as I make a mental note of his use of the word "expatriate" as opposed to "migrant." It's a word that is normally applied to white, Western or at least highly professional foreign workers. Sripala's adoption of it fits the military or diplomatic vocabulary he often uses in describing his career, suggesting a disconnect between how he sees himself and how he's seen by local populations. "They know that [many] vehicles are driven by foreign workers. We have to give way to them. When I see a Land Cruiser that tries to overtake, I let it. Otherwise, they'll take my number and make up some story about my driving." He says he knows of other drivers who were deported for fabricated traffic violations.

But since his youngest daughter is still in college, Sripala has no choice but to stay in Doha for at least one more year. At fifty-six, he's the senior citizen in the room he shares with five young Sri Lankan men. The worst part is the common toilet, which serves several rooms in the same compound. "When it's empty, you have to use it." He shares this and other tips for communal living with his dorm mates, who have come to look up to him as a father figure or "uncle," the generic term for an older man in many parts of South Asia.

Basnayaka, a thirty-year-old mason on his first job outside Sri Lanka after twelve years in its army, is one of the men who seek Sripala's advice. His reasons for leaving his wife and four-year-old twin daughters sound familiar: he needed money to pay off family debts and to give his daughters a better start in life. Through Sripala's translation, I get a sense of what life in the construction sector is like for this novice labourer. As a mason, he works outdoors for up to twelve hours a day—from 7 a.m. to 7 p.m., or later when there's overtime—in what's invariably extremely hot weather. Although he was warned about the heat, nothing could have prepared him for the sun's power in the summer months. He illustrates this point by clenching his fists and pretending to hit his own face to suggest the sun's knockout punch. His foreman allows workers to take ten- or fifteen-minute breaks when they need to drink cold water, which is freely supplied, or to rest in a shady corner. Unlike other companies, this one provides a free lunch in an air-conditioned trailer with tables—all signs of luxury within this sector.

Still, Basnayaka intends to go home at the end of his two-year contract. Although the monthly pay, with overtime, is decent (up to QR2,000, or US$550), he says his life is not: "From site to room and room to site." For over a year now, he has not left the general vicinity of the Industrial Area except to go to a local beach for a quick swim on days when he can gather enough workers to split the taxi fare. He can't afford the cost of even a shared taxi to such attractions as the Corniche or Doha's traditional markets (*souqs*). This explains why, on my way to meet Basnayaka and Sripala, I kept seeing men walking down the desert roads and highways in the blistering mid-afternoon sun. They were trying to cut costs by walking from one part of the Industrial Area to another instead of paying for a seat in a shared taxi. Money may have been what drew these workers to Doha, but spending it on themselves is not in the budget. Of his monthly pay, Basnayaka sends QR1,900 back home and keeps the remaining QR100 for incidentals. His wife wants him back home, but she also keeps asking for more money to feed and clothe the twins.

"He's always crying," Sripala says, taking it upon himself to describe his roommate's emotional state. "I see tears coming from his eyes." The older worker tries to comfort him, but it can be difficult to find moments for heart-to-heart conversations. The all-male environment provides its own comforts and shortcuts (like walking around the common area in underwear), but it also creates some sexual frustrations. On the rare occasions when Sripala and Basnayaka run into women at the Grand Mall on the eastern edge of the Industrial Area, they may flirt a little and ask simple questions—"We're human beings away from home," says Sripala—but neither man would think of having an affair, even if it were possible. "We send all our money to our families. There's nothing left to buy presents [for] the ladies. There's no time for an affair."

It's getting late and both men need to go back to their camp and prepare for the start of the long workweek. (As part of his duties, Sripala must wash the company car on his one day off.) As we approach the main gate of their camp, I can no longer hear Sripala, the chattier of the two men. The noise coming from the generators outside the entrance drowns out his voice. I note that the first row of dorms overlooks the generators, and I wonder aloud how it feels to work all day and come home to such droning. "You get used to it," says Sripala as he and Basnayaka say their goodbyes and rush back to their room.

I guess you have to get used to many things as a migrant worker: the heat, the lack of privacy, the social isolation, the unpredictability of work. Things like personal space and comfort, which so many of us in Western countries take for granted, mean little to brown workers in Doha and elsewhere. I'm convinced that most experience slavery-like conditions, but I walked away from the Industrial Area thinking of these men less as slaves and more as heroes—to their families and communities back home. Much like ancient Greek soldiers, they approach their lives with a heroic resignation. But unlike those fabled fighters, these men will not be immortalized in verse and dramas—despite what their stories reveal about the uneven (to put it mildly) distribution of wealth in the Global South.

*

THE DISPARITY BETWEEN THE lives of local Qataris and those of the migrant workers who execute their vision for a world-class centre of trade and entertainment hits home on the ride back to my hotel. We drive by the Al-Sailiya Sports Club, a grand and gated private establishment for wealthy Qatari men and expatriates. It's one of those places that will probably host some lavish World Cup celebrations in 2022. Just beyond it, in a stretch of desert, several Sri Lankan and Pakistani men play cricket, or at least some improvised version of it. They're making the most of the last few minutes of daylight. When it gets dark, they'll have to walk back to their camp and wait until next Friday for another game.

PART III

CHAPTER 8

The United Kingdom: British Values

The irony of hosting the 2015 annual general meeting of the Muslim Council of Britain at the Muath Trust in Birmingham didn't escape some of the more opinionated members of both organizations. The trust, established in 1990 by the Yemeni community, the oldest Muslim presence in the multicultural city of Birmingham, has flourished over the years. It runs a slick operation—day nursery, adult education, a banquet and conference hall—out of a heritage building in the Bordesley Centre, a ten-minute walk from Birmingham's New Street train station. Prime Minister David Cameron visited the centre to shore up the Muslim vote in the lead-up to the 2015 elections. You can see a photo of the visit on the homepage of the centre's website. Granted, the men's bathroom on this Sunday in June left much to be desired (toilets that didn't flush properly, missing hand soap and leaky water taps), but the centre and the trust that runs it tell the kind of community-based success story Muslims in Birmingham love to share.

The Muslim Council of Britain (MCB), on the other hand, is struggling to stay afloat financially and to remain relevant politically. Upon its establishment in 1997, this umbrella body with over five hundred affiliated mosques, charities, social groups and schools set itself the mission of speaking to and on behalf of British Muslims. Media outlets and various political parties in Britain considered it the go-to organization whenever they needed a comment about or input on a policy relating to Muslim issues. In the early years of Tony Blair's New Labour reign, the then predominately moderate MCB enjoyed both patronage and prestige, securing its reputation as *the* voice of Muslims in Britain.

Then 9/11 and the US-led, UK-backed wars in Afghanistan and Iraq disrupted this co-dependence. The MCB, under pressure from its affiliate organizations, dissented from the government's positions and protested what it (and millions of other Britons) viewed as an unjustified war in Iraq. The organization also voiced concerns about the rise of the security state, which ethnically and culturally targeted the Muslim population as if terrorists lurked behind every home or business owned by a family of that faith. As it fell out of political favour, the MCB struggled to build a new identity amid a rapidly changing landscape of fundamentalism, terrorism (in particular after the July 7, 2005, attacks in London) and, in the last two years, jihadist Salafism as a wave of British Muslims and converts joined the Islamic State in parts of Iraq and Syria. The British government—no stranger to the divide-and-conquer strategy that served it so well during its empire days—switched its support to what it viewed as moderate or mainstream Muslim groups, such as the Quilliam Foundation and the Sufi Muslim Council, both of which echo and help craft the official narrative of combating Muslim extremism.

The MCB has become an organization with an identity crisis for a community facing a political crisis. I would go further and describe it as a community under siege, judging from the chatter in the Bordesley Centre and the topics of the multiple panels and workshops at the AGM (they range from discussing responses to counter-terrorism legislation to brainstorming strategies for promoting Muslim youth activism). "The community needs direction. Our shops and businesses are attacked. Our names are dragged in the media as killers and executioners," I'm told by an attendant from a Yorkshire student group who asks not to be identified. "I'm here to see what this direction might be." He doesn't sound terribly optimistic, and it's a lot to expect from a day-long conference, but this sense of a community simultaneously adrift and under attack permeated the conference hall. Never have I seen so many anxious brown faces in one room.

I lived in England for nearly eight years in the late 1980s and early 1990s, when I decided to move to Canada to seek a better life and to escape what I felt was a particular kind of English racism. But with hindsight, I see that most debates about Muslims in Britain back then had an innocuous quality. They dealt with issues of social cohesion or alienation within the parameters of the European multicultural model. The discussions centred on immigration quotas, the changes in the ethnic makeup of inner cities, and racial tensions between Asian and black communities on one side and far-right groups and conservative media on the other. Race defined the substance and tenor of the argument. Muslims were part of a larger community of "others" that included immigrants from the Caribbean and former British colonies in Asia and Africa.

Two decades later, the Muslim community stands more or less alone as the über-other, ostracized and stigmatized. A group of people who come from different racial, cultural and regional backgrounds have been fused into a single questionable minority: the unassimilated, the enemy within, the hotbed for radicalization. Muslims (those born into or practising the tenets of the faith) and Islamists (those who advocate for jihad, or holy war) have become one in the eyes of the mainstream. In returning to England for the first time in almost eight years and nearly two decades after living there, I find a country quite different from the one I thought I knew, and in whose culture and literature I had specialized. Islam has become a *racially* and politically charged identity, and as a result the vast majority of Muslims now have to confront a double whammy of racial and cultural attacks. The line between race and culture or race and religion has been crossed and possibly even erased. The changing fortunes of the Muslim Council of Britain confirm this theory.

In delivering the 2014–15 state of the union, Shuja Shafi, the newly appointed secretary general of the MCB, summed up his first year in office in apocalyptic terms: "The evils of terrorism overshadowed then—and continue to darken now—the image of our community." The rest of Shafi's overview of the past twelve months in the life of the MCB (and by extension, all Muslims in Britain) served as a pep talk to the community and a laundry list of the challenges it faces. In the past year, he said, the MCB had produced a major study on British Muslims based on an analysis of the 2011 census data, and the news was good, at least from a "strength in numbers" perspective.

Muslims now represent 4.8 percent of the population in England and Wales, more than all other self-identified non-Christian faith groups put together. The Muslim community is one of the youngest in Britain: about 33 percent of Muslims are fifteen or under, compared to 19 percent for the general population. Only 4 percent of British Muslims are sixty-five and over, compared to 16 percent for the overall population. Although

Shafi doesn't address it in his talk, the numbers his organization has distributed to the media have led to alarmist headlines ("UK Muslims Population of 26 Million by 2051?") and predictions of a Muslim majority based on current rates of growth.

But problems are growing almost as fast as people. The David Cameron government has couched its counter-terrorism legislation in terms that set those who oppose it as lacking "British values." This insistence on shared values signals a shift in the British government's attitude toward multiculturalism (which, in the neo-conservative narrative, has increased the segmentation of society into smaller, more isolated cultural units). Commentators from the political centre and left interpret attacks on multiculturalism as proxy criticisms of the Muslim community's perceived unwillingness to adapt to Western values. When conservatives talk of the "failures" of multiculturalism, they mean the failure of Muslim communities to integrate. Cameron's own definition of British values remains vague even when the prime minister liberally applies the word "muscular" in championing them. But these values do include free speech, support of the rights of women and sexual minorities, upholding the rule of law and accepting social responsibility. "A genuinely liberal country believes in certain values, actively promotes them and says to its citizens: this is what defines us as a society," Cameron wrote in an article for the *Mail on Sunday* in the summer of 2014.

In effect, Cameron's British values single out Muslims not just as outsiders but as threats to the country's stability. Shafi disagrees. "As a community we face many challenges in overcoming marginalization, prejudice, discrimination, demonization, disadvantage, ignorance and suspicion," he tells the crowd. "It's these obstacles, not Islam or Muslims, that stand in the way of our full participation in society." To address the "plight of Muslims in this country," the community needs to unite behind a new vision and a new direction.

If Shafi entertained any hopes of fostering unity while delivering his report, the Q&A period that followed must have crushed them. Given the wide spectrum of ideological, social and religious views found in the affiliate groups, it was probably naive to believe in the possibility of a dialogue around this so-called united vision. And doing all that within an organization that's down to two and half full-time staff—not to mention faced with chronic budgetary woes due to unpaid affiliation fees—struck me as doomed from the start.

The following week, when I meet the MCB's Talha Ahmad in London's Whitechapel, an Asian and Muslim enclave in the borough of Tower Hamlets, I get a better sense of how the organization that still likes to think of itself as the voice of British Muslims operates. Ahmad, its spokesperson and public face, earns his living as a solicitor but volunteers his time and media expertise to the MCB. (He says he's also a de facto spokesperson for the Bengali community.) Judging by the royal treatment he receives at the Indian/Bengali restaurant on Whitechapel Road, I get the sense that the venue serves as his unofficial second office.

Ahmad dismisses my "doom and gloom" reading of the AGM. The atmosphere had more to do with the location than any actual sentiment in the hall. After more than a decade of hosting the AGM in London, MCB began to take it outside the capital in an attempt to "reach out in a serious way" to British Muslims in regions like the West Midlands, the northwest and Yorkshire, where they're concentrated. AGMs outside London always feel "depressed and less upbeat," he says. "In London there's more confidence. . . . MCB is at its best in London, in its historic roots." (About 12.5 percent of Londoners identify as Muslims.)

Taken as a whole, Ahmad says, the Muslim community does suffer discrimination from government policies, particularly in the counter-terrorism arena, where they are "under the spotlight, targeted" at all times. Add issues of concentration in low-income, high-unemployment boroughs (especially among youth); violence and a lack of voice in public life; and constant vilification by most mainstream media outlets, and you have an idea of what it feels like to be a Muslim in Britain today.

By and large, my sense of a community under siege checks out, but I'm still not sure if this new form of culturally determined racism is as colour-blind as it appears. To me, it sounds like an elaborate scheme to target racialized communities, especially brown people. The fact that Sikh and Hindu businesses and homes occasionally get attacked by far-right groups with anti-Islam messages suggests that charges of a so-called Muslim threat are in fact a run-of-the-mill racial attack.

Anshuman Mondal, the chair of creative writing and English at Brunel University London and author of *Young British Muslim Voices* and *Islam and Controversy: The Politics of Free Speech After Rushdie*, believes that this shift in public attitudes toward Muslims started with the general backlash against multiculturalism. It's also happening, ironically, at a time when younger members of the community feel more British than their parents ever did.

While researching his book on young Muslims in Britain, Mondal—who spent two years travelling throughout the United Kingdom, talking with and listening to his target demographic—witnessed how the vast majority of them have created a hybrid cultural space where Islam merges with their British identity. However, that doesn't square with the neo-liberal politics of the Labour and Conservative parties, Mondal tells me during a late-morning tea break in central London. Both parties have discovered the political advantages of demonizing one community to rationalize curtailing personal freedoms for everyone else. "How do you distract your working class from the fact that you are running an economy that debased their work, undermined their collective bargaining [rights] and introduced precarity?" Declaring Islam culturally incompatible with values that are intrinsic to British society is one way of doing just that. Free speech, for example, becomes "the banner to marshal all the arguments against Islam. The conjuring trick here . . . is to articulate a new form of racism without being racist." Mondal refers to this strategy as a discourse of euphemism, or "not saying what you mean and not meaning what you say." In this context, Muslims in Britain (who predominately hail from South Asia and the Middle East) are seen as inferior "not because of their skin but because of their culture."

Although the word "brown" as a racial and social identity is widely used in British popular culture and in street language—for an example of both, read Gautam Malkani's recreation of London's South Asians and their brown-on-brown inner fighting in his novel *Londonstani*—it hasn't gained the political traction of "black" or the politically correct term "BME" (black and minority ethnic). "People here don't like to talk about brown because it's a racialized term. We're not supposed to talk about race," Mondal says.

In addition to creating this "racism without racists" culture, British society has divided Muslims into two sets: good and bad. The good ones, in broad strokes, are the middle- and upper-middle-class Muslims who have Indian origins and work as doctors, lawyers, judges and politicians, and in the creative industries. The bad Muslims tend to be largely Pakistani, Bengali and more recent immigrants from the Middle East—working-class asylum seekers and others who have entered the United Kingdom illegally. The media, who conflate race and class as much as they do race and culture, don't always make the same distinction. The divide between the two sets of Muslims, like the economic divide between the one percent and the rest of the population, is growing.

My conversations with a retired family doctor and a young fashion designer brought this contrast in the economic and political fortunes of both sets of Muslims into focus. It also illustrated a huge shift in mainstream British society's perceptions of brown Muslims in Britain over the past forty to fifty years. They live by their faith and in their skin, never knowing which part of their existence sets them outside the British value system.

*

IN HIS EARLY TEENS, Rahemur Rahman (known to his friends as Ray) excelled in Islamic studies and recited passages of the Koran in a soft, melodious but commanding voice that his parents thought would be ideal for a career as an imam. "I was the chosen one," says Ray, now twenty-five, as he recalls evenings spent in Shadwell Ford Square Mosque in London's East End, studying religious texts and living up to his "very strict" mother's image of her son as a devout Muslim. But as a fourteen-year-old in London, Ray was more interested in Western music, fashion and popular culture than the company of stodgy old religion instructors and other brown Muslim boys. (And they were always just boys, since religious schools frowned on mixing the sexes, especially as students entered adolescence.)

And so began a rebellious phase in Ray's life. It started with the time-honoured teenage tradition of ditching school and heading to the West End of London to browse record stores. While he wasn't the only teenager of colour sifting through the R&B and vinyl remixes on Tottenham Court Road on a school day, Ray was probably the only one to tuck his traditional Islamic *thoub* (dress) inside his baggy jeans in an attempt to blend in with fellow truants. Ray's creative way with his wardrobe didn't come by accident. His father had migrated to the United Kingdom from Bangladesh in the 1970s to work as a tailor in a clothing factory, a job he holds to this day. It was the father who took Ray—the third child in a family of nine—and some of his siblings to museums and galleries to foster their appreciation of art, colour and design. When a social worker at Stepney Green School in the East End suggested that Ray nurture his love for clothing and design by applying for the prestigious fashion program at Central Saint Martins, the then eighteen-year-old didn't even think it was within the realm of possibility for a working-class, brown Muslim man living with his parents in a council flat in Tower Hamlets. Isn't that school for the likes of John Galliano and Stella McCartney? wondered Ray, thinking of two of its internationally renowned alumni. Despite some misgivings and a one-year deferral, Ray enrolled in the school in 2009 and graduated in 2014. His journey from an imam in training to a budding menswear designer illustrates both the promises and setbacks of young Muslim working-class men in Britain today.

"Being a Muslim made it very hard to find my place," says Ray as he recalls his early days at the school. While his instructors were supportive and directed him to use his heritage and his "story" for inspiration, life as a London fashion student presented cultural challenges for someone raised on Koranic verses, prayers five times a day and, largely, male-only friends. "It was my first time seeing openly gay people, cross-dressers and full-on drag." Parties would take place in warehouses in Soho and other trendy parts of London, where drugs (heroin) and alcohol were freely available. "It was not a real life." At home, his mother told friends and family that Ray was studying art in order to become a schoolteacher. The very idea of her son designing clothes—even in a household where the main breadwinner was a tailor—struck her as un-Islamic and unmanly.

Ray's outsider status was confirmed on the first day of a six-month internship, part of a year-out program option, at the headquarters of Louis Vuitton in Paris. When he asked an employee for directions to his workstation, she pointed him to the closet where they kept their cleaning supplies. "She thought I was a cleaner because of my brown skin," recalls Ray, with a smile but also some bitterness. The rest of the internship followed a less racially stereotypical path, in part because he remained largely invisible. "I was the kind of brown person they can take to the white world and I can blend in. I wasn't overly *desi*," he says, using a term derived from the Sanskrit for "country" or "province" that has been adopted by the South Asian diaspora. For his social life in Paris, Ray found himself gravitating to other Muslim designers.

Back in London, he returned to the divide between the glittery world of fashion and the gritty one of the tower blocks, where tensions between Bengali migrants and right-wing extremists often took a violent turn. (A teenage Ray was attacked as he left a halal fried chicken diner—and there are too many of them in Tower Hamlets—and a man on a bicycle clubbed him with a metal bar for no other reason than his skin colour.) Bengali youths fought each other for control of drug-trafficking zones. At one point, Ray's father found himself in a "group fight" between Bengali and white parents.

Even the journey to and from school plunged him into the world of racial profiling, where his looks and young age set off alarms. On Fridays, Ray dressed in his traditional *thoub* and rushed to school after his weekly prayers. Without fail, he says, police at Canary Wharf tube station would stop him for a "random" check of his bags and question him about the tools in it (box cutters, scissors, pins). Every week he'd have to show his student ID and explain that the items were part of his toolkit. "No white student has ever gone through this."

By the time he finished his degree in 2014, having been through numerous instances of stop and search, Ray could understand why many Muslim men and women of his generation reconnected with their religion and culture and began retreating from or lashing out at British society at large. "You can't blame them. The world has put Muslims in a pen. The only thing they can do is fight back." He himself identifies not as Bengali but as Muslim British. "Everything comes back to it [Islam]. Bengali only means that my skin is brown."

Ray's views confirm a popular theory among political commentators that for Western-born children of immigrants, identification with Islam serves as a negotiation tactic between the world they know at home and the one they encounter outside it. Doug Saunders eloquently describes this generation's "default affinity" to the faith in *The Myth of the Muslim Tide*: "That was their identity, their fate, and sometimes the only handhold they could grasp during the difficult climb into the centre of Western life."

My conversation with Ray has taken place inside a local coffee shop, and now I ask him to take me for a walk through the council estates in the Whitechapel area and the gentrified but once purely ethnic (and rough) Brick Lane. I'm embarrassed to admit to him that I've never seen a London council estate before. He's not surprised, and remarks that I sound pretty middle class to him. This last comment is said not with resentment toward me but with pride in himself for being working class. As we weave in and out of low-rise blocks in Hanbury Estate, I see a part of London that I've encountered only in novels and indie British films. Brown faces stare back at me. With one or two exceptions at a sunk-in playground—Ray claims it to have been the site of organized fights among Bengali gangs during his teens—every resident seems to be South Asian. The only white person we see is a postman who's struggling to explain to a woman over the intercom that he needs to leave a package for a neighbour with her. I'm guessing that the woman on the other end is someone's mother or grandmother and doesn't speak English. "I've never seen a white family living here," says Ray.

Until his men's fashion line takes off, Ray works part time in Selfridges department store in central London. He is one of several Asian, Latino and Middle Eastern men he describes as roughly the same shade of brown. Customers invariably mix them up. Now that men's beards are trendy—that hipster, Brooklyn look—locals and tourists find it hard to differentiate Ray's beard, a symbol of his faith, from that of a South American sales assistant for whom it's merely a fashion statement. For now at least, Ray thinks it's funny that his brown face blends in with his status as a shop assistant. Once he goes back to his work as a designer, he knows that his skin colour and his faith will likely set him apart again.

*

OTTERBOURNE, A HAMPSHIRE VILLAGE of about fifteen hundred residents, is the kind of quaint English setting that calls attention to itself precisely because not much happens there. Its village hall offers tango lessons and hosts sewing circles. The drama group stages an annual pantomime in December and a summer variety show. The village sits about six kilometres west of Winchester, which you can reach in just an hour from London's Waterloo station. It's one hour and a world away from the reality of Bengali Muslims in Tower Hamlets and the Muslim terror threat, but I'm here to discuss these very issues with one of its residents: Dr. Reefat Drabu, a semi-retired general practitioner.

I met Reefat at the Muslim Council of Britain's AGM, where she made clear her feelings about the organization's tacit support of a small but vocal segment of Muslims who insist on their rights (religious accommodation) but think little of their responsibilities or the rights of others. Is the MCB's fall from grace in part the result of accommodating too many unreasonable demands? I approached her during the lunch break and suggested that we should talk more. After a few email exchanges, we made a plan for me to visit her in Winchester. In the two hours or so of our conversation, I got an introduction to a slice of brown Muslim life in England that is rarely seen in media representations of the community. Over tea in the kitchen of Hillside, Reefat's Edwardian home, I begin by telling her how the image of a patrician country doctor who doesn't wear a hijab or any other symbol of her Muslim faith contrasts with what I've just seen in London's East End.

"The image of Islam [in the media] is mostly a lady with a hijab. I find that offensive because there are more women who don't wear the hijab than do." Reefat thinks that this image helps perpetuate a misleading narrative about gender oppression within Islam. (For the record, she doesn't see the hijab as the symbol of discrimination that critics of Islam claim it to be.)

Growing up Muslim and brown in Britain in the late 1950s and early 1960s brought Reefat face to face with racism. But coming from a well-to-do family—her father was a doctor, and she and two of her four siblings followed in his footsteps—gave her a host of other advantages. "I had a lot of confidence growing up. I could say, 'I'm different.' I came from a family that's sympathetic, prided itself on the value of being truthful, honest." And yet this privileged upbringing became the source of early hardships, setting Reefat apart from the largely working-class South Asian immigrants in the northwest of England, where she came of age. "More people have gone the route of shopkeepers to middle class." Her parents arrived as middle class, and it's a privilege she passed on to her own children.

The family did not shy away from Islam in those early years, but they also didn't see it as a political identity. As Reefat recalls, it was just there. Muslim. Full stop. While working-class Muslim families instituted strict laws on what their daughters could and couldn't do, Reefat and her sister simply adapted aspects of British culture to fit their faith. They played sports, participated in school dances and wore whatever they wanted (as long as the clothes "didn't stand out or attract attention"). They didn't go out with boys, she acknowledges, but "nobody told us don't do it." The family didn't eat pork or drink alcohol, but also "didn't rely on mullahs to tell us what to do." David Cameron would applaud: British values at work, he'd point out.

Life wasn't always so idyllic in North Manchester Grammar School, however. Reefat recalls day-to-day discrimination and racial taunts. A games teacher (of Russian background, she clarifies) always picked on her at netball because of her skin colour. Many years later, Reefat's first child had to deal with constant teasing about her brown skin. Other seven-year-olds would say that she had "poo on her," and that's why her skin was brown. "It left her with a desire not to be brown. To be white." Still, Reefat views this type of schoolyard bullying not as race-specific but as an example of how cruel kids can be; overweight children are called fatties and those with glasses four-eyed, she adds.

I can't help wondering if Reefat's own light brown skin has shielded her from some of the nastier aspects of race discrimination, or if it has acted as a get-out-of-race-jail-free card. Her husband, a founding member of the MCB and a human rights authority, is much darker. "Being light-skinned didn't give me any advantages," she insists. "My husband being darker, it didn't give him any disadvantage." Her ethnic name, she says, has played a bigger role than skin colour in her professional life, with some patients indicating a preference for a non-ethnic (and that's largely understood to be non-Asian) physician.

That last observation is a rare example of Reefat directing her experience with racism onto the laps of white Anglos. For the most part, she believes that the Muslim community has had a hand in creating the drama of its own alienation from society. Democracy requires give and take and an acceptance of the concept of the "common good." The MCB's current way of thinking about Muslim identity in Britain is more of a problem than a solution to the problem, she explains. "The MCB types are typical of us brown people. We're very good at criticism. Everything is rubbish except what we're doing." She cites demands for prayer rooms or separate bathrooms for ablutions as examples of how Muslims insist on special treatment from schools or local authorities. "If we don't get them, we shout and scream about it. We forget that other people have demands of us."

Another example is wearing the niqab, the Muslim veil that covers all of a woman's face except for the eyes, a custom Reefat finds particularly grating. "It means you're withdrawing from society. I see it as a threat to my future liberty as a Muslim." In civil terms, a woman in a niqab gains an unfair advantage: she can see the person she's talking to, but that person can't see her. To Reefat, it symbolizes a community that has become more demanding about its rights and less interested in its responsibilities to fellow citizens of all faiths and ethnicities.

Despite espousing views that will be considered "secular" by most religious scholars, Reefat still identifies strongly with Islam. When I ask her what the faith means to her personally, she responds promptly, as if she's heard this question before, that she wants her children to be able to read the *sura,* a verse from the Koran, when she dies. That's all. When she asks me in return, I reply that I'm from a Muslim family but I don't necessarily identify as Muslim, except when I have to defend the religion of my forefathers against racial or cultural stereotypes. She is not convinced. Islam to her means having a spiritual relationship with God. If I don't have that, she insists, then there's no circumstance in which I should call myself a Muslim.

This final part of our conversation took place as she drove me back to Winchester station to catch the train to London. It left me thinking about why I always end up involved in issues that relate to being Muslim and Arab, despite my uneasy relationship with both identities. I realize that I don't have a choice. The religion forms part of how I'm perceived in the world. Just like my brown skin, it's a fixture of who I am, no matter how much my relationship with it changes.

If you need proof of how Islam and brown skin intersect, or at least of how Muslim communities in Britain live under suspicion for both, look no further than the government's recent attempts to crack down on violent extremism. The 2015 Counter-Terrorism and Security Act covers four areas: (1) Pursue, to stop terrorist attacks; (2) Prevent, to stop people from becoming terrorists or growing sympathetic to violent organizations; (3) Protect, to guard against terror attacks; and (4) Prepare, to mitigate the impact of such attacks if and when they happen. (The act builds on the British government's strategy for countering terrorism, officially known as CONTEST.) While the government insists that all four tentacles of its strategy have equal weight, media outlets and civil liberty groups—not to mention Muslim organizations—have zeroed in on the second *P*, Prevent. In essence, the policy presupposes a link between thinking about extremism and committing violent acts (the so-called conveyor belt theory), and assumes the Muslim community is guilty of acting against British values until proven otherwise.

In the middle of the worst economic crisis since the Great Depression, when austerity became *the* defining government policy, officials threw money at Prevent. The initial 2005 budget of £40 million has long since doubled. Between 2005 and 2011, at least £80 million has been spent on a thousand schemes spread across ninety-four local authorities. Many of these schemes would have been considered wasteful spending if undertaken by a left-leaning city council or the old Labour Party. They include cricket, boxing and judo clubs; camping trips; fusion youth singing; and other initiatives that a commentator in the *Daily Telegraph* described as "many steps away from dealing with what drives young Muslims into extremism." Prevent turned into a cash cow for local authorities and many Muslim groups. Anyone with a proposal that targeted Muslim youth and engaged them in an activity or structured learning had a good shot of receiving government funding. Critics argue that it's very difficult to assess the effectiveness of Prevent initiatives. (Will a newfound love of boxing change the mind of a young person watching videos of or reading articles on the atrocities committed by the Assad regime?) But supporters insist that despite some growing pains, Prevent is moving in the right direction.

I need to look deeper into Prevent.

*

THE QUESTION MARK IN the title of the day conference—"Preventing Violent Extremism?"—seemed redundant. Organized by the Islamic Human Rights Commission (IHRC) in London, the conference was intended to challenge the assumptions of the British government's anti-extremism policies, including the Counter-Terrorism and Security Act, which passed into law in January 2015. The act turns the many previous iterations of the Prevent program from policy guidelines into laws. What began, in the wake of the 7/7 attacks, as a strategy to win the hearts and minds of Muslims in Britain "by promoting a narrative that would counter extremist violence carried out in the name of Islam" has over the course of the decade that followed super-sized into what the IHRC describes as a "social-engineering exercise." Other commentators describe Prevent as the largest program snooping into the lives of British citizens in modern history.

Prevent's most troublesome aspect obligates teachers, doctors, nurses, social workers and community activists, among others, to report anyone they suspect of harbouring thoughts or feelings that might be described as extremist, or as not in line with British values. The program rests on an assumption that violent extremism is a natural progression of nonviolent thought. Prevent officers have descended on campuses and schools, using soft and hard pressure to force student groups, local authorities and businesses to cancel events hosted by or featuring speakers deemed either extremist or not in line with British values of tolerance and free speech.

Indeed, the June 13 IHRC conference started later than originally scheduled to accommodate participants who had registered online before a change of venue was posted on the website. A few days before the conference, IHRC staffers were told by the owners of the original venue, the left-leaning Water Lily group, that it could no longer host because one of the participating organizations (Cage UK, a vocal critic of government anti-terrorism policies) hadn't passed the Prevent test. IHRC relocated the conference to the Amanah Centre, a private banquet/function hall in London's Whitechapel district, which had another event booked for the evening of the same day but agreed to host the conference as long as everyone cleared the premises by 5 p.m. On the positive side, the clock-watching meant that speakers had to shorten their talks and the Q&A period after each session—usually a platform for the long-winded and the incoherent—had to be kept to a minimum. But not even the harried pace of the day could stop attendees from sharing horror story after horror story from the Prevent files.

At the community activism workshop I attended, the reports from the frontlines of being a Muslim in today's Britain were almost indistinguishable from satirical stories in *The Onion*. The words "Orwellian" and "McCarthyist" came up a few times, too. I simply listened and took a few notes. Much of what I heard reminded me more of the Middle East police state I grew up in than the England that gave birth to John Stuart Mill's *On Liberty*.

A teacher reports an eight-year-old Muslim girl to Prevent officers for telling a classmate that nail varnish is a bad idea since Muslim women can't pray with painted nails. A doctor asks a young boy about his views on the "global caliphate" during a routine examination of a foot injury. When another young student tells a teacher about the anti-whaling movement in Japan, he's reported to Prevent—although he may not even be Muslim. (Environmental activism apparently struck the teacher as a harbinger of extremism.) A workshop for Muslim mothers to educate them on Prevent policies gets called off when Prevent officers hear of it. A bus company cancels a contract with a Muslim university organization that has set up a tour of British campuses to educate and advise students on the Prevent program.

If a student expresses sympathy for Palestinians and criticizes or calls for a boycott of Israel, he or she risks being reported to Prevent officers. One of the indicators of nonviolent extremism, a senior Muslim policeman told the media, is youth who avoid shopping at Marks & Spencer, which is "mistakenly perceived to be Jewish-owned." Other signs of radicalization include not drinking alcohol and not wearing Western clothes. Most Prevent interventions happen without any formal documentation—officers simply and suddenly appear at an event or company office and use "persuasion"—so there's no paper trail that activists can use in a complaint or legal challenge.

Arun Kundnani, author of *The Muslims Are Coming!: Islamophobia, Extremism, and the Domestic War on Terror*, a critically lauded analysis of the security state in both Britain and the United

States, is facilitating a workshop that's quickly turning into a click-bait listicle: "Twenty Really Outrageous Stories from the Prevent Files. Number Nine Had Us Floored." Born and raised in West London, Kundnani now calls New York City home and teaches media as a sessional instructor at various academic institutions. He's keeping his cool, and the discussion on time, even as the number of participants climbs with the arrival of those redirected from the original venue to the current one. As Kundnani and others point out, Prevent is tasked with stopping all forms of extremism—including far right-wing extremism—but it seems to target the Muslim community almost exclusively. The IHRC characterizes the British government's attitude to a slew of attacks on Muslim homes, businesses and mosques—the violent extremism that Prevent aims to stop—as a form of "silent acquiescence."

As an example of the different treatment accorded far-right extremists, the IHRC cites the case of Glasgow's Neil MacGregor, who in 2009 threatened to blow up Scotland's largest mosque and behead one Muslim a week. He was charged with breach of peace and sentenced to three years' probation in a lower court, but he should have been charged under anti-terrorism laws and tried in a high court. The police allow the English Defence League to stage marches in Muslim-heavy neighbourhoods in Birmingham and Luton, even when chants of "We hate Muslims" or "No more mosques" can regularly be heard. One march in Luton ended up with Muslim homes and businesses torched or vandalized. No one involved in those attacks was ever charged under anti-extremism legislation, the IHRC claims.

Given this, it's not unreasonable to conclude that Prevent and other anti-terrorism initiatives reinforce a form of cultural racism. Because most Muslims in Britain come from core brown countries—South Asia and the Arab world—it becomes difficult to separate cultural from colour-based racism.

When I meet up with Kundnani in New York's East Village a month later, he warns me about making a direct connection between Muslim and brown skin, even though he argues in his book that reactions to signifiers of Islam (veil, halal meat, beards) indicate a trend toward the racialization of the religion. There's nothing fixed about racial categories, he tells me. "The same person in the 1960s was known as a coloured immigrant. In the 1970s as Asian. In the 1980s as Pakistani or Bengali." Only in the 1990s, and certainly after 9/11, he says, did the same person become "Muslim."

The Salman Rushdie affair in 1989 was a turning point in the transformation of brown identity. The reactions to the fatwa exposed a fault line in British multiculturalism: the existence of a secondary society that doesn't subscribe to the main narrative of peaceful co-existence and in fact is willing to risk life and limb to defend its beliefs. The creation of a two-tier Muslim community began soon after—"good" Muslims were cast as moderate and silent, "bad" Muslims as religious and vocal. The idea of "British values" has permeated society since after the Second World War, when immigrants from South Asia and the Caribbean started to arrive in England and Wales to take on manufacturing and infrastructure jobs left vacant by the war dead.

Kundnani got his first taste of this argument as an undergraduate at Cambridge University, where he took a class with John Casey. The name sounded familiar to me, but I couldn't remember why. Kundnani reminds me that Casey argued, in an infamous 1982 article in the *Salisbury Review*, for the repatriation of brown and black immigrants, or at least their restriction to guest worker status in England. "He was talking about shared cultural values being corrupted by immigrants," Kundnani explains. According to Casey, these immigrants, largely from the Asian subcontinent and the West Indies, had failed to assimilate in the way that earlier groups (Jewish people and southern Europeans) had. "It blew my mind," recalls Kundnani, who has a European mother and a South Asian father but is visibly brown. "It's a more sophisticated way to hate me. I wouldn't even know what the response would be." Casey's writing put Kundnani on the path of racial politics just as the whole debate of shared values began to dominate discussions of Muslim integration and isolation.

Even after 9/11, when Islam and terrorism became interchangeable in the minds of many in the West, the Muslim community could at least say that such threats came from individuals and groups outside Britain—by then, the blame had shifted to Arab Muslims in particular, based on the origins of the nineteen hijackers (most of whom came from Saudi Arabia, with the others from Egypt, the United Arab Emirates and Lebanon). But when the 7/7 attackers in London were revealed to be British born and bred, Muslim voices were lost for words. In the wake of their silence, the government of Tony Blair raised the volume on the idea of British values as a counter-terrorism strategy. "If only [the 7/7 attackers] had been more British, they wouldn't have been inclined to murder fellow citizens," Kundnani says, summing up the official party line. And that thinking gave birth to Prevent, which defines terrorism and British values in a way that casts a wide net for the former and reduces the latter to a caricature. As Kundnani reminds me, former British prime minister John Major once described his idealized version of Britain as a place where old ladies cycled to church on a Sunday. It's the idea of Forever England, a land that never changes, even when its inhabitants, and their skin colours, are forever morphing, browning.

But perhaps what makes Prevent particularly troubling as a form of racial profiling and targeting—a de facto control mechanism of brown political thought and activity—is that it operates in the "pre-criminal" space. In that sense, it's similar to programs designed to warn the public (youth) about gang culture or drugs. But unlike such programs, Prevent assumes that the contemplation or exploration of hard-core Islamic doctrine is a prelude to violent crime. This leaves Muslim youth vulnerable to biased interpretations of their thought processes. It also opens the door to entrapment and a kind of police state where neighbours or individuals in positions of power (the teachers, doctors, social workers who are now obligated to report to Prevent officers) may rat on people against whom they have a grudge.

But it's what comes after such reporting that seems to back up the IHRC's characterization of Prevent as a social-engineering program. Once a person has been identified by a Prevent officer as at risk of becoming a violent extremist, she enters the Channel phase—one-on-one mentoring designed to deprogram her and rewire her social circuits. These programs assume that every Muslim who shows an interest in his or her faith is a potential mass murderer. If left alone, the beast will awaken, but if channelled properly, the Muslim person will not only renounce extremism but also act to stop others from it. This view perpetuates a cycle of mistrust and suspicion. The term "MI5 Islam," referring to the state's interference in matters of faith, has entered the political discourse in Britain.

I can't help wondering if these policies are designed to stigmatize brown communities at a moment when out-and-out racial discrimination has run its course. It made me long for the days when people like me were just called Pakis and spat at or chased down the streets by a bunch of yobs. Back then, my brown skin set me apart as none other than an other. Now it's a shield that hides my desire to destroy British values with a killing spree—or a Marks & Spencer–free shopping spree. Prevent can't always tell the difference.

CHAPTER 9

France: Another Paris

Vendors and customers at the fruit-and-vegetable market in Barbès seem particularly frazzled this Wednesday afternoon in June. It's one day before the start of Ramadan, the Muslim month of fasting, and shoppers have descended on this twice-weekly market with a plan to stock up for thirty days' worth of culinary excess at the end of each full day of fasting. Veiled Muslim women, more than half the shoppers, stuff their carts with large bags of peppers, okra and eggplant. Men of African descent dominate on the vending side, running back and forth between the stalls and nearby trucks to replenish their stock. Arabic and French flow interchangeably, with the odd English word here and white French person there.

Nestled below the arches of the Barbès-Rochechouart above-ground metro station, the market has acquired two contradictory but ultimately complementary reputations: it's where migrants from North Africa (the Maghreb) congregate, and therefore it's a part of Paris that tourists, particularly women, are advised not to visit alone. "Don't take your wallet with you," cautioned Emmanuel, my charming Airbnb host, when I asked for directions from his Marais apartment in the centre of Paris. "And don't go at night," he added, explaining that pickpockets, gangs and other undesirables operate in the area. But Barbès enjoys a second reputation as a funky, "colourful" intersection where visitors can see the "real" Paris. The usual caveats about vigilance and street smarts apply but are quickly followed with "as you would anywhere in Paris." (It's a short stroll away from the tourist trap of Montmartre, but there's little foot traffic between the two.)

A heavy police presence on the periphery of the market and at the gates and pay barriers of the metro station confirms the first view of Barbès as a dangerous place, while also betraying the heavy-handedness with which such threats are acted upon in public spaces. Like Whitechapel in London, Barbès is a handful of subway stops from the heart of a major European capital, but it might as well be a galaxy away.

Scurrying through the market and then walking more leisurely on the side streets around it, I immediately experience both aspects of Barbès. I get funny looks from two police officers who see me scribbling a few words on my notepad. I'm not carrying any proof of my identity with me, having taken Emmanuel's advice and left my wallet at home, so I keep walking. Just up the street from the market and at virtually every street corner, I encounter a glut of brown, unshaven and gruff-looking men hustling me to buy cigarettes, mobile phones, fake perfumes, tacky T-shirts. Their tone is sometimes aggressive, certainly persistent, but nothing here scares me or would stop me from visiting again. When I try to engage one of the cigarette sellers in a conversation in English, he simply responds with "*En français?*" As I don't speak French, I switch to Arabic to see if that will loosen his tongue, but the change does little to comfort him. He tells me to keep walking.

I don't know why I assumed that our brown skin and Arabic heritage would create a bonding moment. My life and his couldn't be more different, and he has thousands, if not millions, of other brown North Africans to chat with if he wants.

Licensed vendors of grilled corn husks and Arabic sweets show relatively more hospitality when I approach with questions in Arabic, but they make their wariness clear. They don't really like to talk to journalists. "How much do I get paid?" jokes an Algerian-born man in his late twenties who works behind the counter at a fast food eatery specializing in halal grilled chicken. Because he's "*sans papiers*," or without official residency papers, he declines to share his name, but that doesn't stop him from venting. "Every day, you don't know if you'll sleep in your bed or in a prison cell," he tells me. He has taken up a string of low-paid jobs, mainly in retail or catering, for almost a decade now and sees no sign of getting out of the rut of underemployment. If it weren't for his two Paris-born children, he would return to Algeria. "The French hate us. Arabs hate us. And I hate them, too," he says in Arabic, ending his sentence with a cuss word or two. A customer, also of Algerian origin and probably in his seventies, listens in on part of our conversation. He tells the younger man to stop talking (or to stop wasting his breath, if I hear him correctly). I'm asked to buy something or leave. As I'm a vegetarian, I choose the latter.

There's an unmistakable sense of doom, of futility and of all-round suspicion in the lives of many Muslims of North African origin in France. Over the next few days, I listen to more stories—some have positive notes, but most are bleak—from people with various educational and social backgrounds, and those stories collectively help me grasp what it means to be brown and Muslim in a country that continues to struggle with racial and cultural difference within and outside its borders. In France you can still detect traces of the colonial mindset that began with Napoleon's invasion of Egypt in 1798 and continued with the occupation of Algeria in 1830, among other imperial acquisitions. My visit to Paris took place five months after the January 2015 attacks on the satirical magazine *Charlie Hebdo* and a kosher supermarket, which left seventeen dead, and five months before the November 13 coordinated attacks on a concert hall, a sports stadium, and bars and restaurants, which claimed the lives of 130 people. I had assumed that relations between mainstream French society and its largest ethnic and religious minority would be intense, inflamed after the January events. But I didn't anticipate this level of despair or loathing, which, my contacts in France tell me, only intensified after the November killing spree.

I got a taste of the white French side of the argument from a conversation with Emmanuel, a classical musician who plays the oboe in a local orchestra. I asked him if he would be able to introduce me to any colleagues in the orchestra who happened to be of North African or Muslim heritage. I live in Toronto and always assume that any music or theatre group nowadays includes artists from different ethnicities. Emmanuel's response shot down that theory. His orchestra doesn't include a single Muslim or African person. "It's a European art. How can they understand it?" Muslims cannot comprehend, let alone play, the notes of a classical score. When I pressed him to explain his personal views on Muslims and Arab immigrants in France, it became clear that I'd touched a nerve. He seemed on the verge of tears, his face suddenly ashen and his eyes fixed on a cloud formation to avoid contact with mine. After a few moments of silence, he told me that he didn't think his English was good enough to engage in this conversation. Instead, he promised to put his thoughts into a letter in French that he'd send me in a few days.

It'll be a long week in Paris, I thought.

*

NO ONE KNOWS FOR SURE how many Muslims live in France. The last census in which the government asked respondents to indicate their religion was taken in 1872. The separation of Church and State, written into law in 1905 by the Third Republic, meant that the government had no right to ask people to reveal their faith. Current estimates—and they are just that—of the Muslim population go as low as three million and as high as ten. Most reputable studies within the last decade settled on a middle ground of five million or so. A report from the Brookings Institution suggests that both the extreme right-wing National Front and local Muslim organizations tend to inflate the numbers—the former as scaremongering, the latter to lobby for more funding. It's safe to say that at least three-quarters of the Muslim population comes from Algeria, Morocco and Tunisia; the remaining quarter comes from as many as 123 different countries, including nations in West Africa and the Middle East. Paris, Marseille and Lyon are home to the majority of Muslims in France.

The first wave came from French Algeria in 1924, when at least a hundred thousand men relocated to France—where they were subjects and not citizens. The first mosque in Paris opened its doors to the community two years later. A second wave of North African migration to France began immediately after the Second World War. The migrants in both waves were homogenous: single male workers taking on manufacturing, mining, construction or sanitation jobs left vacant after the wars. In that, these early Muslim migrants were no different from the millions of brown workers before and since who uprooted themselves to perform jobs that native populations would not do. Only after the colonial wars of independence in the Maghreb, which ended French rule over Algeria in 1962 and the protectorate status of Tunisia and Morocco between 1954 and 1956, did the demographics shift to include families. Residences designed for single workers roughing it on the fringes of cities were retrofitted into family dwellings, with the pursuant problems of overcrowding, noise and poor hygiene.

North Africans joined a long list of people who, over the previous century, had settled in France: Italians, Greeks, Eastern European Jews. Unlike those groups, and despite France's long political and cultural dominance in the Maghreb, North African immigrants experienced alienation and more than the standard French xenophobia. Their skin colour set them apart physically, and culturally their non-European origin and religion acted as barriers to one of the lofty ideals of the Republic: integration. The low economic status of most early immigrants—as well as stories of a lawless and physically aggressive male population—did little to change public perception of them as undesirables and their religion as distinct, separate.

This separation unfolded on not only an ideological level but, more significantly, a physical one. The history of North African immigrants is one of ghettoization and housing apartheid. As British historian Jim House notes, Algerians in particular were "at the bottom of the queue for social housing, and many local authority agencies openly discriminated against them." Housed in what in effect were shantytowns outside Paris, Lyon or Marseille, these immigrants countered the social stigma of their living conditions by developing tightly knit communities that provided a system of support but inadvertently accentuated their separate existence. The *banlieues*—the housing projects that ring big French cities and are largely occupied by black and brown immigrants—may have been materially better, but they continue to be thought of by native and immigrant French alike as symbolic of urban alienation and violence. A youth riot that rocked Paris in 2005—and a relatively smaller one in 2007—originated in the *banlieues* and fed off residents' sense of social injustice and neglect. The riot's racialized, Arab roots can be gleaned from the media's shorthand for it: the French Intifada. International reporters who descended on the *banlieues* to learn more about the two brothers responsible for the *Charlie Hebdo* attacks often described them as living a "parallel existence" from the rest of the country. The most startling description of the *banlieues* appears in Andrew Hussey's history of the "long war" between France and its Arabs, also called *The French Intifada*: "For all their modernity, these urban spaces are designed almost like vast prison camps. The *banlieue* is the most literal representation of 'otherness'—the otherness of exclusion, of the repressed, of the fearful and despised."

Nearly a century after that first wave of North African migrants, questions of integration and cultural incompatibility dog a community that has grown by the millions—thanks, in part, to family reunification laws, a higher birth rate and an insatiable need for cheap labour in France during the economic boom of the late 1940s to the early 1970s, or what historians refer to as the country's Glorious Thirty Years. When the oil crisis of 1973 led to a worldwide recession that hit France's economy hard, the presence of the North African community, once an inevitable consequence of French imperialist expansion, turned into a localized problem. Brown immigrants were welcomed (or at least tolerated) until the first sign of financial trouble, when they became a burden. Like South Asians in the United Kingdom, children of another empire, North Africans in France faced discrimination for their cultural incompatibility and not necessarily for their skin colour, religion or ethnicity. (Immigrants from the region included Jews and Algerian Berbers who didn't identify as Arabs or Muslims.) What these immigrants ate, what they drank (or didn't drink), what they wore and how they treated women—all were (and still are) stumbling blocks on the road to integration.

For many commentators, the focus on cultural difference serves as a distraction from the larger economic and social toll of marginalization. Unemployment for brown and black citizens in France sits at 20 percent, double the national average. The Muslim population in French prisons, which studies put at 50 to 80 percent, is staggeringly out of proportion with the general demographics. While this may reflect limited opportunities for North African youth in particular, it also suggests a systemic bias within the judiciary. According to one study, "Crimes involving young Muslims are prosecuted more vigorously than those of their peers." The legal system, social justice activists believe, focuses its energy on youth of non-French origins.

The transformation from immigrant other to Muslim other began in subtle, slow measures in the 1980s but gained speed and turned confrontational in the 1990s. The uptick coincides with the civil war in Algeria, which began in 1992 and lasted throughout the decade, forcing thousands of Muslim—and perhaps even Islamist—refugees and immigrants to settle in France. The 9/11 attacks in the US helped propel what was up until then a series of provocations and counter-provocations between the state and its Muslim minorities into a full-scale cultural war. In 2004, citing the *Laïcité* principles (which ensure the neutral role of the state in matters of religion), the government of Jacques Chirac passed a law that would ban all religious symbols in schools. Despite language that included the cultural insignia of all major religions, the law was understood as an attempt to stem the tide of Islamic religiosity. Advocates believed the law would uphold the principles of secularism and send a strong message about an intolerant version of Islam that discriminates against women. Critics pointed out the law's potential to inflame the militant tendencies of a younger generation of Muslims, increasing their sense of alienation, and argued for flexibility (modernization) of the century-old *Laïcité* laws. A cultural war and a war of cultures beckoned.

Even kebab has become a battleground in this war. The grilled meat sandwich, which entered French cuisine through its Muslim Turkish population in the 1990s, has become a €1.5 billion industry, with as many as three hundred million sandwiches served at an estimated ten thousand (and rising) outlets. In the 2014 French municipal elections, candidates from the far-right National Front campaigned against what one politician called the "kebabization of France." In certain segments in French society, the popularity of kebab tapped into anxieties about Muslim culture: halal meat served by swarthy, low-paid immigrants in what some claimed were unhygienic conditions. In a heavily syndicated Reuters story by reporter Alexandria Sage in 2014, the owner of France's first chain of kebab houses summed up the underlying emotional tenor of the war on kebab: "We're not asking anyone to sing the praises of kebabs or to make kebabs a French dish, as we know that will never happen. . . . But it's just like the image France has today with its own immigrants. . . . They bring a richness to France and yet France doesn't embrace that."

The Collectif contre l'islamophobie en France (CCIF) was set up in 2003 to document transitions and disruptions in society's views toward Muslims, and to offer support and legal advice to those affected by them. It's a small but highly effective organization operating out of a nondescript office behind a printing house in the city of Saint-Ouen, outside Paris.

Because of the sensitivity of its business—read: to avoid getting attacked or torched by right-wing extremists—the CCIF doesn't share its address with people it doesn't know well. When its spokesperson, Yasser Louati, invites me to visit the office and talk to staff, he asks me to call him when I exit the metro station so he can meet me there. We walk together to the office, which I may have had a hard time finding even with an address and a map. I get a glimpse of the CCIF's paranoia from the first image I see inside its doors: a painting of a shooting target superimposed on a veiled woman. A more nuanced poster for an ad campaign by CCIF reproduces a famous painting from the French Revolution but reimagines the models as Muslims, immigrants and other underprivileged groups. The caption translates to "We (too) are the nation." Yasser tells me that the Paris metro authority banned the poster because it considered it religious in tone. By and large, French officials have not embraced the CCIF, which has repeatedly stated that most of the discrimination cases it tracks—up to 66 percent in the first half of 2015—have been carried out by government agencies (housing, education, security and policing).

Yasser, thirty-five, embodies the many challenges facing younger Muslim men in France. The son of Tunisian parents who have lived in France since the 1960s, he trained as a pilot in the United States and worked for almost a decade in the Gulf for commercial and private airlines. In 2011, after the financial crisis clipped the wings of the private aviation sector, he returned to his hometown of Paris and a brutal unemployment reality. Despite his ten years as a pilot, he couldn't secure a job in aviation. Instead, the father of two made ends meet by working the night shift in a three-star hotel in downtown Paris, abandoning an earlier dream of starting an MBA. "Either I am overqualified or my resumé is too atypical," he says, looking back at his years of job hunting. A work history largely in the Muslim world didn't help either.

But it looks like the former pilot has found his true calling with this new job as the CCIF's public face. It suits his personality as a big mouth. He recalls his mother, fearful of the attention he was drawing to the family, warning him to stop arguing with other students and teachers at school about Muslim issues. His parents were typical of early Arab immigrants who kept themselves to themselves. "My parents lived with fear. . . . They always had a fear toward authority—whatever was said to them was true." They also didn't identify as Muslims but took pride in their Arabic heritage, sending ten-year-old Yasser back to Tunisia for a few years to learn his native language and culture. Their motives were strictly nationalist and not religious, but things didn't play out that way. When Yasser was about sixteen and back in Paris, in 1995, he began to pray in his school. At first, he was the only one. Not long after, friends of North African origin began to follow his example. "As the years went by, people my age started to return to their Muslim identity," he explains. French society showed hostility to these young people, and they in turn were hostile to it. Religion became the ammunition each side used in this war.

Elsa Ray, a white Frenchwoman, converted to Islam in her twenties and began working with the CCIF not long after it was set up. Her veil and loose-fitting clothes, which adhere to Muslim notions of female modesty, trump her white skin when it comes to being on the receiving end of racial harassment on the streets or in dealings with local authorities. Her experience, like that of many converts, confirms the hypothesis that the new discrimination in France targets Muslims for being identifiably Muslim. Symbols of Muslim identity have a way of projecting a darker hue onto her skin, to the point where she receives ethnic-specific taunts. It's no wonder that women—because of the veil or niqab, or perhaps because they're seen as weak or helpless—were the targets of about 73 percent of the Islamophobia incidents recorded by the CCIF in the first half of 2015. In the life of a French Muslim woman, Elsa tells me, there are "many chances" to face discrimination. "When she's going to high school or university. As a wife, mother, worker. When she plays sports or if she wants to go the cinema, she can experience racism."

Elsa's list is drawn not from theoretical possibilities but from actual data the CCIF has collected over the years. In one case that the CCIF took up, a gym denied membership to a Muslim woman because she wore a veil. The gym owners backtracked when they were threatened with a lawsuit. Several schools up and down the country have sent female students home or suspended them for wearing veils or (as I'll explain later) long skirts that cover their legs. A supermarket refused to rehire a checkout clerk who returned to work after a maternity leave with her hair covered.

Most of these cases involved younger members of the Muslim community, who, Elsa argues, refused to repeat the mistakes of their parents. "After [decades], the kids born in France realized that being invisible is not the solution to integrate to society. . . . One explanation for [rediscovery of Islam] is as a way to confirm their identity." They're French but they're also Muslim, the thinking goes.

Racism has evolved as well. In the past, many French displayed a xenophobia and a "post-colonial state of mind" that claimed to know what was best for everyone. Nowadays racial anxieties have shifted to one religious and ethnic group: Muslim North Africans. This is not an Arab or ethnic thing. Lebanese and Syrian immigrants in France tend to be lighter in skin and more middle class, and they include a larger proportion of Christians. They hardly factor in the anti-immigration rhetoric of far-right groups or pro-integration hardliners. In fact, politicians often hold them up as the model of Arab immigration (just as they single out North Africans as a problem population). The world of immigrants is not complete until it's divided into the good brown people and the bad brown people.

*

AFTER MORE THAN A decade as a career diplomat, working in French embassies and consulates in Yemen, Korea and Spain, Samira returned to Paris with the hope of finding a job that draws on her extensive experience in media and international relations. The thirty-something Lyon-born woman of Algerian descent also wanted to get married and start a family—something she achieved shortly after returning to France, when she met her husband, Hisham, on her way to a job interview. She asked him for directions, he gave her his phone number and the rest is history (or rom-com meet-cute fodder). But finding love in Paris proved much, much easier than finding work.

Despite submitting application after application, Samira rarely received more than a short email message or a cryptic voicemail to the effect that her resumé didn't meet the job description. She often got no response of any kind, even when, in her opinion, her qualifications seemed like a perfect fit. Something doesn't add up here, she thought. So as an experiment, she sent out two resumés with the next job application: one with her own name and the other with a very French-sounding name, Mathilde. (Samira asked me not to reveal her last name or that of her resumé doppelgänger. Whitefacing is something she's not proud of.) She used her landline number for one and her mobile for the other. Within a week of applying to a Paris-based media company looking for a spokesperson, Samira received a call on her mobile from a woman asking to speak to Mathilde.

"It took me a second to process her request," says Samira during a Ramadan *iftar* (the meal that breaks the fast) at the apartment she shares with her husband and one-year-old son in the suburb of Montfermeil, about eighteen kilometres from the heart of Paris. The human resources person on the other end of the line told Samira that Mathilde's work history had left such a strong impression that she wanted to conduct a pre-interview on the spot and possibly invite her for an in-person chat the following week. Samira agreed to the interview, which focused on her previous work experience and ideas for the new job. A degree in political science and her experience in the diplomatic core had taught her to handle any situation with classic grace under pressure. By the time the phone call ended, Samira—or Mathilde—had been invited for that second interview. To extricate herself from this awkward and potentially illegal situation, Samira called the HR person a day before the scheduled interview to tell her that she had accepted another position. She sent no more resumés with Mathilde's name—there was no need to do so.

Whatever point Samira needed to get across, to herself at least, had been made. Job applicants with non-French-sounding names face discrimination that goes beyond the "so many applicants, not enough jobs" explanation. Studies back up Samira's resumé experiment, suggesting that those with Muslim-sounding names—regardless of their ethnic origin—are more likely to be passed over by employers. In a preview article of their upcoming book, *Why Muslim Integration Fails in Christian-Heritage Societies*, Claire Adida, David Laitin and Marie-Anne Valfort conducted a similar experiment, sending out two nearly identical resumés on behalf of people from the Senegalese community, which includes both Muslim and Christian members. Muslim candidates were 2.5 times less likely to get an interview than their Christian counterparts.

When Samira, as Samira, eventually landed a job interview at a TV station, her interviewer asked her to show papers that proved her French citizenship—despite the fact that her resumé listed her all-French education and included a history of representing the country in diplomatic missions around the globe. "I remember thinking, This is not happening to me. It's become a joke." She thought that while she was working abroad, a law had been passed requiring candidates to show proof of residency during job interviews. Somehow, the woman interviewing Samira still thought of her as illegal because of her name and skin colour.

Samira didn't get that job—or another one at a community radio station. She now believes it's impossible to get work in Paris if she wants to keep her Arab identity and religion. Her friends advise her to play the game: hang out at restaurants and social events where she can network with potential employers over a drink, but she says that she "can't fit into those kinds of situations." To make ends meet, she has accepted work as an office cleaner. I'm so surprised at this twist that I ask her to repeat herself in case I've misheard her. "A cleaner. Emptying the trash," she tells me with a note of defiance.

My normal reaction to a dinner conversation that gets to this point is to reach for my glass of wine. But this is a strictly Muslim household and no alcohol is permitted. Before we sat down to eat, Hisham (Samira's husband) and Elias, a law student friend of the family, had completed the fourth of the five daily prayers that Muslims are required to perform. It was just past ten in the evening and everyone in the apartment, except me and the toddler, had been fasting all day. All were between twenty-five and thirty-five, and their adherence to Islamic rituals started as part of the rebellion against both their parents and French society at large that Yasser and Elsa from the CCIF had talked about.

"Our parents told us to be quiet," Samira explains as the two other men in the room nod in agreement. "This is how we've been raised—seeing our parents humiliated and seeing our parents seeing us humiliated and telling us not to talk about it." Hisham describes the humiliation of his parents' generation as a trauma. "If you talk to anyone—Tunisian, Algerian, Moroccan—it's the same," he says. "Parents telling us, 'Please don't say anything.'" Earlier generations of North African immigrants tried to deal with racism by not showing signs of their ethnicity or religion. Very few women wore the veil or any other traditional items of clothing, while men avoided political discussions and gatherings. But their children and grandchildren face a new kind of discrimination, in which a volatile mix of race, religion and culture sets them apart from society and brings them into nasty confrontations with the police and the judicial system.

Elias, who grew up in the coastal town of Marseille to working-class Moroccan parents, has experienced a series of such confrontations with the police. As a teen he would get stopped routinely when he used a jet ski on the Mediterranean, with police officers assuming it was stolen and adding insult to suspicion by telling him that he looked like someone who eats too much *shourba* (Moroccan soup). After a football game one evening about six years ago, Elias found his car blocked in by two police officers sitting idly in their cruiser. When he asked one of them—politely but firmly, he insists—to move so he could get out, the situation escalated within minutes. In front of multiple witnesses, one of the officers hit Elias in the face. Eventually, he moved his car just enough to make it possible for Elias to get out. Elias knew that were he even to brush against the cruiser, he could be arrested for damaging police property. Somehow he managed to squeeze out and drove home. He didn't report the incident. "Even if you report it, nothing is done. When an Arab speaks, his word is worthless for the police."

Instead of giving up on life in France or following some of his hometown friends in joining ISIS or rebel groups fighting Bashar Assad's regime in Syria, Elias focused on his law studies. He's currently preparing for his bar exam in Paris and plans to specialize in discrimination and penal law. But even this transition from perceived lawbreaker to law practitioner came with its own racial overtones. When he was articling for a Paris-based law firm and accompanying senior members to court appearances, he would often find himself blocked from entering areas where other lawyers prepared for trials or met with clients. Court officers assumed he was the accused or a gang member. "Even if you're doing something with your life, they [French society] put obstacles."

As I listen to Elias and Samira, one thought comes to mind: Why don't they leave France and perhaps come to Canada, or go somewhere in Europe where their ethnicity doesn't carry the same baggage? "We *are* French," Samira shouts back from the kitchen when she hears my question. "They have to accept us. We're not fleeing. If we leave, that means they're right. I want to make them accept us." While she says she hopes things will get better for her son's generation, at the moment she's not optimistic. "It's getting worse." You don't need to be a mind reader to guess that she's referring to the post–*Charlie Hebdo* atmosphere.

Everyone at the dinner table agrees that the attack was a horrific crime that portrayed the entire Muslim community in France in the worst possible light. But they also believe it gave the French licence to say that they don't like Muslims in their midst and get away with it. Samira remembers crying uncontrollably when the news broke and wishing she could get away from France for a while. In the days after the attacks, she paid her respects to the family of Ahmed Merabet, the Arab police officer who was killed as he responded to the gunshots. (This is the Ahmed in the hashtag #jesuisAhmed, which trended on Twitter as an alternative to the more universal #jesuischarlie.) "He was a really good guy," says Samira. "When you enter his mom's house, it's like you've entered your grandmother's." What irked her, though, was a comment from former president Nicolas Sarkozy, who wondered why the women in the officer's family wore veils for a public ceremony. "Instead of saying [Merabet] gave his life for his country, [Sarkozy] focused on what his mother was wearing. This is Islamophobia." Samira says that the secretary of ecology was the only official government representative at Merabet's funeral. Even members of the police union and politicians from the officer's home municipality were outraged by this slight. "He died in his uniform. What more can he do? *He died in his uniform.* He died a hero," continues Samira, holding back tears. "He died for nothing. Muslim life here is like black life [in the US]. It's worth nothing."

It's almost 2 a.m. and Elias offers to drive me home. I'm extremely grateful, as I'm not entirely sure I can get back to my apartment in the Marais at this hour by public transport. He and I chat in the car about his experiences growing up in Marseille, and I hear more horror stories. But I don't need to delve into his past to get a taste of his present life, with its fears of police brutality and discrimination. As we leave the quiet streets of Montfermeil and head toward the highway that will take us back to central Paris, we hear a siren. Elias becomes nervous, thinking that a police car is following him. He pulls aside and starts looking for his papers. When it turns out to be an ambulance, he keeps driving. Internalizing suspicion has become a daily routine for brown youth in France.

When I contacted Samira the morning after the November 13 attacks at the Bataclan concert hall and other venues, she told me that everything had changed again. "You should see Paris. It's like everyone is mourning. Everyone [is] looking and suspecting everyone. It's just awful." Her resolve to stick it out in Paris after the *Charlie Hebdo* attacks seemed much weakened now, especially as the mother of a baby boy. Who wants to raise a child in a country where his faith and brown skin would be associated with the worst terror attack, to date, in its history?

*

SAMIRA'S ASSERTION THAT Muslims in France have much in common with black Americans danced in my head as I got off at the Père

Lachaise metro stop the next day. I was there to witness a demonstration against the acquittal of a police officer who shot dead an unarmed black youth named Lamine Dieng in 2007. "Ferguson, Detroit, Baltimore . . . Et aussi [and also] Paris en France," read one of the leaflets distributed before the march. Scheduled for a Saturday afternoon, the demonstration started outside 58, rue des Amandiers, where Dieng was gunned down. The murder (and the march) took place in a working-class and migrant-heavy residential area with numerous businesses catering to African and Muslim people: Islamic burial, halal meat, women-only hairdressers. One of the protest's sponsors was the Coalition Against Racial Profiling, whose public face, Sihame Assbague, has emerged as a trenchant critic of institutional and societal Islamophobia.

Sihame grabbed worldwide attention in April 2015 when she started the hashtag #jeportemajupecommejeveux (I wear my skirt as I please). It was a response to a headteacher in the northern French town of Charleville-Mézières who sent home a fifteen-year-old Muslim student for wearing a long black skirt. The skirt, the teacher believed, revealed the girl's religious affiliation, thereby violating the country's secularity laws.

When Sihame woke up to the news, she thought, "First they came after the head scarf and now the skirt?" She searched the Internet to find photographs of white women sporting similar outfits. Within minutes she found images of two female government ministers and an actress, and in a tweet, she asked the teacher to explain why the student was singled out for wearing such a fashionable item. International news agencies picked up the story after the hashtag went viral, and some ran posts featuring other women in long skirts, including the character Elsa from the animated feature *Frozen*.

As a report in the *Guardian* noted, the region's education officer considered the skirt a "provocation" on the student's part, an attempt to bring her faith into a secular space. Even the *New York Times* weighed in on the incident with an editorial that ended with a harsh message to French society: "The principle of laïcité originally arose in the struggle against the dominant role of the Roman Catholic Church, but that battle was decisively won a long time ago. No religion poses a serious challenge today to secular rule in France, and to invoke so lofty a principle against a girl wearing a long skirt only makes a mockery of it."

I catch up with Sihame and about one hundred demonstrators at the twentieth arrondissemont amid chants of "*Justice pour Lamine*" and "*Vérité* [truth] *pour Lamine*." Sihame believes brown and black French citizens must work together, since both often find themselves the target of racial profiling or heavy-handed (to put it mildly, given the circumstances of Lamine's death) police tactics. However, she agrees that French people of Muslim and North African descent like her—her parents hail from Morocco, but she was born and raised in Paris—face the added stigma of their religious identity and integration issues.

Our conversation takes place as we walk alongside other protestors. The mood is surprisingly celebratory, and the real interruptions come from friends saying hello to Sihame. I get a sense that I'm walking with a community of professional protestors, or at least people who have done this so many times that they've mastered the art of the political demonstration. Aside from one argument between two activists and a motorcyclist who tried to cut across the pedestrian-only demo route, the protest is peaceful. Police officers in plain clothes direct traffic onto alternative routes. As I scan the crowd, I see an overwhelmingly large number of bearded men and veiled women, all in their twenties and thirties. I casually remark to Sihame that I'm not surprised so many young Muslims in France are "retreating" to religion in order to escape the harsh realities of life. I have barely finished my sentence when she darts a glance my way, as if to say, "I can't believe you, too, have bought into this narrative."

"It's an insult to think that people choose their religion because of the weakness of the state," she cautions me. "That doesn't respect the choices of people. If I choose to come back to Islam, it's because I believe in Islamic values." In fact, it was Sihame who, when she was fourteen or fifteen, insisted that her family buy only halal meat. Up until then, her mother, a house cleaner, bought whatever meat she could find in the supermarket nearest to their apartment building. Sihame did some research and found a butcher not that far away, and from that point on the family bought only halal meat. At around the same time, Sihame's history teacher began to make disparaging comments about Muslims, and she found she couldn't defend her faith because she didn't know much about it. Her parents, like many of their contemporaries, considered themselves largely secular. (Her father came to France in 1972 to work on the railways and married her mother in 1984.) Sihame began to read the Koran and educate herself on Islam, and she ultimately found a sense of belonging and comfort in its teachings. She admits that her parents at first expressed concern for this newfound religiosity, but they have since come on board.

Like Samira and Elias, Sihame is forging an identity for herself—and her generation—as both Muslim *and* French. She doesn't buy into the dichotomy that even some Muslim public figures have advocated: to be truly French, Muslims must relax their faith and sign on to the secularity model. Or the idea that to be Muslim, a woman must cover her hair and act submissive. Sihame doesn't wear the veil but understands why some women choose to put it on—to take control of their own bodies, to give themselves a say in a society that otherwise limits their right to choose how to present themselves.

I'm not sure I agree, so I change the subject and tell Sihame about my experience in Barbès, where several Muslim business owners declined to talk to me, and about a failed attempt to engage a group of Muslim students at the Institut du monde arabe. "They're afraid they'll get profiled for something they tell you," she explains. One of her friends chimes in: "I don't believe free speech exists. You can say whatever you want, but there are consequences." Sihame believes that the *Charlie Hebdo* attack led to an "explosion" in Islamophobia. "It became completely natural." This wave of Islamophobia has swept across other immigrants from South Asia, including Sri Lankan and Indian newcomers who are assumed to be Muslims until proven otherwise. While they're less targeted than North Africans, they're not as organized and therefore tend not to document their encounters with racism. It's this expansion in the scope and vocabulary of racism that keeps Sihame marching in the streets on a Saturday that she could have spent at home with her husband and first-born.

"The struggle is vital. It's a matter of life and death," she tells me. "We need to do this for the next generation. We have no choice."

*

THREE DAYS BEFORE I leave Paris, I receive an email from Emmanuel while I'm having lunch at a café near the Gare du Nord. Emmanuel says I can find the letter he promised when we first talked if I look under the mat outside his apartment. Six weeks after my return from Paris, my friend Antony, a French immersion teacher in Toronto, translates it for me, and with Emmanuel's permission, I include it below with only one paragraph (related to the issue of gay marriage) deleted. I had expected a rant about Muslim violence and incompatibility with European values, but instead the letter placed the blame for the current cultural impasse on the French majority. It didn't offer solutions or even hint at a reconciliation. Instead, its note of resignation echoed what, I suspect, many moderate French people feel about the Muslims in their midst and the politicians who use them as an election issue.

You had asked me what the French thought of the Muslim community and what my thoughts were about the subject.

Paris is a left-wing city (politically socialist), as is France. The French believe themselves to be "open" politically, socially, culturally and religiously. But this is false and superficial. Even our political leaders do not believe what they say and what they recommend.

Fundamentally, historically, we the French are right-wing, but without honest and competent leaders, we have elected a left-wing man [Hollande], one who speaks of tolerance and integration but one who is incapable of putting his words into action.

Laws have been created to punish anyone punitively (or financially) who is xenophobic or homophobic. However, what is the reality? People say they follow these laws; however, their actions speak otherwise.

Historically, the French do not have any consciousness of this:

- *The Crusades, where the Catholic kings set out to conquer the world, in order to destroy the Muslim world.*
- *The Inquisition, when in the name of religion we burned all heretics! (It is understood that we burned anyone who did not conform to social norms, anyone who was different.) A ton of innocents were sacrificed.*
- *Later: colonialism. For example, in 1962, Algeria became independent, but France had used up all of its riches and petrol for many years.*

Later, France was happy to have North African Muslims "work" in coal mines in northern France (cheap labour, completely exploited). In short, this use of man by man gives the impression that "slavery" has not disappeared. This is why we can understand protests and revolts. . . .

France continues, due to its pride, to believe that it is a strong country, powerful and dominant. It is thus becoming the prey of a radical Islam. The security of the country has become a major stake for our political leaders; the subject of terrorism supplants all others (social issues, unemployment, and loss of purchasing power). . . . It's ultimately a bonus for our political leaders to maintain this daily fear. And the best way to control Islam is to control all of the Muslim world: no Muslim man will ever have access to the key ring of our state.

No one will admit to this, but it's a fact: the Muslim person sweeps, picks up the trash, fixes cars—and the luckiest of them all can teach Science.

It's all an illusion and appearance!

CHAPTER 10

The United States: Undocumented

For Mexicans and Mexican-Americans, the summer of 2015 will be remembered as the Summer of Trump. The real estate mogul and TV personality declared war on immigrants from Mexico when he announced his presidential bid on June 16. In a now infamous speech, Trump proclaimed: "They're bringing drugs. They're bringing crime. They're rapists. And some, I assume, are good people." In the following weeks, he refused to apologize for his statements and even, in the parlance of the TV talk shows on which he made frequent appearances, doubled down on his attacks. By mid-August, Trump's platform included promises to force Mexico to pay for a wall that would stretch across three thousand kilometres to "keep itself out" of the US. He also claimed that if elected, he'd ban remittances from illegal immigrants to their families in Mexico and deny children born on US soil their "birthright," or claim to citizenship, even though that right is enshrined in the Fourteenth Amendment to the Constitution.

Not to be left out of the Mexican-baiting games, other Republican candidates—including Ted Cruz, Rick Santorum, Scott Walker and Bobby Jindal (the only brown man among them)—echoed Trump's policy statements in their own campaigns, or at least agreed with the sentiment behind them. Ben Carson, at the time Trump's closest rival for the Republican Party nomination, suggested that only Mexicans working in the agricultural sector should be allowed to stay in the US. "After we seal the borders, after we turn off the spigot that dispenses all the goodies . . . people who had a pristine record, we should consider allowing them to become guest workers primarily in the agricultural sphere," he said during a Republican presidential debate in September. In the 2016 race to the White House, it looked like Mexicans (and Latinos in general) would be the scapegoat of choice, perhaps knocking their fellow brown people, Muslims and Arabs, from their perch as America's favourite ethnic group to hate. As a member of the latter group, I breathed a sigh of relief—even if, deep down, I knew our (next) turn would come. (Sure enough, by the end of 2015 Trump said he would consider requiring Muslim-Americans to register in databases or carry special identification cards, among other measures to combat terrorism.)

Sitting in a corner booth that doubles as his office in one of two Mexican restaurants he owns in the Bronx, New York, Antonio laughs off the Republican candidates' demonization of undocumented Mexican immigrants. "Republicans know that immigrants make them money," he tells me on a Sunday morning, just before the brunch crowd descends at noon. Many tycoons, including Trump, built their fortunes on the sweat and tears of immigrants. But maybe Mexicans have allowed themselves to be boxed into this corner, he adds. "We come from somewhere else, so we accept lower wages. It's the price immigrants pay to come to the States—work hard and get paid less. . . . We're less educated. That's why we came here. We get paid by the hour and we've accepted that." Restaurant owners and fast food chains depend on this system of exploitation. In 2008, the Pew Hispanic Center released a study suggesting that about 20 percent of cooks and chefs in America were illegal immigrants, mostly from Mexico.

Antonio fits into his own profile of the hardworking and exploited immigrant, but he also stands out as a prime example of a capitalist success story: those illegal immigrants who bust their humps for years, save enough money to start their own businesses and offer employment to others—all while paying their taxes ($11,000 every three months, in Antonio's case) and remaining undocumented, subject to deportation or criminal charges for living illegally in the country. After a number of years when the net immigration rate—the number of Mexicans who left the United States versus those who came in—fell to zero due to the weaker US economy and an increase in deportations, the trend reversed in the first half of 2015. Latest immigration data show the number of Mexican immigrants to the US rebounded to 740,000 in 2014–15, or 44 percent of the 1.7 million newcomers. According to 2015 figures, nearly 12.1 million migrants live and work in the US illegally, and just over half (52 percent) come from Mexico.

In 1997, twenty-two-year-old Antonio joined this six-million-people-and-counting club. Looking back, he's not sure why he immigrated. "It was an opportunity. I just packed and left." His first impressions of New York City didn't match the images he saw on TV growing up in his hometown of Puebla, in the centre of Mexico. "I found it dirty. It wasn't the city I expected," he says, adding that he envisaged a city that looked more like Central Park and the Upper West Side than the Bronx or Harlem. He spoke very little English at the time and lived in Corona, Queens, but commuted to Upper Manhattan for his first job: stocking fruit and vegetables in a delicatessen. The job didn't require much interaction with customers, which suited him just fine. Despite the long shifts, he carved out a few hours a week to take English classes at a community college in Queens. "I wanted to learn how to speak, how to write. I was watching lots of English channels and programs." He sharpened his colloquial English through dialogue he heard on soap operas and afternoon talk shows, including the peak years of the *Oprah Winfrey Show.* (He remains a big believer in Winfrey, whose gospel of self-help and reinvention he follows to the letter.)

As his spoken English improved, Antonio felt comfortable seeking work in the restaurant business. He started as a dishwasher alongside a rotating brown cast of Hispanic and South Asian illegals. In a few years, he'd climbed the restaurant ladder by working first as a busboy then as a bartender and a waiter at an Italian joint in the theatre district. "Whatever I wanted, I worked hard for it. It was hard with the long hours and not having the education. I watched everybody and tried to learn the business."

Despite the pressure of juggling three part-time jobs and working eighteen-hour days, Antonio knew that once he'd learned the ropes of managing a restaurant, it wouldn't be long before he opened his own. The fact that he was still undocumented after more than ten years in New York didn't stop him from investing his entire life savings in his first restaurant in the Bronx in 2008. That taqueria—"I wanted to bring a piece of my Mexico to New York"—fell victim to the Great Recession and closed its doors within two years. Antonio regrouped and learned his lessons, and in 2011 he opened a new restaurant on 149th Street in the Bronx that was successful enough to finance a second outlet in the more residential area where I caught up with him.

Americans love tales of self-made men, and Republicans adore small-business owners. But they seem to draw the line when the self-made man is made in Mexico or Central America, and when his business becomes an extension of that identity. Federal agents routinely raid businesses in the food industry—chicken farms, doughnut factories, ethnic (especially Mexican) food chains—as part of a crackdown on illegal labour. I don't need to guess at the level of angst that Antonio feels from a possible immigration raid; I saw it with my own eyes. When I showed up at his restaurant for our scheduled meeting, I asked a cook in the semi-open kitchen to let him know I'd arrived. A few brown men were cutting vegetables and preparing guacamole, and they included Antonio, who was within earshot of my conversation with the female cook. Only when she and Antonio were satisfied that I was indeed the writer with an appointment and not an undercover immigration officer did he identify himself, asking me to wait for him in the corner booth.

The possibility of deportation weighs heavily on a man who says he feels he's "home" and "very integrated" in New York City. "I would be very sad if I left. It's unfair because I worked so hard. For the moment, I'm not planning on going anywhere else. I feel like I've achieved something. . . . If I die tomorrow, I can die very happy." I tell him that he's living as close a version of the American dream as I can think of, a perfect example of that can-do spirit so essential to the country's perception of itself and its history. That endorsement does little to alleviate his anxieties. "I don't know about the American dream," he shoots back. "Everybody has his own version of it. My American dream is giving jobs to twenty people, feeding their families."

As soon as the clock strikes twelve, the restaurant begins to fill up. Although weekdays attract multi-ethnic workers from nearby businesses and factories, the Sunday brunch draws an exclusively Latino crowd. Waiters take orders or answer questions about the specials in Spanish despite the English-only menu. As the kitchen is short one cook, Antonio lends a hand between taking phone orders for delivery and checking in on me. No wonder he looks older than his forty years. As a fellow gay man who is a decade older, I don't share that last observation with him. However, I do ask him how and if his sexuality and race ever intersected. "I felt more discrimination as a gay man from other Mexicans because of their machismo," he reveals, "than I felt from white people because of my skin."

Earlier in our conversation I had asked Antonio to identify his own skin colour; to me, he fell somewhere in the middle of the spectrum of light to dark brown. After saying that he never thought about his own colour (and opting for "mulatto" when pressed), he added that he "very much refer[s] to other Mexicans as brown"—at least in a political sense, in order to verbalize ongoing tensions between Hispanics and blacks. He recalls being on friendly terms with the black community during his early years in New York. "African Americans were more welcoming [then]. But when Obama came to power, they became very aggressive." Latinos—and in particular day labourers working off the books and receiving their wages in cash—became a favourite target of gangs of (predominantly black) youth. Many African Americans believe that the influx of Mexican immigrants has changed the texture of traditionally black neighbourhoods—erasing personal histories and diluting political legacies.

The community of Port Richmond in Staten Island bears witness to this ethnic shift. Between 2000 and 2008, the number of Hispanics living on Staten Island grew by about 40 percent, and many of them relocated to the Port Richmond area, once a predominantly black and low-income community. Within a few years, according to local news reports, the area became known as Little Mexico, with bars playing Spanish-language heavy metal music and shops selling chillies and tomatillos. Local black businesses closed their doors. Encounters between the two communities ranged from the indifferent to the tense to the deadly as the number of racially motivated assaults increased—at least according to Hispanics; many black commentators describe the crime wave as opportunistic. (Latin gangs also operated in many formerly black neighbourhoods, perpetuating a cycle of black-on-brown and brown-on-black crime.)

Staten Island became the latest setting for a long-simmering dispute between African American and Hispanic communities over the issue of illegal immigration. Many blacks believe that Hispanic newcomers undercut their chances at finding employment by accepting lower wages. Sociologists use the term "black flight" to describe how African Americans are ceding ground to Hispanic immigrants in places such as Los Angeles, where between 1993 and 2008 the black population fell by about 125,000 while Latino numbers rose by nearly half a million. Studies suggest that blacks in neighbourhoods with a large Hispanic presence tend to vote more consistently for anti-immigration politicians than those in mainly black neighbourhoods. A study from Harvard suggested that between 1980 and 2000, immigration from Latin countries caused black employment in the low or unskilled sectors to decline by about 7.4 percent. Work in sectors such as construction underwent a general lightening of complexion at the turn of the twenty-first century, with Hispanic workers replacing blacks. As an op-ed in the *New York Post* in 2008 described it, "The rising tensions between African-Americans and Hispanics render the old hopes of a black-brown coalition chimerical, especially as blacks realize that Latino political gains come at their expense."

On this Sunday in July, most black residents simply walk by Antonio's restaurant. They know that Sunday brunch is Latino family time. Even I, as a brown-skinned man, feel like an intruder, and so I leave this little slice of Mexico in the Bronx for another slice of Mexico in Queens.

*

LETICIA AND HER BROTHER Daniel both started their respective one-child families on money earned while working off the books in the service industry. They sidelined their creative aspirations in order to survive in one of the most expensive cities in the United States.

Both moved to New York in the 1990s—Daniel in 1993 and Leticia two years later. They came from Mexico City, where the family ran an upholstery and furniture business. Daniel, now forty-one, specialized in sofa covers, while Leticia, thirty-nine and a trained graphic designer, managed the company's advertising and promotion. When an older brother invited Daniel, a self-taught artist, to join him in New York, he thought of it strictly as an "experiment." When no jobs opened up in the furniture business, Daniel joined the long line of fellow undocumented, for whom the cash-only payments of the restaurant business provided a way to earn a living without leaving a paper trail. "Italian, Greek, Mexican [restaurants]—I worked in all of them." Eventually he settled on Italian, working at pizzerias in Manhattan and Queens for fourteen years. Leticia initially worked as a seamstress at a clothing factory in Brooklyn, but she quit that job—"I didn't like how they treated the workers"—and found herself in the kitchens of several restaurants in Manhattan. When she became pregnant, the daylong shifts no longer suited her, and she returned to her first love of graphic arts, finding work as a tattoo artist, a career she has been practising for sixteen years now.

I met each sibling separately on two different days and in two different work environments. Leticia and I chatted in the Jackson

Heights smoke shop and tattoo parlour where she works the day shift during the week. Daniel picks up the late-night and early-morning shifts at the same place. During the day he works on large-scale ceramic and papier mâché creations inspired by Mexico's pre-Hispanic history; he rents studio space in an artists' warehouse in Long Island City, and that's where he and I met to talk. Each sibling now has one child: Daniel a fourteen-year-old daughter from a previous partner, and Leticia a sixteen-year-old son from a husband who died in an accident in 2006.

At first, Daniel thought that art would bring in enough income for him to quit restaurant or tattoo work. It didn't. "I keep trying," he says as we sit in his studio, surrounded by his unsold creations. Despite some critical acclaim and support from folk art curators, buyers remain scarce. Some pieces rent out to festivals and decorate altars in Mexican community centres, but that hardly covers the cost of moving them around town in a truck. So why does he insist on working with this art form and these cultural references if the market is limited? "I have to bring my own Mexico here," he responds. "I miss it." This statement of national pride doesn't mean that Daniel and his daughter—who waited in the lobby while her father and I chatted, despite my best attempts to bring her into the conversation—have cut themselves off from the multicultural aspects of life in New York City.

"Here you see people from everywhere. I have friends from everywhere—black, brown, white." Most of the buyers (and curators) are in fact white Americans who collect Mexican art and "appreciate it more." At home, Daniel celebrates Thanksgiving and the Fourth of July because they're "good holidays." With his burly physique and long beard, he looks identifiably Mexican, but his daughter passes for white, since her mother is very light-skinned. If the daughter makes a decision to distance herself from her Mexican heritage and opt for mainstream white

American culture, Daniel says he'll be cool with that. "That's her life," he remarks, before pointing out that she's "kind of curious about Mexico."

When the daughter turns eighteen, she'll be able to sponsor Daniel, giving him his best shot at changing his undocumented status. In November 2014, President Obama announced a series of immigration reforms, including the Deferred Action for Parents of Americans and Lawful Permanent Residents (DAPA). This gives parents of children born in the US a three-year work permit and an exemption from deportation. Daniel seems as indifferent to the immigration debates within the Republican Party as he is to the Band-Aid solutions coming out of Washington. After twenty-two years without leaving New York City, he's carved out a new hybrid identity for himself: "A Mexican but a New Yorker. A new identity."

Leticia shares some of her brother's hesitancy around citizenship laws. Moving from undocumented to legal would be a welcome step, but it wouldn't solve all her problems or change her life priorities. "It depends on circumstances," she explains as she shows me sketches of some of her tattoo art, including Aztec, Mexican and traditional American ink. "With my son, it's more important that he grows to be a good person. If I do that, then I'm happy." This is why she works Monday to Friday, sacrificing the busier weekends to spend time with him. Like his cousin, Daniel's daughter, the son is light-skinned. He's also more than six feet tall and passes for white on the street—which is more than can be said for his mother. "I don't think I can pass for white. I start talking and people know I'm Mexican," she says, pointing out her accent and also her black hair. She's even wearing a dress that features embroidered flowers typical of traditional Mexican garments. But she's aware of a generational and cultural gap growing between American-born children and their migrant parents, and she goes through it with her son. "He wasn't born in Mexico, but his parents were. His blood is purely Mexican."

Another gap is growing within the Mexican community in New York. Some migrants, like Daniel and Leticia, hold on to aspects of their culture out of a desire to bring part of Mexico into their daily lives. Others, especially middle-class Mexicans and those with lighter skin, focus their energies on passing for white or adopting a more all-American lifestyle of baseball and suburban living, avoiding Hispanic media and, in extreme cases, forbidding their children from speaking Spanish in public. People in this category tend to look down on the likes of Leticia, and she has some words for them: "If you want to be American, that's fine. But never forget where you're from. That's part of you. I don't know why you want to hide it."

Perhaps some acculturated Mexicans struggle with women like Leticia because of her status as a single-mother breadwinner in a community where men call the shots. Keeping a roof over her own head and her son's gets harder as the years go by and their needs change. The siblings don't earn a regular salary from their work as tattoo artists; they get paid by the client, with the Bangladeshi shop owner taking a cut from each job. Some seasons are busier than others, with the winter generally slow. "The winter is long," Leticia tells me. "We have to save money for rent and bills." I notice that no customer has set foot in the shop for at least an hour, and when I sneak a peek after lunch, the place looks just as empty. This is on a Wednesday afternoon in July, the peak of the busy season.

Daniel and Leticia face tremendous financial hardships, but they pale next to the fear that the lives they've built up over decades may vanish if hardline politicians are successful in deporting the parents or denying the children their citizenship rights. That's a very brown experience in the United States. Whatever problems African

Americans face—and they are legion—deportation will never be one of them. Still, the mood of the undocumented in New York, like the city itself, struck me as resilient, defiant—optimistic in the face of doom and gloom from the Republican candidates and even Obama, on whose watch deportation figures have shot up. (In some Latin corners, Obama is known as Deporter-in-Chief.)

For the flip side of the brown undocumented life, I head to Phoenix, Arizona, a city and state that have turned anti-immigration legislation into a blood sport. I wanted to experience for myself the differences in the lives of brown Mexican migrants in New York, the ultimate blue state, and those in red states that are geographically closer to Mexico. Recently, Phoenix has also witnessed a "mysterious surge" in illegal immigrants from India, according to the *Arizona Republic*'s immigration reporter, Daniel Gonzalez. They fly from India to Central America before setting off on a five-thousand-kilometre journey through many countries and entering the US via the Arizona–Mexico border as asylum seekers. Arizona is becoming a gateway to America for more than one brown group.

*

FRANCISCA PORCHAS KNOWS HOW to whip her audience into activist shape. To the sixty or so Mexicans and a handful of white and African American supporters in the auditorium of Puente, a migrant justice organization based in Phoenix, her wishes and her commands go hand in hand. After all, her business card says "organizing director" for a reason. And there's a lot to organize during this weekly Monday night membership meeting.

But first, Francisca asks everyone in the room to stand up, identify themselves and share their idea of a perfect summer day. This breaking-the-ice-in-the-desert exercise may seem so high school or so corporate retreat, but to an outsider like me, it reveals the simple dreams of a community of predominately undocumented Mexicans in one of the most anti-immigrant cities in the United States. No one here dreams of a spa retreat or a shopping spree. They will settle for a quiet day at home in the comfort of the A/C. It's July and the daytime temperature hovers around the mid-forties.

"I'd like to be locked away in my house, doing nothing. Not to go out at all into the street," one woman in the second row tells a room full of people who understand instantly why someone's idea of perfection is self-incarceration. The chances of being racially profiled and taken into a detention centre increase when you step outside your front door. Another woman—and the majority of those present are women—says she wants to be "tucked away" at home (also with the A/C on) with her children, whom she doesn't get to see enough of because she works long hours. The recurrent motif of the air conditioning is partly about the heat, but it also betrays the fact that some members of this community can't afford to keep it running twenty-four hours. It remains a luxury.

If this is the "pleasantries" portion of the evening, I wonder what the heavy stuff will sound like.

Sure enough, Francisca moves on to tonight's real agenda, which is about organizing her base over the last week of September and the first week of October to attend a high-profile trial involving Maricopa County Sheriff Joe Arpaio. Known as America's toughest sheriff, Arpaio, over six terms in office, has earned a reputation among brown people in Phoenix as their biggest enemy. Francisca asks members to think of the kind of presence they'd like to have outside the courthouse. Perhaps some artwork and music to draw media attention? How about a legal table where people can come and ask questions about their immigration status? Do they need one week of activities or two? And should they do it daily or only at the start of each week, when the media are most likely to cover court procedures?

The trial rests on the allegation that Arpaio and his officers conducted several racially motivated inspections and traffic raids between 2011 and 2013, despite a federal court ruling that declared such moves unconstitutional. A man in his thirties tells the crowd that, the previous week, he recorded on his mobile phone an incident in which a policeman pulled over a Mexican driver simply because of the way he looked. Other people in the room chime in, suggesting that racial profiling of drivers continues unchecked. The tone of the discussion changes even more dramatically when Francisca explains the details of Kate's Law, just passed by the Republican-dominated House. Representative Matt Salmon introduced the law after the death of Kate Steinle, a thirty-two-year-old white woman who was killed by a stray bullet while walking along San Francisco's waterfront with her father. The shooter, a Mexican illegal who spent sixteen of his twenty years in the US in jail or addiction treatment centres, had been deported several times but always managed to sneak back in. The law establishes a mandatory minimum sentence of five years for illegal re-entry to the United States. It also challenges city-level immigrant-rights policies in three hundred municipalities—commonly know as sanctuary cities—and punishes them for not cooperating with federal immigration forces.

It was the "perfect crime" in terms of stirring up anti-immigrant hysteria, Francisca tells the room: a white victim and a brown shooter with a history of mental illness, a long criminal record and multiple violations of the immigration laws. (When Francisca and I talked about this incident the previous week, she told me that her first thoughts upon hearing about the shooter were: "Please be white, please be white." It's the same reaction that Muslims in North America or Europe have whenever stories of lone-wolf attacks break. We brace ourselves for the inevitable backlash.)

"If he [the Mexican shooter] had been an American, they would have said, 'He's just crazy,'" opines one attendee, earning a round of applause from the room. "How many Mexicans have died or are on death row?" Such laws don't protect victims but separate families, a sad but familiar experience for some people in the room. Indeed, this otherwise humbly furnished room is filled with children's artwork emblazoned with slogans like "Don't Separate Our Families."

And all that before the name Trump comes up! But inevitably the presidential hopeful makes his way into the conversation. Not surprisingly, the reactions are visceral. "I feel humiliated," says one woman, referring to Trump's comments about Mexicans as rapists and drug pushers. "I was really mad. We try to help them [Americans] and work for them. We came to this country not to take anyone's money. We work hard for what we have. Lots of people humiliate us." Only when a particularly large woman says that she'll do anything to fight social injustice except go on a hunger strike does the mood in the room revert to the pre-Trump, pre-Arpaio lightness.

When I speak one on one with Francisca, I learn more about her personal stake in the social justice movement. Like many in the room, she came to the US with her family as a child, in 1988. "Phoenix has always been a very racist place, always been reactionary," she tells me as we sit in Puente's administrative office. "I remember thinking I would like to go back to Mexico or go somewhere else." The somewhere-else wish came true, but not until she'd finished her degree in Phoenix in justice studies. In 2003, she landed in Los Angeles, where she spent a decade learning the theory and practice of community organizing. In 2013, she returned to Phoenix and started volunteering for Puente, taking over the role of organizing director in 2014.

As I talk to Francisca, I remember hearing a caution about Puente from Daniel Gonzalez of the *Arizona Republic.* He described its politics as falling on the "radical left" of migration activism when I met him for a chat. That does seem to be a fitting description of the organization, but the tilt to the left can also be explained as a defence mechanism against what has come to be known as "respectability politics"—the idea that the way to earn acceptance and understanding from mainstream Americans is to convince them that immigrants are "nice" people just like them, and to avoid engaging in any activities that perpetuate ethnic stereotypes. This approach dates back to the civil rights movement of the 1950s and 1960s but has largely fallen out of favour. Despite having some champions—and several see President Obama as a perfect product of it—respectability politics has been criticized by the likes of author Ta-Nehisi Coates and Georgetown University's Michael Eric Dyson as, respectively, one of the "most disreputable traditions in American politics" and the misguided belief that "good behavior and stern chiding will cure black ills and uplift black people." Within the Hispanic community, advocates of respectability politics tend to distance themselves from the criminality of other members.

"What we're saying is that we're not throwing anyone under the bus," Francisca tells me. "We're not going to buy into the 'undeserving' and 'deserving' politics." The divide, echoing the ones I saw in New York, is not just between the middle- and working-class immigrant but also between the recent and long-established one. As Francisca explains, acts of racial profiling go beyond picking on people with brown skin. How someone is dressed, what car he drives and what accent he has all play into whether he gets stopped, and once stopped, if he is arrested or let go. "Our members are aware of the fact that the way we look is why we're targeted," she says, adding that the darker a person is, the greater are his or her chances of getting stopped.

But there are other issues and people to engage with at the moment, and Sheriff Arpaio tops the list. "He terrorized the community for a long time. He created a culture that's racist. It's time for him to go, time for his legacy to go." Puente would also like Arizona to shut down all the immigration detention centres and stop cooperation between the police and Immigration and Customs Enforcement (ICE), an agency of the Department of Homeland Security with, according to its website, "a unique combination of civil and criminal authorities to better protect national security and public safety in answer to the tragic events on 9/11."

Puente's list of demands seems long and uncompromising, but as Francisca points out, the organization has seen some progress—or at least signs of progress—on several of these issues, including the election of several Latinos to the nine-member city council. (Phoenix is the sixth-largest city in the United States, but its entire council consists of one representative for each of its eight districts, plus the mayor.) And at eighty-three, Arpaio can't run for office much longer, so what activism can't accomplish, the Grim Reaper will take care of. The next leaders of the city—and by extension the state—*are* being identified and groomed. Twenty-four-year-old Viri Hernandez is making sure of that.

*

WHEN VIRI LOOKS BACK at her life as an undocumented immigrant, one encounter of the many she's had with authorities stands out. It happened when she was in high school and living with her family in a barrio in West Phoenix. When she and her siblings opened their front door after school one day, they immediately realized that they had been broken into. Even though the family lived modestly in a neighbourhood of largely poor migrants and day labourers, the number of burglaries had been rising over the years. When Viri knocked on the doors of twelve neighbours, nine of them admitted that they, too, had been robbed. No one reported the incidents to the police because they feared that any encounter with law enforcement, even as victims of crime, could lead to detention or deportation. The Hernandezes could either follow their neighbours' example and let the incident go, or break the pattern of fear and report it to the police. They chose the latter.

"I never realized how afraid I was until that moment," Viri tells me as we sit down for a lunchtime conversation in the offices of the Center for Neighborhood Leadership, an organization that develops civic leaders in brown and black communities. When the police officer asked her for proof of identity (her parents were at work), she handed him an ID card issued by the Mexican consulate, a red flag for the police. Her fate and that of her family rested on the officer's reactions in the moments that followed. Fortunately, he handed her back the card without pursuing the immigration line of inquiry. Viri breathed the biggest sigh of relief in her life. However, it soon became clear that the officer also wouldn't do more than write a report of yet another burglary in a bad neighbourhood—one reason crime rates remain high. "They [criminals] go to our communities because we are poor and brown. And because we live in fear. These stories weren't unique. In every neighbourhood, people are afraid, being targeted and not calling the police." For all Viri knows, the thieves were also brown and undocumented. "We're left fighting for the crumbs."

Until 2014, when she got married to a US resident and attained her legal status, Viri lived her life in constant fear. And it was fear of a different kind that brought her to Phoenix in the first place.

When Viri was just one year old and still living in Cuernavaca, south of Mexico City, her mother woke up one morning, packed a few things, grabbed her daughter and left a violent and abusive husband. The mother didn't let stories of women getting raped while crossing the Mexico–US border dissuade her from trying to create a new life for herself and her daughter somewhere else. Fortune, if you can call it that, smiled on her, and she managed the crossing without incident. A few years later, the repentant father joined them, and the family grew by more children born in the US. Both parents worked as office cleaners at first, but the mother eventually quit to look after the children while the father, like many undocumented, went into the construction business. To this day, only Viri lives in the US legally, which means she belongs to a mixed-status family. Currently, immigration rules do not offer the Hernandezes any reasonable way out of their situation. "The only possibility is if they are detained, arrested, stopped," Viri explains. "Then they can petition to stay here."

In January 2014, that nightmare scenario-cum-only hope almost came to pass when Sheriff Arpaio's men raided the construction company where Viri's father worked, arresting people with no IDs and confiscating files with employee information. Her father happened to be working off-site that day, but he knew that the company kept his home address and contact information on file. "Within three days, my family moved," she tells me, adding that her father has not held a full-time job since. Because he didn't have (and wouldn't have qualified for) any employment insurance, the family relied on their home-based business renting party supplies—chairs, plates and cutlery, and the like—to survive. Both parents refuse to go back to working under the table because they can no longer tolerate employers who take advantage of the undocumented. During her stint as an office cleaner, Viri's mother complained to her bosses about the toxic cleaning products she was forced to use. They did nothing, knowing very well that if she continued to complain, they could find another Mexican illegal who would do the job quietly.

The narrative of fear and exploitation is one that the Center for Neighborhood Leadership wants to change by "empowering" members of the Hispanic and black populations on a community level. The centre works on several concurrent initiatives, including an anti-bullying and safe schools campaign; a community policing program that is focused on changing police relations with the community; and the "Good Things Grow" campaign, which aims to increase access to fresh food and vegetables in barrios with no places to buy fresh groceries. The centre also campaigns for blacks and Latinos running for positions in city hall and on school boards. At the time of our conversation, Viri and her colleagues at the centre were immersed in a campaign for a city-issued ID that Phoenix residents (legal and illegal) can carry as proof of identity. Not having ID prevents many vulnerable citizens—homeless, domestic abuse victims, runaways from the LGBTQ community—from accessing such essential services as housing or food stamps. While it sounds like a no-brainer, even a simple initiative like this can't be untangled from Phoenix's colour lines.

"How do we not make it into a scarlet letter?" Viri says. "How to make older, white communities want to have it?" The answer was to load the ID with value-adds to streamline city services: library card, museum card, public transportation pass, etc. So far, there seems to be little support for the card from those in the white Phoenix community *or* from Hispanic people who have lived in Phoenix for decades and have worked hard at building a fence between themselves and the illegals. Viri finds their attitude understandable but frustrating. Invoking the "white privilege" mantra to describe members of the Hispanic community who are light-skinned, she believes that their lack of accent and more sophisticated vocabulary give them licence to be less sensitive to newer immigrants, whose accents and mannerisms give them away. Viri is rephrasing Francisca's "deserving and undeserving" divide within the community. The more people I talked to in Phoenix, the more of these internal divides I noticed.

Lydia Guzman, a sixth-generation Mexican-American, shifts the blame from her own community and places it where she thinks it belongs: on white voters who have moved to Arizona in the past few decades from states where little racial mixing existed. "They have this thing about brown people," she tells me. "They don't know what to do with them. Just by looking at the colour of my skin, they think I have no rights." Lydia and I are meeting at the headquarters of Chicanos Por La Causa, a Mexican- and immigrant-rights organization in Phoenix with more than four decades of social work in the housing and employment sectors. She volunteers a few days a week to suggest solutions to or recommend experts for immigration problems or employment discrimination cases.

More recently, she has started to focus on issues of youth alienation. Hearing her speak of the experience of Hispanic youth reminded me of the many conversations I had in Paris about French Muslims and in London about their British counterparts. There's a brown continuum of disaffected youth. "Some of the kids from the barrios have a chip on their shoulder. They're always harassed by the police. They want to push back. They have the anger, and it victimizes them even more." The combination of combativeness and being brown can be explosive, she says. Lydia then takes me on a tour of Guadalupe, a barrio that she feels captures how lives in the city are divided along colour lines. The barrio is literally segregated by a stream and a purpose-built wall that separates it from Tempe, home to the main campus of Arizona State University. With street signs in Spanish and hardly a white person anywhere in sight, the barrio looks more like a Mexican border town than part of a city as prosperous as Phoenix.

Of all the divides in the Mexican community, the one that operates along the lines of sexual orientation most hits a nerve with me, since it echoes a similar argument I've always heard about Muslims' intolerance of sexuality. Brown people are often presumed to be reactionary or homophobic.

*

THE FAIR TRADE CAFÉ in Phoenix offers its progressive and alternative clientele a refuge from a city known for its reactionary and mainstream politics. It's the kind of place that hosts weekly poetry slams and serves organic, ethically sourced coffee. On a late Monday afternoon, the branch off Central and Roosevelt was teeming with students, NGO workers and the tattooed, bearded and pierced. Finding the two working-class Mexican gay men I'm supposed to meet may be harder than I thought. As I scan the large indoor and patio spaces, I notice but look past two men talking. One of them is too all-American and preppy to be my interview subject. But the white-looking man, Jonathan, waves me over to his table, and soon I realize that I had bought the stereotype that all Hispanics are brown, especially the working-class among them. (The friend, Dago, looked more traditionally Mexican.)

I apologize for being late, but I'm not sure that's really what I'm apologizing for. "Sorry, I thought you were a white guy," I blurt out, "and I was expecting someone with dark skin." Jonathan has heard this before. While both of his parents are Mexican, his ancestry includes mixed Spanish and Italian blood. His brother and sister, he tells me, are darker in skin colour. He is white, even though he works outside in the agriculture and forestry sectors. The family grew up on the eastern shores of Maryland and in

Virginia in multicultural, working-class neighbourhoods where a person's skin colour determined his or her social progress.

"My sister is nine years older than me. She took care of me when I was born," Jonathan tells me, adding that casual observers often assumed her to be his Hispanic nanny. "There was a stage in my life when I realized I was white. We talked about the idea of brown a lot. That's something important to me. . . . It's important for [those of] us who are white or light-skinned to understand the privilege of our skin colour." When the darker-skinned brother visited Phoenix, he was arrested on Jonathan's front lawn by a police officer patrolling the neighbourhood. "They didn't feel like he should be there."

Jonathan also believes that his status as an out gay man within the Mexican-American community hews him closer to the white label. "Gay has been identified as white" in American society, he tells me. This can sometimes give mainstream America licence to pat itself on the back as enlightened and point the finger at minorities for their perceived reactionary views. "We forget that there are places in the US where I can be beaten to death for being gay."

The marginalization of LGBTQ members within the undocumented community traps them further in a brutal immigration system. That's why both Jonathan and Dago volunteer for the Arizona Queer Undocumented Immigrant Project and the Arcoíris Liberation Team, two organizations trying to keep a spotlight on LGBTQ people who face immediate deportation or have been in detention centres for years. Many illegal LGBTQs have come to Phoenix without families and can't count on that system of support. For Jonathan and Dago, simple acts of moral support for detained LGBTQ people go a long way toward sustaining their hope and spirit. Members of both groups write letters to the detained and pay them visits on some Saturdays. I had hoped to tag along with Jonathan and others, who were scheduled to visit the infamous Eloy Detention Center the previous Saturday, but unfortunately, the trip was cancelled.

"Conditions are so bad [in Eloy]. People lose hope; they give up and want to go back. When they feel that way, they open our letters and read them," says Jonathan. "It helps us, too, because we believe these places should be shut down." According to Jonathan and Dago, internees at the Eloy Detention Center recount horror stories of rape, guard abuse, medical neglect, food and clothing shortages. At least five detainees have committed suicide since 2003 (the average rate, nationwide, is one per detention centre). Eloy also accounts for 9 percent of all deaths in detention centres across the country since 2003, with 14 out of 152.

The idea of starting a conversation between the family-oriented and Catholic anti-deportation groups and the gay ones came to Dago about two years ago, when he noticed that the two solitudes, so to speak, had campaigned separately against Bill 1062, which gives individuals the right to refuse services on religious grounds. (It was passed by the Arizona legislature but vetoed by the state's governor.) By combining the energies of sexual rights activists and brown rights activists, "something more powerful" can be created, Dago says.

I tell Jonathan and Dago that racial politics in Arizona strikes me as extraordinarily toxic. Jonathan agrees that it's a "fair assessment" but doesn't think the wave of anti-immigration laws of the past ten years is exclusive to the state. It's just that the laws here come fast, furious and crazy enough that they make other states look reasonable. "I don't think we should underestimate racism and xenophobia in other places," says Jonathan. Dago chimes in, citing Alabama as a state that has its own race-based laws but doesn't make the news as often as Arizona. "Arizona plays the Donald Trump of politics," he says. "We always need somebody that's loud. That opens space for other states" to do the same (or worse) but quietly.

Dago's life in Arizona is representative of the ongoing struggles in the life of the undocumented. He arrived in Phoenix in 1994 or 1995—he can't remember which—when he was seven or eight. The family "walked through the desert" from their hometown of Guerrero, in southwest Mexico, and snuck across the border, eventually making their way to Phoenix. Although Dago had a brother and some relatives in Georgia, the family found it easier to stay in Phoenix (crossing state borders would have made them vulnerable to police inspection). At the time Arizona's economy was booming, and employers in the service and construction industries, struggling to keep up with demand, often overlooked the immigration status of new hires. Once Dago was admitted to a local elementary school, he stayed in the system until his high school graduation.

Access to higher education was not so automatic, however. Shortly after he started a program in transborder studies (sometimes known as Chicano/Chicana studies) in Phoenix College, Proposition 300 came into effect. The referendum, approved by Arizona voters in 2006, denied in-state tuition or financial aid to students who were not US citizens, permanent residents or lawful immigrants. Two years earlier, Proposition 200 (the Arizona Taxpayer and Citizen Protection Act) restricted voting rights and access to public services for anyone without legal status. It in effect cut off health insurance for large numbers of immigrants. Regardless of the language these propositions used, they clearly targeted Mexican immigrants. To Dago, this singling out of his people carries historical echoes of other migrant groups that had "to put up a fight to find a place" in the American story. "I suffered so much, I experienced so much discrimination. But I'm committed to continue working to have a space for [Mexico] here, to have access to basic human rights and resources. My biggest issue is not having access to basic needs." Living in Phoenix without health coverage means that any trip to a doctor—or worse, a hospital—can lead to financial ruin. Despite all these obstacles, Dago sees himself living in Phoenix for quite some time. "I was brought up by a woman who is a fighter. If I want something, I have the power to create it."

Some of that resolve shows up his passion for performing in drag on the political-cabaret circuit. It's how he chose to come out to his parents. "I came out of the shadows as a Mexican and from the closet as a drag queen." After his first performance, he knew that he had to come out. He suspected that his parents knew he was gay because of the telltale hint whenever he snuck home after his shows: "They heard the heels going down the hallway."

*

I SPENT JUST UNDER a week in Phoenix, but by the end of my time there, I felt like I had internalized some of the fears of the brown community. I was late to my meeting with Jonathan and Dago because I got confused between First Street and First Avenue in the downtown core. As I was making my way through the main downtown bus station, a police cruiser pulled up and the officer waved to me. For a second, I thought that I was being racially profiled and automatically reached for my wallet to fetch my Canadian ID. But the officer was simply motioning for me to cross the street before he drove on. It was an innocent—gentlemanly, even—gesture.

When I returned to Toronto, I made a point of looking at police cars and even smiling at some officers during a local food festival in the neighbourhood known as Greektown. It became my way to wash the confrontational relationship between the authorities and the brown community in Phoenix out of my hair. But as the next chapter will show, things in Canada aren't always that rosy either. Living while brown carries risks even in my liberal hometown of Toronto.

CHAPTER 11

Canada: The Wedge Issue

In the annals of Canadian terrorism investigations, Project Thread falls somewhere between a gripping episode of *24* and an amateur production of *A Comedy of Errors*.

Most Canadians, including many in the Muslim community, barely recall what happened in Toronto in August 2003, when a "possible Al Qaeda sleeper cell" was identified in the suburb of Scarborough. Or so thought the RCMP as they arrested twenty-two Pakistani students and one Indian—all Muslims and all taking courses in a diploma mill by the prosaic name of Ottawa Business College—on suspicion of planning a terrorist attack.

At first blush, the activities of some of the men did seem to echo parts of the 9/11 plot. One of them, for example, took flying lessons, and his flight plan covered such sites as the Pickering Nuclear Generating Station east of Toronto. Another had covered a wall in his room with a poster for Lufthansa, the German air carrier. The RCMP alleged that several "unexplained" small fires broke out in apartments some of the accused shared. These apartments, investigators revealed, were sparsely furnished, which suggested that the students followed a plan of moving around to avoid discovery, or that they never intended to live in them for an extended period. A taste for minimalist decor formed part of the case against the men: it would cut down on the packing when the time came to run away.

In a media backgrounder handed to journalists immediately after the arrests, the RCMP cited the students' age, regional background and religious affiliation as further evidence of their terrorist leanings. All the men were between eighteen and thirty-three, and all but one had "connections to Pakistan's Punjab province, noted for its Sunni Muslim extremism." Stories of a network of terrorists in our midst soon made their way to Canadian media outlets, which played on the public's fears of our date with terrorism. But this time, the stories came with a happy ending: "Canada's 9/11 Moment Averted." Phew!

Within a few weeks of the arrests, which attracted international headlines, the case against the men began to crumble and allegations that the investigation was mired in racial stereotypes from the start gained credibility. Of the four hundred students taking courses at the unregistered business school, the RCMP pulled out names that sounded Muslim or included "Muhammad." (A 2003 article in the *Toronto Star* about the aftermath of the operation featured the startling headline "They Only Arrested the Muhammads.") The terrorism investigation devolved into a case of immigration fraud. It was revealed that the owner of the now defunct school, who never faced criminal charges, issued registration papers to students to the tune of $700 apiece. Almost all the students were eager to stay in Canada by any means.

Canada deported thirteen of the targeted twenty-three back to Pakistan—despite protests from activists and lawyers that their lives would be in danger—while ten claimed refugee status. All have their names now forever associated with a "terrorism" investigation; the odd media reference here and there shows they were still trying to rebuild their lives more than a decade after the arrests. An internal RCMP review in 2004 absolved the force of any wrongdoing and described the investigation as "sound and logical." History has added insult to reputational injury by relegating the men's ordeal to a footnote in Canada's war on terror. The more high-profile (and more legitimate) case of the Toronto 18 broke in June 2006, dominating headlines and the national conversation. The plot to storm Parliament Hill and detonate truck bombs in downtown Toronto led to convictions against eleven men under Canada's post-9/11 anti-terror laws.

Still, Project Thread remains significant because it has created two blueprints for the treatment of brown Muslim men of a certain age within the Canadian security system. The first involves racial profiling, which casts these men as potential mass murderers just because of their names, their skin tones or their national origins. The second builds on the first by sacrificing the human rights and dignity of suspects, including the presumption of innocence, in the name of keeping Canadians safe and secure. The fact that some of these men shared accommodations or got together for meals turned the basic right of free association into guilt by association. The string of assumptions and errors took a strange turn when one of the accused claimed that the RCMP had mistaken him for his brother, with whom he shared an apartment. He was found hiding in a pile of laundry, according to a *Globe and Mail* report. Some of the students spent a few weeks in detention while others languished there for several months, facing verbal abuse from other inmates and prison guards for crimes they hadn't committed or were unlikely to be convicted of. In the twelve years that followed, that preview turned into the main feature in the Canadian government's relationship with its Muslim citizens, and Islam in general.

*

AS CANADIANS WE OFTEN talk about ourselves and our institutions in a language that sets us apart from, and makes us feel superior to, our more militaristic neighbours to the south. We pat ourselves on the back for refusing to take part in George W. Bush's folly in Iraq in 2003, but often overlook how far we have followed in Washington's footsteps in that other war with no end in sight: the war on terror. We've issued security certificates for permanent residents and foreign nationals, placing them under house arrest or detaining them in a holding centre in Ontario for years. The accused and their defence lawyers don't get access to all the evidence against them—just a summary decided upon by a federal court judge. Since 9/11, five men (all brown and Muslim) have been issued security certificates and have been fighting deportation to Algeria, Morocco, Egypt and Syria—countries where their safety cannot be guaranteed.

In fact, with the all-encompassing Bill C-51 passing into law in 2015, Canada may have matched, if not surpassed, the most draconian provisions of anti-terror laws in the US and Britain. What the Liberal governments of Jean Chrétien and Paul Martin started between 2001 and 2006, the Conservatives of Stephen Harper continued (and then some) in their near decade in power—an era that came to an end on October 19, 2015, when the Liberals won a majority under the leadership of Justin Trudeau. Both parties, in varying degrees, predicated their anti-terror legislation and the operation of their security services on the blueprints created by Project Thread: racial profiling on the one hand, limiting rights of the profiled (or accused) on the other. In their book *False Security: The Radicalization of Canadian Anti-Terrorism*, law professors and commentators Craig Forcese and Kent Roach describe Bill C-51 as "the most radical national security law ever enacted in the post-*Canadian Charter of Rights and Freedoms* period." The bill, they write, transforms the judiciary "from a protector of *Charter* rights into a pre-authorizer for *Charter* violations."

And while C-51 and the string of anti-terror laws that have passed through Canada's Parliament since 9/11 never explicitly target one ethnic or religious group, they "have become code for anti-Muslim legislation," declares constitutional and criminal lawyer Nader Hasan during an interview in his downtown Toronto office. "It's a bit gauche in this day and age, or not socially acceptable, to be a complete racist or bigot."

Instead, and for a host of complicated political and ideological reasons, the Conservatives have used Arab and Muslim Canadians as a wedge issue, mastering the art of "xenophobic demonization," as one journalist put it, whenever they needed a boost in the polls. This echoes the "racism without racists" strategy in the neo-liberal politics of the United Kingdom, especially in its focus on values. The Conservative messaging constructs Muslim and Arab Canadians as inherently inimical to Canadian values of free speech, transparency and human rights, especially of women, through two interrelated narratives: security and culture. Arab and Muslim men have found themselves caught in the security zone (Project Thread, the Toronto 18, the October 2014 attack on Parliament Hill), while women are entrapped by cultural assumptions (the hijab and niqab debate, and the "barbaric cultural practices" hotline that the Conservatives came up with during the 2015 federal election as a way for Canadians to snitch on their Muslim neighbours). While these security and culture narratives often relate to Muslim- and Arab-specific issues, the cumulative effect of this baiting is a generally more anti-immigrant and less tolerant society. Anti-brown discrimination drags down the whole country.

A March 2015 survey from EKOS Politics suggested that in Canada, opposition to immigration had reached heights not seen in twenty years. Running alongside this bump was a sharp increase in race-based discrimination as the number of Canadians who thought that too many non-whites were being allowed into the country reached the 40 percent threshold for the first time ever. Frank Graves of EKOS tied the disappointing results to areas where the Conservatives had seen a resurgence under Harper. Of those who identified themselves as Conservative, 51 percent believed that too many visible minorities live in Canada (compared to 32 percent for Liberals and 35 for the NDP). And while the same survey showed that 64 percent supported banning the niqab at citizenship ceremonies, Graves suggested that the issue had emerged as the "first really explicit" debate about values in Canadian politics for some time. "The Conservative movement has been very successful in using values to secure emotional engagement for its supporters."

To be fair, the Harper Conservatives didn't cast all Muslims or Arabs as enemies of the state. According to Nader Hasan—the Canadian-born, US-educated Muslim son of a Bengali father and Norwegian mother—the Conservatives felt compelled to prove that they were not categorically anti-Muslim by cherry-picking which segments of the community to be seen with in carefully orchestrated photo ops that featured "dark-skinned Muslim men." Hasan suggested that some of these men had little connection to the community and didn't understand the issues their fellow Muslims were protesting, specifically the more hawkish aspects of the government's foreign policies in the Middle East (whereby any criticism of Israel was interpreted as anti-Semitism or hate speech). Former immigration minister Jason Kenney cut federal funding for the Canadian Arab Federation (CAF) in 2009 for what he believed to be the organization's anti-Semitism and support of terrorist organizations in the Middle East. While many in the Arab community, myself included, would argue that CAF failed to control the more radical voices within its base, few would go as far as suggesting that it condoned terrorism or incited anti-Semitism. Like many Arab and Muslim organizations, CAF took a strong position on what it believed to be the annexation of Palestinian lands by Israel since 1967—a position also held by many social justice and progressive groups, as well as churches and unions. I would even describe some of these views—including a desire to end the suffering of Palestinians in the West Bank and Gaza—as mainstream among Arabs and Muslims in Canada. But the mainstream of this particular brown community had no traction among the Conservatives.

Someone from an Arab community group (who spoke on condition of anonymity) told me that the Harper government had established strong connections to what it believed to be "persecuted" minorities within the Muslim faith—the Ismaili and Ahmadiyya sects. Harper built alliances with, in particular, the more affluent but small Ismaili community, a hundred thousand of whom live in Canada. Harper expressed his personal admiration for the Aga Khan, the hereditary leader of the Ismaili Muslims, during the latter's visit to Canada in early 2014. (Harper singled out the Aga Khan's dedication to pluralism, then went on to belittle the "food and festival multiculturalism of recent decades" and invoke a "frontier" spirit in which character mattered more than lineage.) The two men announced a $100-million joint venture between Canada (which will cover 75 percent of it) and the Aga Khan Foundation for development projects in Asia and Africa. That's the kind of brown the former prime minister seemed to like: moneyed and apolitical.

In finding themselves afoul of the Conservatives, Arab and Muslim Canadians joined an ever-expanding list of communities whose interests clashed with the party's agenda. The Harper government set its sights on environmental groups and indigenous populations, for example, as each presented a threat to its fantasy of unfettered expansion in the energy sector. Even a consciousness-raising movement such as Idle No More became a target for spying and surveillance by the Ministry of National Defence in 2013 for perceived threats to military personnel or possible interception of weapons shipments. It was not a coincidence that when a Cree woman from Alberta won a Mrs. Universe beauty contest in August 2015, she used the platform to denounce the Conservatives' attacks on Native people. "With the bills that have been passed, we are being treated like terrorists if we're fighting for our land and our water," Ashley Callingbull-Burnham told a CBC News program.

In the weeks leading up to the 2015 federal election, when most of the reporting for this chapter took place, several members of the Arab and Muslim community talked of a collective chill. Fear of government, suspicion of one another and reluctance to talk to the media (or me) about aspects of, as one of them described it, the "hate-hate relationship" between the government and most Muslim communities didn't surprise me. A decade of a political culture that considered scapegoating Arabs a viable strategy for political survival would do that to a community.

Sophie Harkat has lived with this culture of fear for more than thirteen years now. Her husband, Mohamed Harkat, an Algerian refugee in Canada, is one of the five men issued a security certificate. In December 2002, he was arrested and detained without charge for more than three years in solitary confinement. Since 2006, he has been under house arrest in Ottawa with what Sophie describes as the harshest bail conditions in Canada. (He wears a GPS tracking device at all times and must be under the supervision of his wife or mother-in-law twenty-four hours a day, among other restrictions.) During Mohamed's trip through the

Canadian judicial system, the Harkats received little support from the Muslim community in Canada. "After Mo[hamed] got arrested, I got a lecture in front of a Muslim group," she told me during a phone conversation. The standard response, recalled Sophie, went something like this: "We'd love to help, but we're scared to be associated with you." (Mohamed declined my request for an interview, as he had just received his deportation papers around the time I approached Sophie to facilitate a conversation with him.) "It's the white people who are fighting our battles," she said, citing a number of lawyers and civil liberties experts who have lent a hand over the years. "I can count the number of Muslims [who've helped] on one hand." For Sophie, the experience of "people of dark skin" tells a bigger story about Canada's loss of compassion for the vulnerable. "I feel bad for the refugees who are coming," she tells me. "If you're a refugee coming to this country, you're going to face a lot of discrimination."

After talking to Sophie, I realized that I'd underestimated how upsetting on a deep and personal level hearing variations of the same story could be. Was this really happening in Canada in 2015?

Let me say clearly that my anger was also directed at the wannabe jihadis and the Muslim leaders who have tacitly, if not explicitly, indulged their sense of grievance and injustice. I accept that some Arabs and Muslims in Canada have a lot of soul-searching to do, but that doesn't justify the collective treatment of this community of brown people as suspects in a conspiracy against Canada.

In reporting on brown experiences in Hong Kong, Trinidad, France or the United States, I was able to maintain a certain emotional distance between myself and the people I talked to. Admittedly I was more engaged in stories from the Muslim community in Britain because I had lived and studied there, and I maintain a (perverse) cultural and emotional connection to the former empire in whose shadows I was born and raised. But in writing about Canada, I'm writing about my home, my self, my skin, my now and tomorrow. I have nowhere else to go, no other place to run to. The people I talked to shared my native tongue, were born or raised in Arab countries I have lived in or visited, and often looked a lot like me—at least to an outsider. When I arranged to meet men I didn't know, I'd tell them to keep an eye out for a brown, Middle Eastern–looking middle-aged guy. They often replied,"Ditto." I thought it remarkable how some of the women I met reminded me of my own sisters and nieces.

In short, what happens in Canada is too close for comfort. The lives upended by unfounded suspicions, smear campaigns or secretive policies during the past decade could be mine or those of close friends who share my Arab and Muslim heritage—as well as my brown skin, our calling card to the world.

I have lived in Canada for two decades now, one of which predates the Conservatives under Stephen Harper. I can't say that I've experienced any direct racial prejudice or Islamophobia. I consider myself well educated and middle class, and therefore I transcend some of the racial encounters that are all too familiar to, for example, my students from struggling immigrant backgrounds. "We don't live in the same Toronto," one of them told me when I talked about how I thought the city was one of the most accepting places in the world. I've never identified as Muslim in a public way, although I have taken it upon myself to write about issues relating to that faith community. Yes, when I worked as a drama critic I had minor xenophobic encounters with a small segment of the reading public or with members of the theatre profession, who referred to me as "Ali Baba" behind my back (as I discovered toward the end of my time on the job). It rankled not for personal reasons but because it tested my assumptions about race relations in Canada. I suffered through the odd "Have you taken any flying lessons lately?" jokes from friends who thought they were being funny and clever without realizing they were neither. In short, living in downtown Toronto shielded me from the more pernicious aspects of racism in Ontario or the country at large. Which is not to say that I haven't kept an eye on anti-brown sentiments brewing as far afield as British Columbia in reaction to a perceived South Asian invasion.

In early 2014, I followed (and later wrote about) a controversy in Brampton, Ontario, a city whose population has turned increasingly brown in the past decade or so. An anti-immigration group, Immigration Watch Canada, distributed a flyer that juxtaposed a vintage black-and-white picture of citizens of European descent against a recent colour photo of Brampton's largely Sikh, brown community. "From this . . . to this," ran the caption. Although the flyer featured additional textual content about the "changing face of Brampton"—in plainer words, the collective darkening of skin tones—and some census data suggesting the squeezing out of the white population, the two images reduced the demographic shifts of suburbia to one of pre- and post-multiculturalism. "Pre" means good, white. "Post" means bad, brown.

A few months later, another flyer urged (white, presumably) Brampton residents to "Say 'No' to the Massive Third World Invasion of Canada." This flyer featured an image of a stop sign imposed on a picture of a single brown Sikh man. (Immigration Watch Canada denied any involvement with this second flyer.) Charles Davenport, the American eugenicist and anti-immigration advocate we met in chapter 1, would have been thrilled. Taken together, the two flyers build on his sense of white siege to a brown invasion.

In an interview with *Global News*, one of the spokespersons for Immigration Watch Canada explained the racial divide in the community, one of several in Ontario and British Columbia that are becoming brown, in language that recalled opponents to non-white immigration to America in the early twentieth century: "The people of a European-based background who had lived in Brampton all their lives, their parents and grandparents and way further back than that, had become a minority in Brampton in a very short amount of time—from 2001 to 2011, the percentage of people of European background had dropped from 60 percent to about 30 percent. So the flyer was pointing out . . . is this a good thing to be happening? Is becoming a minority in your community an issue Canadians should be talking about?"

A similar sense of brown versus white could be detected in the words of John Williamson, the former Conservative MP for New Brunswick Southwest. While talking to delegates at a conference in Ottawa in early 2015, the one-time director of communications for Stephen Harper said that it made no sense to pay "whities" to stay home while companies brought in "brown people" as temporary foreign workers. Although he prefaced the remarks by saying he was going to "put this in terms of colours, but it's not meant to be about race," it was hard to see how one could separate the two. Williamson later apologized for his "offensive and inappropriate language," calling his comments the biggest mistake of his career, but that did little to satisfy some of his fellow Conservatives, who feared that the statement would alienate the ethnic voters the party had been courting for years. Local brown people weren't amused. The president of the New Brunswick Filipino Association told a CBC reporter that she was "hurt" by the comments, since members of her community worked hard and paid their taxes.

As the 2015 federal election entered its last ugly stage, the Brampton and New Brunswick incidents played out like minor provocations. The election felt too personal, too close to the skin, as not all brown people were thrown under the Conservative election bus—just Arabs and Muslims. Each report of a veiled woman getting attacked on the streets of Toronto or Montreal took me back to Paris, where such crimes happen regularly. Each editorial appealing to Canadians' sense of decency and tolerance scared me more than it reassured me. Have we come to this? Throughout most of September and early October, I feared that Canada would be sucked into the kind of divisive racial politics that have been earning far-right parties wider support among European citizens.

Watching a panel discussion hosted by the Organization for Islamic Learning in mid-September at a banquet hall in north Toronto brought back memories of the day I spent in Birmingham attending the AGM of the Muslim Council of Britain. There I was again, surrounded by a sea of brown men and women, mostly of South Asian origin, wringing their hands over how Muslims had been cast in the role of enemy within. Same angst, different city. Whatever smugness I'd felt in Birmingham was knocked out of me as one speaker after another talked about how Canada no longer "had their back." Panellist Kamran Bhatti, a software engineer by profession and a part-time de-radicalization activist of Pakistani origin, discussed how Bill C-24 strips dual citizens and immigrants of their Canadian citizenship. Our right to citizenship can be taken away based on information collected in the countries we fled. "Our lives, our bodies, our very place in Canada are under threat," Bhatti said. The no-fly lists on which many Muslim names appear designate brown folks as "too guilty to fly, too innocent to charge." I noted the same level of anxiety in other events organized by Muslim or Arab groups in the countdown to the election. If there was a bright spot, it came in the form of a far more engaged Arab and Muslim electorate, something I had not seen in my twenty years in Canada.

Like many immigrants, I came to Canada to escape the political repression and dictatorship of several Arab regimes of my early years.

It was depressing to find such blatant Islamophobia in a country that was once a beacon of democracy to the world—a country that had welcomed me with open arms only two decades earlier. I often muse to my Canadian and American friends about the unfair deal they got whenever political leaders talk of missions to bring civilization and democracy to countries they are about to invade or bomb. Western governments have failed to export freedom and instead have imported some of the more repressive systems they sought to destroy, including ethnic baiting and the security state. Brown bodies have paid the ultimate price for this exchange.

So you can imagine the collective sigh of relief of many Arab and Muslim Canadians when, on the evening of October 19, the Liberals ousted the Harper Conservatives from power. Although Prime Minister Justin Trudeau voted for Bill C-51 (and despite some misgivings about his party's penchant for campaigning from the left and governing from the right), I felt better that night about my future in Canada than I had for the previous decade. At the time of writing this, it was too early to tell whether the narrative of Muslims as a wedge issue would be replaced by one in which, as Trudeau said in his acceptance speech, "A Canadian is a Canadian is a Canadian." But the omens look good. The new Parliament is racially diverse—according to one report, the Liberal caucus alone includes thirty-eight of forty-six recognized visible minorities. The list includes a record ten Muslim MPs, with an Afghanistan- and Somalia-born among them. Trudeau named four Sikh MPs and one Afghan Muslim woman to a cabinet that also featured an equal number of women and men.

On a lighter note, I—and millions around the world, I suspect—delighted in a video that emerged after the election in which Trudeau was seen dancing bhangra with a group of brown women at a 2009 event hosted by the India Canada Association of Montreal. It seems silly now how happy that made me. After all, it was probably an attempt to court the brown vote by the then new MP. But after the toxic racism of the election campaign and all the anguish of a country on the brink of intolerance, I allowed myself to be optimistic and rejoice in the sight of my prime minister dancing brown.

*

YOU CAN SAY, WITHOUT fear of sounding reductionist, that Hussein Hamdani's life has unfolded as one encounter after another with the colour line: black, brown, white. Even when we sat down to talk at a Tim Hortons in his hometown of Appleby, an hour away from downtown Toronto by commuter train, I found myself marvelling at the diversity of his community of choice. What I had assumed would be a white, suburban setting—what could be more mainstream Canadian than a Tim Hortons on a Saturday afternoon just before a Blue Jays game?—turned out to be a catalogue of skin colours and ethnic affiliations. Hussein, who claimed to have a finely tuned "Muslim radar," could identify the brown contingent by religion: Muslims, Sikhs, Hindus.

It's both a party trick and a survival gene sequenced in the DNA of the Hamilton-based lawyer, anti-radicalization activist and (until early 2015, when allegations about his "radical past" surfaced on an anti-Muslim website and in a news report in Quebec) member of the Canadian government's Cross-Cultural Roundtable on Security. Born in Kampala, Uganda, to a Yemeni family, Hussein learned from an early age that skin colour means belonging to one community and feeling excluded from another. The East African nation and former British protectorate once hosted a thriving, economically dominant minority of Arabs, Indians, Pakistanis and Bengalis, commonly known to the black majority as Muhindis. "It's a catch-all term for anyone who's brown," Hussein tells me.

(The same people are more generally referred to as Asians.) At about 5 percent of the Ugandan population, this demographic group controlled nearly 85 percent (some say up to 90 percent) of the country's economy. The Hamdani family owned Uganda's largest chicken and cattle farm and spoke the lingua franca of the local brown communities: Gujarati or a derivative of it. Everyone knew their place. "At birth you were imprinted with an identity, a community—a clear fence, border, where who you were was defined by your religion and skin colour [with] little transgressing of these borders." It wasn't an apartheid system, but it acted as one.

Then came Idi Amin. In 1971, Amin, a military officer who came to be known as the Butcher of Uganda, orchestrated a coup, declaring himself president and chief of the armed forces. The next year he expelled all Asians who were not Ugandan citizens, giving an estimated sixty thousand people up to ninety days to leave the country. He then expropriated their businesses, including the Hamdanis' farm, claiming that Asian control of the economy stood in the way of native black development (an opinion many Africanists shared). After five unhappy years in their ancestral home of Yemen, Hussein's family sought refugee status in Canada, settling in St. Catharines in 1977. This time, they had to define themselves in relation to a white majority.

While the Hamdanis didn't interact much with the mainstream community, Hussein knew he needed to act white if he wanted to make a life for himself in Canada. He learned to play hockey and lacrosse, and performed most of the roles that a teenager in Southern Ontario in the 1980s was supposed to. "My girlfriend was white . . . [and] I was prom king," he tells me. "But I knew *I* wasn't white. No matter how well I spoke English or played hockey and lacrosse, I was somehow different."

Only a handful of non-white students were enrolled in his high school, but four of them got together to form an informal club: the Brother Brown Club. The members came from different parts of the world—India, East and South Africa, the Middle East—but all shared the experiences of a common and, for St. Catharines at the time, distinct skin colour. The club marked the beginning of Hussein's social awakening as a brown man in a country that was still adjusting to its changing complexion. (News of skinhead gangs and white supremacist groups operating in the Niagara region at the time, Hussein recalls, only intensified his and his family's sense of colour anxiety.)

Only in 1991, when Hussein started his degree in political science and history at McMaster University in nearby Hamilton, did this hyper awareness of his skin colour transform, gradually, from a social to a religious phase. In his third year, through a series of coincidences and student-housing bungles, Hussein ended up sharing a house off campus with six other brown Muslim men. "That's when we felt our Muslim consciousness," he recalls. Looking back at those years, Hussein finds it hard to determine if the men bonded because of their common faith or their skin colour. "It's about coming to a new world that we all felt at home in," he explains. "We all came from a white world . . . into an ethnic, brown world where, even if you weren't religious, you felt a bond." Indeed, Hussein doesn't describe his early years in McMaster as overtly religious. He remembers seeing Muslim students hanging out and enjoying themselves at various school cafeterias and thinking that he'd like to be part of this happy community.

During his two years at the University of Toronto (1995–97), studying for his master's in international relations, Hussein became more and more observant, organizing religious events and study circles for the Muslim Students Association. He was and remains particularly vocal about Palestinian rights and the Israeli occupation, but not in any way that would encourage violence or terror. "We were at the vanguard of this new Muslim way. We were not angry old Muslims," Hussein says, describing his circle of friends.

While they didn't see themselves as angry, they did have a desire to live in isolation from white Canadian society. On the morning of September 10, 2001, Hussein and a small group of his friends got together at a café in Toronto's business district to discuss plans to move en masse to an Ontario town like Milton or Brampton to form "some type of a commune" where they could live a holistic Muslim lifestyle. Others suggested something less cult-like: targeting a community, buying up houses and living as close as possible to one another. Hussein had already started informal conversations with the mayors of several smaller Ontario towns. The question was not *whether* to break away from the mainstream but *where* to do so.

Within twenty-four hours, that self-segregation plan was shelved. Permanently. With the terrorist attacks in the US the day after their meeting, Hussein and his friends realized that retreating into an insular world would not help anyone, least of all Muslims. "We realized that our role is not to disengage from the whole country but to build bridges with non-Muslim Canadian society. Our role here is to be fully engaged with the whole Canadian population as Muslims." As part of this new engagement strategy, Hussein began volunteering with immigration and shelter organizations and advising the chief of police in Hamilton, where he works, on issues of security and youth radicalization. In 2005, when the Liberal government invited applications from various minorities in Canada for seats on the fifteen-person Cross-Cultural Roundtable on Security, he put his name forward. Hussein was an obvious and easy choice.

For a decade, he served on this federal body and focused on bridging the gap between RCMP and CSIS on the one side and

Muslim youth on the other. And although the makeup of the roundtable changed during the Conservative term in office, from community applicants to political appointees—"people who had no real knowledge of the issues," he says—Hussein remained an active, if prickly, member. "I was very sensitive if I heard any type of racial or religious racial profiling in policy development. . . . I tried to change the language of the RCMP and the Canadian Border Services." As an example, he cites his discomfort with prefacing the word "terror" with either "Islamic" or "Islamist"—or Harper's coinage, "Islamicist"—preferring instead to call it Al Qaeda–inspired terror, at least in those pre-ISIS years.

In the winter of 2015, Hussein's work as part of Hamilton's anti-radicalization movement received praise from Public Safety Minister Steven Blaney. Just a few weeks earlier, in late January, he'd made a guest appearance on *The Agenda with Steve Paikin* on TVO (Ontario's public television network), where he was treated like a hero who'd stopped many radical youths from boarding planes for Syria or committing terrorist acts on Canadian soil.

By the spring, the model citizen was a fallen hero. Acting on information that first appeared on an Islamic-watch blog called Point de Bascule (the Tipping Point), a French television network in Quebec suggested that Hussein had once espoused radical views. The main evidence against him seemed to be a 1996 document from the Muslim Students Association of the US and Canada, an umbrella organization for Muslim groups on campuses across North America.

The document is more of a survival guide for campus politics than a radical manifesto, but in it, twenty-four-year-old Hussein urged Muslim students to get involved in all aspects of campus life—or what he termed "the Islamicization of campus politics and the politicization of MSA groups." Both the blog and the TV report also alleged a hidden connection to Ahmed Yassin, the founder-leader of the Palestinian group Hamas, even though in 2004 Hussein had written openly about his visits with representatives of several Islamic movements in the West Bank, including Yassin. As Hussein made clear to the media (and to me), he had been vetted by CSIS and the RCMP in 2005 and given security clearance. He'd contributed to the Canadian government's anti-radicalization initiative longer than Harper was prime minister.

In late April, Minister Blaney suspended Hussein from the roundtable "pending a review of the facts." In a statement released to the media at the same time, a spokesperson for the minister made it clear that a decision had been made ahead of said review: "While questions surrounding this individual's links to radical ideology have circulated for some time, it was hoped that he could be a positive influence to promote Canadian values. It is now becoming clear this may not have been the case." There soon followed news reports with such headlines as "Hero or Extremist?" By July, Hussein had received a letter thanking him for his work on the roundtable and informing him officially that he was no longer part of it.

Hussein believes that his vocal opposition to Bill C-51 and his personal support for the Liberals (he was involved in a fundraiser for Justin Trudeau that collected more than $130,000 from members of the Muslim community in Ontario) are behind his removal from the roundtable. The allegations have caught the attention of the Law Society of Canada, which, at the time of writing, was conducting its own review. If it supports the government's position—an unlikely but possible outcome—Hussein may be disbarred. "I'm very, very upset," he tells me, adding that his livelihood depends on his reputation.

Without realizing it, Hussein had become another casualty of what, in an interview for the *Montreal Gazette*, he called "the fear industry." "There's a campaign to make Canadians afraid of

Muslims and the religion of Islam," he told reporter Catherine Solyom. "The corollary is that only the Conservatives can save us from the Muslims, so they frighten people before the federal election." The Tipping Point blog is one of a growing number of Muslim-bashing websites that have become a "lucrative business" in the United States and are now a reality in Canada, according to the author of a US report that tracks funding for anti-Muslim organizations.

If someone like Hussein no longer felt safe, what would that have meant for the future of Arabs and Muslims in Canada had the Conservatives stayed in power? Who would have been next?

*

YOU DON'T HAVE TO be Muslim to feel excluded, experience discrimination or be constantly on the radar of the security state.

Farid (not his real name), a science teacher, took early retirement in 2012 after a particularly nasty encounter with his school board in which, he believes, his Arabic identity figured prominently. A Catholic of Lebanese origin with a history of involvement in his local church, Farid came to Canada in 1990 with his wife and their young daughter. Within months they had changed their minds about moving to Quebec and settled in the Greater Toronto Area, where Farid landed a job as a biology, physics and chemistry teacher in a French-immersion school. His first impressions of Canada were favourable compared with his native Lebanon, then in the final stages of a vicious fifteen-year civil war. "I remember the freedom of opinions, the sense of security," he told me over coffee at yet another Tim Hortons in suburban Toronto.

The freedom of association and thought in Canada convinced Farid to resume his political activism as a new member of the

Canadian Arab Federation and a long-standing one of the Syrian Social Nationalist Party (SSNP). The latter's main goal is uniting the Levant countries (Syria, Lebanon, Jordan and Palestine), which were carved up in 1917 and placed under separate colonial mandates. It was this association that led Farid to his first encounter with agents from CSIS, Canada's spy agency, who questioned his application for Canadian citizenship. Farid had not included his membership in SSNP in the forms, but a Lebanese security agency shared that information with CSIS. His wife and daughter received their passports within the standard three- to four-year window of arriving in Canada, but his was delayed by an additional four years. Still, he thought little of it and carried on with his new life.

Shortly after 9/11, he was once again approached by CSIS. This time, the agency asked him, "as someone who cares about Canadian security," to share any information he had about the Arab community. He was expected to be a snitch, or to put it in the euphemistic language of the security state, an informant. He declined the offer. Back at work, however, he began to notice differences in the way some fellow teachers talked to him. The fact that he was Christian and had nothing to do with terrorist groups like Al Qaeda did little to alleviate his sense that he was no longer just another teacher but an Arab-Canadian teacher. "Some questioned why and how these people [terrorists] did that. Is it the culture or the religion?"

Farid felt that his colleagues expected him to interpret the actions of Arab and Muslim extremists—actions that some believed he approved of or at least condoned. When, in 2008, he organized a fundraising campaign for children in Gaza, collecting $5,000 for World Vision, one or two teachers cast doubts on his response to what the United Nations, among other international organizations, had declared a humanitarian crisis. The implied question: Would the money go to help the needy or support terrorism? Previous fundraising efforts for the United Way and other charitable groups that targeted the developing world had elicited very little skepticism. Why was this endeavour different? "Because it's Gaza," Farid insists, citing the growing anti-Arab sentiments of some colleagues as evidence. "One hundred percent because it's Gaza."

The worst was yet to come.

March 5, 2012, started out like another day in Farid's twenty-two-year career as a teacher in Canada. At recess time, he followed his routine of checking the latest international and Arab news from a number of websites, including the Al Jazeera network and other Arabic-language publications. As Farid tells it, a student came to his office to complain about another. As he was explaining what happened, the student, who was standing behind the teacher's desk, could easily see the images on the screen. Farid can't remember the exact story he was catching up on at that time, but he knows it featured graphic images of civilian casualties in the Arab world. It could have been from Syria or Iraq. The experienced teacher dealt with the student's complaint and thought nothing more of what was an everyday encounter between two teenage boys.

"A week to ten days later, I was called by the principal. There [had] been a complaint about me showing kids violent pictures," Farid recalls. "The kid told his family, and the family got upset and called the police." (At this point, he mentions that the kid comes from the Sikh community. I ask if this has any bearing on his sense of anti-Arab discrimination, but Farid doesn't think so.) The school board decided to put Farid on paid leave while it conducted an investigation. "I went back to my class, gathered my things and left." In his mind, it was an overreaction but something that could be resolved in a few days at most.

The next morning he received a call from the Children's Aid Society (CAS) to get his side of the story, a standard procedure. A few days after that call, the police also got in touch. Neither CAS nor the police felt that the case had any merit, and both decided not to follow up on it. The school board took nearly fifty days—"a very stressful period in my life"—to reach a similar conclusion. By then, Farid had decided that it made no emotional sense to continue working in an environment where every action he took, every website he visited, cast him as a suspicious figure, a threat to the safety and security of students and by extension the school. He felt the stigma of being an outsider because of his skin colour and ethnic origin, as well as the paranoia of colleagues around these two racial identifiers. This was a different Canada from the one he had landed in back in 1990. "I was expecting my boss to stand up for me. No one asked what kind of pictures [the student saw]. . . . My guess is that a white teacher in the same situation would have been treated differently." He picks up an occasional teaching gig, but at sixty-two, Farid has taken early retirement.

More than three years after this encounter, he remains distressed about his treatment. "It changed the way I feel about Toronto," he says. He thinks that his personal experience mirrors the political changes in Canada, where bills that limit freedom of speech (Bill C-51) or the rights of dual citizens (Bill C-24) have passed. The laws are creating "a lot of questions, concerns about legislating our words, ideas, thoughts as Canadians."

Time will tell if the new Liberal government repeals or amends these laws.

*

A KNOCK ON MY apartment door jolted me out of my afternoon nap. It was a Friday, about three weeks before the October 19 election, and I assumed it was one of the candidates from the three major political parties doing the usual door-to-door canvassing. I had missed a recent visit from the Conservative candidate and was looking forward to giving her an earful about her party's race politics and references to old- and new-stock Canadians. I had a whole rant rehearsed and ready for the moment she or one of her volunteers returned to my building.

But my spiel would have to wait, as the knock came from my next-door neighbour and friend, Dorene. The evening before, she told me, she had watched a news report on BBC America on the conditions in Yemen, where a war between the Shiite rebels and forces loyal to the internationally recognized post–Arab Spring government had entered its seventh month. The report focused on the humanitarian crisis unfolding in the Arab world's poorest country, a story that had more or less disappeared from most other news outlets. All eyes were on the Syrian refugees trying to make it to Europe by land or sea.

Dorene, eighty-seven, could not sit still and do nothing about Yemen—a country she had absolutely nothing to do with, apart from having a neighbour who hailed from it—but she also wasn't sure what the best course of action would be. Armed with a cheque for a few hundred dollars, she'd knocked on my door for suggestions about which aid organization was doing the most to alleviate hunger or ensure an adequate medical response to an ever-expanding number of casualties. I nearly cried. With so much negativity in the election cycle, I had forgotten that at heart most Canadians are compassionate, kind, generous people who don't buy into the narrative of a Muslim threat to their existence. When Canadians like Dorene—white and "old stock"—see human suffering in a poor country, they feel compelled to lend a hand and share some of their wealth with the less fortunate, without waiting to hear what religion these people believe in or which sect they belong to. At this moment, most of the world's displaced happen to be from Syria, Libya and Yemen, among other countries in the Middle East and North Africa. Most are Arab, Muslim and part of the collective brown.

I take comfort in social media posts and conversations among friends and students about efforts to sponsor Syrian families or individuals. Synagogues, churches and community groups have been pitching in and strategizing about how best to lend a hand. Their actions have proved louder and more compelling than the voices of those who want a foreign policy based on a Fortress Canada model.

In the (almost) two years I spent reporting and writing this book, I witnessed and heard stories of intolerable insensitivity and cruelty to and by brown people. A maid in Hong Kong told me that when her European employers decided to go home, they tried to find a taker for her and the family dog among other expats on the island. She was humiliated. In Dubai, a construction worker from Bangladesh, whose story I didn't have the chance to share here, described how his supervisors made light of his debilitating fear of heights when he first worked on a skyscraper. He nearly fell to his death at least once. (He eventually got some jobs on low-rise buildings, working fewer hours and making less money than many of his colleagues.) Our bodies and skin colour render us dispensable, vulnerable. Whenever I heard these stories—including the many you've just read—I felt relieved to be heading home, to Canada, in a few days, weeks or months. Something else was waiting for me there, something more tolerant and inclusive.

Part of my faith in Canada is Pollyannaism. I choose to think of this country as full of Dorenes and not Stephen Harpers. But I also know that the 2015 election and all the racist fault lines it exposed are not an aberration but an indication of a specific anti-brown feeling that has been gaining momentum, even in liberal

Canada. Arabs and Muslims were offered as the wedge issue, the "them" to the mainstream Canadian "us." Which brown—or for that matter, black, East Asian, Native—community will be next? As historian Erna Paris noted after the October election: "No immigrant-based country can afford to believe that its leaders will never resort to the oldest, most dangerous, tactic in politics: the devaluation of a national minority. Nor can we Canadians afford to imagine that we will be immune to incitement."

To be brown in the world today, you must make time to celebrate narrow escapes from prejudice and hate, even while you prepare for those times when you may not be so lucky. Our skin colour gives us away. Vigilance is imperative. For now, I'm celebrating the return of a Canada I fell in love with when I first arrived as a landed immigrant.

If that makes me a Pollyanna, so be it.

Acknowledgements

First and foremost, I'm hugely indebted to all the women and men who shared their stories and opinions with me. Their tales of joys and heartaches, gains and losses, as well as their generosity and wisdom, have touched and inspired me.

My deep thanks to my agent (and gentle handler of my neurotic side), John Pearce of Westwood Creative Artists, for his support for the past eight years and for believing in a book called *Brown* from the moment I emailed him about it in April 2012. "This seems to call for a meeting," he responded, almost immediately. (Twelve minutes, to be exact.)

This is my second book with Jim Gifford, who continues to be everything a writer looks for in an editor, and then some. I'm grateful to him for reading each chapter individually over the course of a year and then going over the manuscript as a whole in the fall of 2015, suggesting thematic and copy changes in his usual insightful and gentle style. Thanks also to Doug Richmond for taking the time to read and comment on parts of the book. Janice Weaver copyedited the manuscript with astounding attention to detail and an eye on the bigger picture. I'm lucky to have HarperCollins Canada again as my publisher. Thanks also to Beverley Sotolov for a thorough proofread. My thanks go to Noelle Zitzer, Rob Firing, Lisa Rundle and Iris Tupholme, among others, for taking such good care of me (and my books).

Thanks to my dear friend Laurie Lynd, a film and TV director, for reading an early draft in the middle of shooting two TV shows. A consummate storyteller and a sensitive soul, Laurie helped me identify issues of narrative continuity and flow. I rehearsed my arguments in this book on my friend Shane

Smith, who listened patiently and offered encouragement (and sometimes beer).

Thanks to Ryerson University for a 2013 Creative Grant that was instrumental in defraying travel costs to Hong Kong, and to the Ryerson Journalism Research Centre for a project grant that paid for part of my trip to Trinidad.

Many friends, academics, writers and journalists have been generous with their advice and contacts in different countries.

For the colourism chapter, I'm grateful to Dr. Allan Fox in Toronto and Dr. Hasan Abdessamad of Vancouver for putting me in touch with friends in the dermatology field.

For the chapter on Trinidad, I'm grateful to Stephan Tang of Ryerson University for several conversations, and for his many introductions to friends and family in Port of Spain and beyond. Thanks also to Collin Sookoo for driving me to Felicity and showing me around town.

For Thailand, my base in Asia for three months, thanks go to my friend Cary List for recommending places to stay and put ting me in touch with the lovely Wiwan Tharahirunchot, whose sister's apartment in downtown Bangkok I was able to sublet.

For the Philippines chapter, I'm indebted to my Toronto pal Roberto Borra Ulep for decoding Manila for me, and for connecting me with his old school friends, Oliver and Jonas, whose stories appear in the book, as well as a host of experts on labour migration.

In Sri Lanka, Professor (and ace writer) Randy Boyagoda of Ryerson University hooked me up with the Marga Institute, which in turn opened many other doors for me in Colombo.

In Hong Kong, my thanks go to Michael Bruck for a wonderful stay in his apartment in the Mid-Levels and his gracious company. Kevin Sites of Hong Kong University's Journalism and Media Studies Centre generously shared his contacts in the world of advocacy for domestic workers. Special thanks go to Kay McArdle of PathFinders for allowing me to observe the work she and her amazing team of women do to help many mothers and their children.

For the chapter on Qatar, many thanks are owed to New York–based Stephen Northfield of Human Rights Watch for putting me in touch with Nicholas McGeehan in London, who in turn connected me with Laura Bain in Doha. Both Nicholas and Laura were instrumental in helping me break through the world of construction workers in the Industrial Area and its surroundings.

In Britain, I drew on a pool of old friends who offered advice, contacts and places to stay. Thanks to David Payne and Chris Cox for letting me crash at their beautiful flat in Muswell Hill in North London, and for wonderful conversations over many homemade meals. Simon Wright shared his contacts and knowledge of British race and cultural politics. My friends Jago and Alison Morrison (and their daughter, Lilly, and my godson, Bevan) in Petersfield, Hampshire, are my English family. Thanks for letting me stay with you as long as I wanted, again.

In the United States, I'm indebted to Dina Lior for opening up the world of Mexicans in New York City, and to *Arizona Republic* reporter (and now managing editor at *Honolulu Civil Beat*) Bob Ortega for his many suggestions and contacts, including one to Daniel Gonzalez, immigration reporter at the *Republic.* Thanks to Rolf Sjogren in New York City for making me feel at home in his apartment, always.

In Canada, my thanks go to Ben Barry, associate professor at Ryerson's School of Fashion, for his contacts in the world of colour theory, and to Michelle Shephard from the *Toronto Star* for suggesting a few case studies of discrimination against members of the Arab and Muslim community.

I'm fortunate to have many kind and supportive friends, colleaugues and neighbours who confirm why Toronto has been my home and sanctuary for twenty years (and counting). It's a good place to be brown.

Notes

INTRODUCTION: BROWN. LIKE ME?

For the update on Mark Lester's career, see Martin Whittaker, "Long After the Stardom, Another Twist," *Independent*, October 22, 2011, http://www.independent.co.uk/life-style/long-after-the-stardom-another-twist-mark-lester-was-the-child-star-of-oliver-who-asked-for-more-but-1464248.html.

James Joyce's quote appears in Steven Connor, *The Book of Skin* (Ithaca, NY: Cornell University Press, 2004).

The current figures for people living outside their country of birth (and projections for 2050) come from Kim Mackrael and Charles Forelle, "Taming Immigration: Some Countries See Migrants as an Economic Boon, Not a Burden," *Wall Street Journal*, 2015, http://www.wsj.com/articles/some-countries-see-migrants-as-an-economic-boon-not-a-burden-1450881706.

The deportation of illegal Indonesian workers in Malaysia was widely reported in regional media and international wire services, including Agence France-Presse, which also covered the protest over the vacuum cleaner commercial. The latter story appeared online in the *Guardian* on February 5, 2015, http://www.theguardian.com/world/2015/feb/05/protest-as-malaysian-vacuum-cleaner-advert-says-fire-your-indonesian-maids.

For a general overview of the exploitation of migrant labour, including information on domestics not being paid for work at private homes, I consulted a report by the International Labour Office (ILO) titled "Profits and Poverty: The Economics of Forced Labour" (Geneva: International Labour Office, 2014), http://www.ilo.org/wcmsp5/groups/public/---ed_norm/---declaration/documents/publication/wcms_243391.pdf.

For more on the niqab debate and the 2015 election in Canada, see Adam Rasmi, "Canadian Politics, Unveiled: Could a Niqab Ban Decide the Elections?" *Foreign Affairs*, October 15, 2015, https://www.foreignaffairs.com/articles/canada/2015-10-15/canadian-politics-unveiled. For a breakdown of each party's stance on the niqab, see Laura Payton, "Election Issues 2015: A Maclean's Primer on the Niqab," *Maclean's*, October 6, 2015, http://www.macleans.ca/politics/ottawa/election-issues-2015-a-macleans-primer-on-the-niqab.

For information on the Hispanic population in the United States and its growth patterns, I relied on figures in various reports issued by the Pew Research Center: Hispanic Trends; these reports are available at http://www.pewhispanic.org/. The California statistics come from Javier Panzar, "It's Official: Latinos Now Outnumber Whites in California," *Los Angeles Times*, July 8, 2015, http://www.latimes.com/local/california/la-me-census-latinos-20150708-story.html.

For a historical overview on the emergence of Hispanic Americans as model consumers, I'm indebted to Arlene Dávila, *Latino Spin: Public Image and the Whitewashing of Race* (New York and London: New York University Press, 2008).

Demographic details on South Asians in America are drawn from the 2010 census data, as analyzed by the advocacy group SAALT (South Asian Americans Leading Together). See http://saalt.org/south-asians-in-the-us/demographic-information/. Additional information is also available on the Asian American Federation's website at http://www.aafederation.org/.

For Indians in the tech sector and the H-1B visa, see Kenneth Rapoza, "In India, More Workers Off to U.S.," *Forbes*, January 2, 2013, http://www.forbes.com/sites/kenrapoza/2013/01/02/in-india-more-workers-off-to-u-s/. See also Patrick Thibodeau and Sharon Machlis, "With H-1B Visa, Diversity Doesn't Apply," *Computerworld*, August 10, 2015, http://www.computerworld.com/article/2956584/it-outsourcing/with-h-1b-visa-diversity-doesnt-apply.html.

Projections for the US population between 2012 and 2060 come from an analysis by the United States Census Bureau. For an overview, see https://www.census.gov/newsroom/releases/archives/population/cb12-243.html.

Figures for the Hispanic and South Asian populations of Canada are drawn from Statistics Canada's 2011 National Household Survey (NHS). As well, see Statistics Canada's "Projections of the Diversity of the Canadian Population, 2006 to 2031," http://www.statcan.gc.ca/pub/91-551-x/91-551-x2010001-eng.pdf. Also of interest are Simon Houpt, "Targeting Canada's 'Invisible' Hispanic Community," *Globe and Mail*, November 17, 2011, http://www.theglobeandmail.com/report-on-business/industry-news/marketing/targeting-canadas-invisible-hispanic-community/article554684/, and Eva Salinas, "Latin American Immigrants Make Waves in Canada as Generation Ñ," *Financial Post*, February 4, 2013, http://business.financialpost.com/entrepreneur/latin-american-immigrants-make-waves-in-canada-as-generation-n.

I drew information about the analysis of the US census from Ann Morning, *The Nature of Race: How Scientists Think and Teach About Human Difference* (Berkeley and Los Angeles: University of California Press, 2011), 196.

For insights on the Rob Ford phenomenon in the context of the alienated suburbs, read Jeet Heer, "The Divided City," *Toronto Life*, February 13, 2014, http://torontolife.com/city/rob-ford-toronto-rexdale-downtown/.

For a more detailed discussion of construction workers in Doha, Qatar, see chapter 7 in this book.

Part I

CHAPTER 1: A COLOUR, A VANISHED RACE, A METAPHOR

In addition to the websites mentioned in the text, I drew some general observations about colour psychology, and brown in particular, from various books and articles, including Faber Birren, *Color Psychology and Color Therapy: A Factual Study of the Influence of Color on Human Life* (New Hyde Park, NY: University Books, 1961) and *Color in Your World*, rev. ed. (New York: Collier Books, 1978). See also Adam K. Fetterman, Tianwei Liu and Michael D. Robinson, "Extending Color Psychology to the Personality Realm: Interpersonal Hostility Varies by Red Preferences and Perceptual Biases," *Journal of Personality* 83 (February 1, 2015): 106–16.

Information on UPS comes from the company's corporate website, https://www.ups.com/content/corp/about/history/1929.html, and from Greg Niemann, *The Big Brown: The Untold Story of UPS* (San Francisco: Jossey-Bass, 2007).

Details of the Stormtroopers' and the Nazis' preference for the colour brown appear in several sites about colour psychology, including http://www.sensationalcolor.com. For a brief history of the Brownshirts, see Otis C. Mitchell, *Hitler's Stormtroopers and the Attack on the German Republic, 1919–1933* (Jefferson, NC: McFarland & Company, 2008).

For Karen Haller's views on brown, see http://www.karenhaller.co.uk/psychology-of-colour.htm.

For Obama's tan-suit fracas, see John Hendrickson, "One Year Ago Today, Obama Wore the Worst Suit in Presidential History," Esquire.com, August 28, 2015, http://www.esquire.com/style/mens-fashion/a31265/obama-tan-suit/. On a more serious note, read Daniel Strauss, "Rep. Peter King Is Angry President Obama Wore a Tan Suit," *Talking Points Memo*, August 29, 2014, http://talkingpointsmemo.com/livewire/president-obama-peter-king-tan-suit-rant.

For my survey of work by nineteenth- and early-twentieth-century race scientists, I'm indebted to Nell Irvin Painter, *The History of White People* (New York and London: W. W. Norton & Company, 2010). I also drew on Kwame

Anthony Appiah, "Race in the Modern World: The Problem of the Color Line," *Foreign Affairs* (March/April 2015): 1–8, https://www.foreignaffairs.com/articles/united-states/2015-03-01/race-modern-world, and Nicholas Wade, *A Troublesome Inheritance: Genes, Race and Human History* (New York: Penguin Books, 2015).

Lothrop Stoddard's *The Rising Tide of Color Against White World-Supremacy* is available online from Project Gutenberg, http://www.gutenberg.org/files/37408/37408-h/37408-h.htm.

For more on Davenport, see Wade, *A Troublesome Inheritance.*

For the backlash against racialist science and for the various hypotheses on race and ethnicity, I consulted Peter Kivisto and Paul R. Croll, *Race and Ethnicity: The Basics* (London and New York: Routledge, 2012). See also Stephen Cornell and Douglas Hartmann, *Ethnicity and Race: Making Identities in a Changing World* (Thousand Oaks, CA: Pine Forge Press, 2007).

For more on the transformation of some "darker" ethnic groups into American whites, see David R. Roedigar, *Working Toward Whiteness: How America's Immigrants Became White: The Strange Journey from Ellis Island to the Suburbs* (New York: Basic Books, 2005).

Three books that deal with the otherness—and by definition brownness—of, respectively, the South Asian, Latino and Arab communities in an American context have influenced my thinking in the final section of this chapter. They are Vijay Prashad, *The Karma of Brown Folk* (Minneapolis: University of Minnesota Press, 2000); Richard Rodriguez, *Brown: The Last Discovery of America* (New York: Viking Penguin, 2002); and Moustafa Bayoumi, *How Does It Feel to Be a Problem?: Being Young and Arab in America* (New York: Penguin Press, 2008).

On brownfacing and the casting of visible minorities in Hollywood, see Aziz Ansari, "Aziz Ansari on Acting, Race and Hollywood," *New York Times*, November 10, 2015, http://www.nytimes.com/2015/11/15/arts/television/aziz-ansari-on-acting-race-and-hollywood.html?_r=2.

For a summary of political and physical attacks on brown communities in the US, see South Asian Americans Leading Together (SAALT), "Under Suspicion, Under Attack: Xenophobic Political Rhetoric and Hate Violence against South Asian, Muslim, Sikh, Hindu, Middle Eastern, and Arab Communities in the United States" (2014), http://saalt.org/wp-content/uploads/2013/06/SAALT_report_execsum.pdf.

CHAPTER 2: COLOURISM: FAIR IS FAIR?

Agence France-Presse reported on the letter by Myanmar's consul general in a story that ran on several news sites, including that of the *Sydney Morning Herald*, http://www.smh.com.au/world/envoy-calls-refugees-ugly-as-ogres-20090213-8759.html. See also Greg Torode, "Myanmese Envoy Says Rohingya Ugly as Ogres," *South China Morning Post*, February 11, 2009, http://www.scmp.com/article/669529/myanmese-envoy-says-rohingya-ugly-ogres.

For an overview of the persecution of the Rohingyas in Myanmar, see "Myanmar's Shame," *Economist*, May 23, 2015, www.economist.com/news/asia/21651877-poverty-politics-and-despair-are-forcing-thousands-rohingyas-flee-myanmar-authorities. See also Tom Miles, "Bay of Bengal People-Smuggling Doubles in 2015: UNHCR," Reuters, May 8, 2015, http://www.reuters.com/article/us-thailand-rohingya-unhcr-idUSKBN0NT11D20150508.

For the general discussion of shadism and colourism, I've drawn on the following: Evelyn Nakano Glenn, ed., *Shades of Difference: Why Skin Color Matters* (Stanford, CA: Stanford University Press, 2009); Kathy Russell, Midge Wilson and Ronald Hall, *The Color Complex: The Politics of Skin Color Among African Americans* (New York: Anchor Books, 1992); Kimberly Jade

Norwood, ed., *Color Matters: Skin Tone Bias and the Myth of Post-Racial America* (New York and London: Routledge, 2014); and Ashley W. Doane and Eduardo Bonilla-Silva, eds., *White Out: The Continuing Significance of Racism* (London and New York: Routledge, 2003).

Harris-Perry is quoted in Touré, *Who's Afraid of Post-Blackness?: What It Means to Be Black Now* (New York: Free Press, 2011). For a Canadian take on being a light-skinned black person, see Lawrence Hill, *Black Berry, Sweet Juice: On Being Black and White in Canada* (Toronto: Harper Perennial, 2001).

For insights into race and colour (or colour as a substitute for race) in Brazil, I consulted Stephanie Nolen, "Brazil's Colour Bind," *Globe and Mail,* July 31, 2015, http://www.theglobeandmail.com/news/world/brazils-colour-bind/article25779474/. See also Deborah J. Yashar, "Does Race Matter in Latin America?: How Racial and Ethnic Identities Shape the Region's Politics," *Foreign Affairs* (March/April 2015): 33–40, https://www.foreignaffairs.com/articles/south-america/2015-02-16/does-race-matter-latin-america.

For Eduardo Bonilla-Silva and David R. Dietrich's "Latin Americanization" of race in the US, see Glenn, ed., *Shades of Difference*, 40–60.

For more on Bobby Jindal's portrait, see Jack Linshi, "Why a Bobby Jindal Portrait Sparked a Racial Controversy," Time.com, February 5, 2015, http://time.com/3695541/bobby-jindal-indian-immigration/. See also Hillary Crosley Coker, "Bobby Jindal's New Portrait Is White Enough to Win an Oscar," Jezebel.com, February 4, 2015, http://jezebel.com/bobby-jindals-new-portrait-is-white-enough-to-win-an-os-1683700260.

Some details in the section on Dr. Nimal Gamage are from his website, http://www.lankacosmetic.com. For a literary evocation of Cinnamon Gardens, see Shyam Selvadurai, *Cinnamon Gardens* (Toronto: McClelland & Stewart, 1998).

CHAPTER 3: TRINIDAD: GUARDING THE COLOUR LINE

For the discussion on the Indo identity in Trinidad, I drew on Kavyta Raghunandan, "Hyphenated Identities: Negotiating 'Indianness' and Being Indo-Trinidadian," *Caribbean Review of Gender Studies* 6 (2012): 1–19, and Bridget Brereton, "'All ah We Is Not One': Historical and Ethnic Narratives in Pluralist Trinidad," *Global South*, vol. 4, no. 2 (Fall 2010): 218–38, http://www.jstor.org/stable/10.2979/globalsouth.4.2.218.

For the overview and new interpretations of indentured Indian labour in the Caribbean, see Viranjini Munasinghe, *Callaloo or Tossed Salad?: East Indians and the Cultural Politics of Identity in Trinidad* (Ithaca, NY: Cornell University Press, 2001).

General population information on Trinidad and Tobago can be found at the United Nations *Demographic Yearbook 2014*, http://unstats.un.org/unsd/demographic/products/dyb/dyb2014.htm.

For more on Darrell's research into ethnic struggles through chutney music, see Darrell Gerohn Baksh, "Jep Sting Radica with Rum and Roti: Trinidadian Social Dynamics in Chutney Music," *Popular Music and Society*, vol. 37, no. 2 (2014): 152–68. See also "The Indian Community in Trinidad: An Interview with Viranjini Munasinghe" on the Asia Society website, http://asiasociety.org/indian-community-trinidad-interview-viranjini-munasinghe.

For a comparative look at the African and the Indian narrative claim on Trinidad, see Tony Martin, "African and Indian Consciousness," in *General History of the Caribbean*, vol. 5 (Paris: UNESCO, 1996), 258–312.

On aspects of colourism in Trinidad, I drew on Aisha Khan, "Caucasian, Coolie, Black, or White?: Color and Race in the Indo-Caribbean Diaspora," in Glenn, ed., *Shades of Difference*, 95–113.

For an anthropological reading of the kidnappings of people of Indian descent in Trinidad, see Rebecca Prentice, "'Kidnapping Go Build Back We Economy': Discourses of Crime at Work in Neoliberal Trinidad," *Journal of the Royal Anthropological Institute* 18 (2012): 45–64.

Part II

CHAPTER 4: THE PHILIPPINES: AT THE WORLD'S SERVICE

More information on the various programs offered by the Magsaysay Center for Hospitality and Culinary Arts can be found at http://www.mihca.com.ph/.

Details of the Flor Contemplacion case and its national implications are drawn from various sources, including Philip Shenon, "Ramos Calls the Filipino Maid Executed in Singapore a Heroine," *New York Times*, March 19, 1995, http://www.nytimes.com/1995/03/19/world/ramos-calls-the-filipino-maid-executed-in-singapore-a-heroine.html. For the Greek definition of the word "Filipineza," see "Definition of Filipina as Maid Is Correct," *New Straits Times*, August 12, 1998.

For the labour shortage in Singapore's restaurants, see Jessica Lim, "Eateries Turning Away Diners Due to Growing Labour Crunch," Straitstimes.com, January 27, 2015, http://www.straitstimes.com/singapore/eateries-turning-away-diners-due-to-growing-labour-crunch.

For my overview of migration history in the Philippines, I'm indebted to Filomeno V. Aguilar Jr., *Migration Revolution: Philippine Nationhood and Class Relations in a Globalized Age* (Manila: Ateneo de Manila University Press, 2014). I also drew on Sunil S. Amrith, *Migration and Diaspora in Modern Asia* (Cambridge, UK: Cambridge University Press, 2011).

The September 2014 report from the Centre for Migration Advocacy can be found at https://centerformigrantadvocacy.files.wordpress.com/2014/04/working-paper-on-the-mdgs-philippine-migration-and-the-sdgs.pdf.

Lysley Tenorio's short story "Aviary" appears in Jessica Hagedorn, ed., *Manila Noir* (Mandaluyong City: Anvil Publishing, 2014), 17–27.

For a historical analysis of the Filipino transformation from musicians to entertainers and hosts, see Lydia N. Yu Jose, "Why Are Most Filipino Workers in Japan Entertainers?: Perspectives from History and Law," *Kasarinlan: Philippine Journal of Third World Studies*, vol. 22, no. 1 (2007): 61–84, http://journals.upd.edu.ph/index.php/kasarinlan/article/viewArticle/363.

The UN Women report is titled "Contributions of Migrant Domestic Workers to Sustainable Development" and is available for download at http://asiapacific.unwomen.org/~/media/7148BD87A4F7412D8CBD10482146276F.ashx. For more on gendered analysis of migrant labour from the Philippines, see Rhacel Salazar Parreñas, *The Force of Domesticity: Filipina Migrants and Globalization* (New York and London: New York University Press, 2008).

CHAPTER 5: HONG KONG: WORKERS, WOMEN, MOTHERS

For more on karaoke's popularity in the Philippines, see Suemedha Sood, "Karaoke in the Philippines," BBC.com, August 12, 2011, http://www.bbc.com/travel/story/20110812-travelwise-karaoke-in-the-philippines.

The 2014 figures for domestic workers in Hong Kong come from a presentation I attended at Helpers for Domestic Helpers in April 2015. For more, see http://www.hdh-sjc.org. Additional information on the minimum wage comes from the independent HK Helpers Campaign, http://hkhelperscampaign.com/en/, and We Care Hong Kong, http://wecarehk.com.

For the history of Filipina domestic workers in Hong Kong, I drew on Nicole Constable, *Maid to Order in Hong Kong: Stories of Migrant Workers* (Ithaca and London: Cornell University Press, 2007). See also Vivienne Wee and Amy Sim, "Hong Kong as a Destination for Migrant Domestic Workers," in Shirlena Huang, Brenda S. A. Yeoh and Noor Abdul Rahman, eds., *Asian Women and Transnational Domestic Workers* (Singapore: Marshall Cavendish Academic, 2005).

Information on Hong Kong as a society of working women can be found in Miho Goda, "Working Mothers and Foreign Domestic Helpers in Hong Kong," Childresearch.net, November 15, 2013, http://www.childresearch.net/papers/parenting/2013_01.html.

For more on the sexualization of domestic workers, see Kimberly A. Chang and Julian McAllister Groves, "Neither 'Saints' Nor 'Prostitutes': Sexual Discourse in the Filipina Domestic Worker Community in Hong Kong," *Women's Studies International Forum*, vol. 23, no. 1 (2000): 73–87. See also Nicole Constable, "Jealousy, Chastity and Abuse: Chinese Maids and Foreign Helpers in Hong Kong," *Modern China*, vol. 22, no. 4 (1996): 448–79, http://www.jstor.org/stable/189304.

The analysis of the role domestic helpers play in family well-being in Hong Kong is from "Hiring Domestic Help and Family Well-being Among Chinese Couples in Hong Kong: A Propensity Score Matching Analysis," a presentation by Adam Ka-Lok Cheung at the Demographic and Institutional Change in Global Families Conference in Taipei, Taiwan, March 2013, http://www.ios.sinica.edu.tw/dicgf/abstract/p-6-4.pdf.

The breakdown of cases from the PathFinders files comes from the 2014 annual report, available for download at http://www.pathfinders.org.hk/public/wp-content/uploads/PathAR2014_23_6_1650.pdf. For more on domestic workers as mothers and the role played by PathFinders, see Nicole Constable, *Born Out of Place: Migrant Mothers and the Politics of International Labor* (Hong Kong: Hong Kong University Press, 2014).

The most detailed look inside ChungKing Mansions appears in Gordon Mathews, *Ghetto at the Center of the World: Chungking Mansions, Hong Kong* (Chicago and London: University of Chicago Press, 2011).

For a list of activities of the Feast Hong Kong, see https://www.facebook.com/thefeasthongkong.

CHAPTER 6: SRI LANKA: IN THE SHADOW OF THE PHILIPPINES

The figures for migrant workers leaving Sri Lanka annually and foreign exchange earnings are drawn from Bilesha Weeraratne, "Sri Lankan Female Domestic Workers in the Middle East: Does Recruitment through an Agent Minimize Vulnerability?" (Colombo: Institute of Policy Studies of Sri Lanka, 2014).

For reports on the execution of Rizana Nafeek, see "Sri Lankan Maid Rizana Nafeek Beheaded in Saudi Arabia," BBC.com, January 9, 2013, http://www.bbc.com/news/world-asia-20959228. See also Jason Burke, "Saudi Arabia Executes Maid Accused of Murdering Baby," *Guardian*, January 9, 2013, http://www.theguardian.com/world/2013/jan/09/saudi-arabia-executes-woman.

For a summary of migration patterns to and from Sri Lanka, see Nisha Arunatilake, Priyanka Jayawardena and Dushni Weerakoon, "Sri Lanka," in Saman Kelegama, ed., *Migration, Remittances and Development in South Asia* (New Delhi: Sage, 2011). See also Amrith, *Migration and Diaspora in Modern Asia.*

Information about Sri Lankan female domestic workers in the Gulf is drawn from Michele Ruth Gamburd, "Sri Lankan Migration to the Gulf: Female Breadwinners—Domestic Workers," Middle East Institute, February 2, 2010, http://www.mei.edu/content/sri-lankan-migration-gulf-female-breadwinners-domestic-workers. See also Weeraratne, "Sri Lankan Female Domestic Workers in the Middle East," and a report from International Trade Union Confederation, "Facilitating Exploitation: A Review of Labour Laws for Migrant Domestic Workers in Gulf Cooperation Council Countries," November 2014, http://www.ituc-csi.org/gcc-legal-and-policy-brief?lang=en.

For stories of returnees, see Suwendrani Jayaratne, Nipuni Perera, Neluka Gunasekera and Nisha Arunatilake, "Returning Home: Experiences and

Challenges—The Experience of Returnee Migrant Workers of Sri Lanka" (Colombo: Institute of Policy Studies of Sri Lanka, 2014), http://med-mig.ips.lk/handle/789/169.

For a sample of Mangala Raneniya's media exposure, see "Lankans Eyeing Gulf Jobs Warned Against Con Agents," Adaderana.lk, March 23, 2014, http://www.adaderana.lk/news.php?nid=26170. See also Leon Berenger, "300 Sri Lankan Expatriate Workers Die Annually; Most of Them in West Asia," (Sri Lanka) *Sunday Times*, no date, http://www.sundaytimes.lk/140406/news/300-sri-lankan-expatriate-workers-die-annually-most-of-them-in-west-asia-91813.html.

CHAPTER 7: QATAR: BETWEEN MEN

Reports on the marathon fiasco appeared on various news sites, including the following: Lesley Walker, "Qatar Marathon Organizers Apologize After Runners Lament Event Setup," *Doha News*, March 29, 2015, http://dohanews.co/qatar-marathon-organizers-apologize-after-runners-lament-event-setup/; Ben Collins, "Slaves Forced to Run Marathon Shoeless in Qatar," *Daily Beast*, April 2, 2015, http://www.thedailybeast.com/articles/2015/04/02/slaves-to-run-shoeless-in-qatar.html; and Richard Spencer, "Asian Labourers 'Press-Ganged' into Joining Qatar Marathon Record Attempt," *Daily Telegraph*, March 30, 2015, http://www.telegraph.co.uk/news/worldnews/middleeast/qatar/11503669/Asian-labourers-press-ganged-into-joining-Qatar-marathon-record-attempt.html.

The information on death tolls for migrant workers in Qatar comes from the report "Building a Better World Cup: Protecting Migrant Workers in Qatar Ahead of FIFA 2022," Human Rights Watch, June 2012, https://www.hrw.org/report/2012/06/12/building-better-world-cup/protecting-migrant-workers-qatar-ahead-fifa-2022; and from "The Case Against Qatar: Host of the FIFA 2022 World Cup," International Trade Union Confederation, March 2014, http://www.ituc-csi.org/IMG/pdf/the_case_against_qatar_en_web170314.pdf. See also Owen Gibson, "More than 500 Indian Workers

Have Died in Qatar Since 2012, Figures Show," *Guardian*, February 18, 2014, http://www.theguardian.com/world/2014/feb/18/qatar-world-cup-india-migrant-worker-deaths. The *Guardian*'s "Modern-Day Slavery In Focus" series (http://www.theguardian.com/global-development/series/modern-day-slavery-in-focus) features several in-depth looks at Qatar.

The breakdown of Qatar's economy comes from the CIA World Factbook, https://www.cia.gov/library/publications/the-world-factbook/geos/qa.html#Econ.

For a scorecard on Qatar's 2014 pledge to improve the lives of its migrant workers, see Owen Gibson, "Qatar: How Have Conditions for Migrant Workers Changed in Nine Key Areas?" *Guardian*, May 14, 2015, http://www.theguardian.com/world/2015/may/14/qatar-how-have-conditions-for-migrant-workers-changed-in-nine-key-areas.

For details on the arrest and detention of the German TV crew, see Ben Rumsby, "Qatar World Cup 2022: TV Crew Arrested and Has Equipment Destroyed for Filming Documentary About Event," *Daily Telegraph*, May 5, 2015, http://www.telegraph.co.uk/sport/football/world-cup/11583406/Qatar-World-Cup-2022-TV-crew-arrested-and-has-equipment-destroyed-for-filming-documentary-about-event.html.

Part III

Chapter 8: The United Kingdom: British Values

For a brief history of the Muath Trust, see http://www.muathtrust.org/Aboutus.aspx. For information on the Muslim Council of Britain, see http://www.mcb.org.uk.

For a summary of the MCB's changing fortunes, see "No One to Talk To: A Muslim Group Falls from Favour," *Economist*, October 18, 2014, http://

www.economist.com/news/britain/21625867-muslim-group-falls-favour-no-one-talk. See also Arun Kundnani, *The Muslims Are Coming: Islamophobia, Extremism, and the Domestic War on Terror* (London: Verso, 2015).

Figures on Muslims in the UK come from the Muslim Council of Britain, "British Muslims in Numbers: A Demographic, Socio-economic and Health Profile of Muslims in Britain Drawing on the 2011 Census," January 2015, http://www.mcb.org.uk/wp-content/uploads/2015/02/MCBCensusReport_2015.pdf.

For a thorough analysis of the emergence of Islam as a political identity in Britain (and Europe), particularly among youths, see Doug Saunders, *The Myth of the Muslim Tide: Do Immigrants Threaten the West?* (Toronto: Knopf Canada, 2012). See also Ian Buruma, *Murder in Amsterdam: Liberal Europe, Islam, and the Limits of Tolerance* (New York: Penguin Books, 2006).

For more on Cameron's definition of British values, see David Cameron, "British Values Aren't Optional, They're Vital," *Daily Mail*, June 15, 2014, http://www.dailymail.co.uk/debate/article-2658171/DAVID-CAMERON-British-values-arent-optional-theyre-vital-Thats-I-promote-EVERY-school-As-row-rages-Trojan-Horse-takeover-classrooms-Prime-Minister-delivers-uncompromising-pledge.html.

For the popular use of the word "brown" among South Asians in London, see Gautam Malkani, *Londonstani: A Novel* (Toronto: Harper Perennial, 2008).

For the official record on CONTEST, the counter-terrorism strategy, I consulted HM Government's publication *CONTEST: The United Kingdom's Strategy for Countering Terrorism* (London: TSO, 2011). Available in English, Arabic and Urdu from https://www.gov.uk/government/publications/counter-terrorism-strategy-contest.

The British media response to CONTEST and Prevent has been detailed and critical on both ends of the political spectrum. A select list of articles I consulted includes the following: Douglas Murray, "The Prevent Strategy: A Textbook Example of How to Alienate Just About Everybody," *Daily Telegraph*, March 31, 2010, http://www.telegraph.co.uk/news/uknews/terrorism-in-the-uk/7540456/The-Prevent-strategy-a-textbook-example-of-how-to-alienate-just-about-everybody.html; Josh Halliday and Vikram Dodd, "UK Anti-radicalisation Prevent Strategy a 'Toxic Brand,'" *Guardian*, March 9, 2015, http://www.theguardian.com/uk-news/2015/mar/09/anti-radicalisation-prevent-strategy-a-toxic-brand; and John Morgan, "Universities Must Assess Risk of Students Becoming Terrorists, Says Home Office," *Times Higher Education*, March 12, 2015, https://www.timeshighereducation.com/news/universities-must-assess-risk-of-students-becoming-terrorists-says-home-office/2019067.article.

Quotes from the Preventing Violent Extremism Conference are drawn from various handouts in the press kit. Some of them also appear in Faisal Bodi, "A Briefing by the Islamic Human Rights Commission on Tackling Extremism in the UK: A Report of the Prime Minister's Taskforce on Tackling Radicalisation and Extremism" (London: Islamic Human Rights Commission, 2014), http://www.ihrc.org.uk/attachments/article/10904/TEUK%20Report-FV-FB.pdf.

For an analysis of the John Casey article in the *Salisbury Review*, see Michael M. J. Fischer and Mehdi Abedi, *Debating Muslims: Cultural Dialogues in Postmodernity and Tradition* (Madison: University of Wisconsin Press, 1990).

CHAPTER 9: FRANCE: ANOTHER PARIS

On the number of Muslims in France and a breakdown of country of origin, see Jonathan Laurence, "Islam in France," December 2001, http://www.brookings.edu/research/articles/2001/12/france-laurence, and Jonathan Laurence and Justin Vaisse, "Being Muslim in France," in *Integrating Islam: Political and Religious*

Challenges in Contemporary France (Washington, DC: Brookings Institution, 2006), http://www.brookings.edu/research/books/2006/integratingislam. See also Jawad Iqbal, "Muslim Population in France," BBC.com, January 15, 2015, http://www.bbc.com/news/the-reporters-30835554.

For an overview of the early waves of North African migrants to France, see Naomi Davidson, *Only Muslim: Embodying Islam in Twentieth-Century France* (Ithaca, NY: Cornell University Press, 2012).

On the *banlieues,* youth riots and France's complex relationship with Arabs, see Andrew Hussey, *The French Intifada: The Long War Between France and Its Arabs* (London: Granta, 2014). See also Angelique Chrisafis, "Seven Years After the Riots, the Suburbs of Paris Still Simmer with Resentment," *Guardian*, November 3, 2012, http://www.theguardian.com/world/2012/nov/03/estate-racial-hatred-poisoning-france.

For details on the treatment of minorities, particularly Muslim North Africans, in France, see Laurence and Vaisse, *Integrating Islam.*

For more on kebab as a barometer of cultural change in France, see Alexandria Sage, "In France, Kebabs Get Wrapped Up in Identity Politics," Reuters.com, October 28, 2014, http://www.reuters.com/article/us-france-immigration-kebabs-idUSKBN0IH0CQ20141028.

Information collected by the Collectif contre l'islamophobie en France is included in an English-language report covering the first half of 2015, "Report on Islamophobia in France Six Months After the January 2015 Terrorist Attacks."

For an analysis of the attitude of second-generation North Africans toward France and Islam, see Jean Beaman, "As French as Anyone Else: Islam and the North African Second Generation in France," *International Migration Review* (May 2014), http://onlinelibrary.wiley.com/doi/10.1111/imre.12184/abstract.

For more on the resumé experiment, see Claire Adida, David Laitin and Marie-Anne Valfort, "The Muslim Effect on Immigrant Integration in France," *Washington Post*, September 30, 2014, https://www.washingtonpost.com/blogs/monkey-cage/wp/2014/09/30/the-muslim-effect-on-immigrant-integration-in-france-2/.

For contrasting views on *Charlie Hebdo*, see two articles in the same magazine: Jeffrey Goldberg, "The Dangerous Myths About *Charlie Hebdo*," *Atlantic Monthly*, May 5, 2015, http://www.theatlantic.com/international/archive/2015/05/charlie-hebdo-trudeau-pen-garland/392255/, and Scott Sayare, "The *Charlie Hebdo* I Know," *Atlantic Monthly*, January 11, 2015, http://www.theatlantic.com/international/archive/2015/01/charlie-hebdo-secularism-religion-islam/384413/.

For coverage of the long skirt controversy, see the Agence France-Presse story, "French Muslim Student Banned from School for Wearing Long Black Skirt," *Guardian*, April 28, 2015, http://www.theguardian.com/world/2015/apr/28/french-muslim-student-banned-from-school-for-wearing-long-skirt. See also the *New York Times* editorial, "Laïcité and the Skirt," May 1, 2015, http://www.nytimes.com/2015/05/02/opinion/laicite-and-the-skirt.html.

CHAPTER 10: THE UNITED STATES: UNDOCUMENTED

For a summary, and fact-check, of Trump's statements on Mexican immigrants, see Michelle Ye Hee Lee, "Donald Trump's False Comments Connecting Mexican Immigrants and Crime," *Washington Post*, July 8, 2015, https://www.washingtonpost.com/news/fact-checker/wp/2015/07/08/donald-trumps-false-comments-connecting-mexican-immigrants-and-crime/.

Ben Carson explained his policy on Mexican migrant workers during a CNN debate. A transcript of the various candidates' views on the issue from the same debate can found at http://www.ontheissues.org/Archive/2015_CNN_GOP_Immigration.htm.

For an overview of undocumented immigrants in the US, including workers in the service industry, see Jeffrey S. Passel and D'Vera Cohn, "A Portrait of Unauthorized Immigrants in the United States," Pew Research Center: Hispanic Trends, April 14, 2009, http://www.pewhispanic.org/2009/04/14/a-portrait-of-unauthorized-immigrants-in-the-united-states/. On the use of illegal immigrants in the fast food industry, see Lisa Baertlein, Mary Milliken and Ed Stoddard, "U.S. Fast Food Caught in Immigration Crosshairs," Reuters.com, February 8, 2011, http://www.reuters.com/article/us-usa-immigration-fastfood-idUSTRE71664T20110208.

For the drop in net immigration from Mexico during the Great Recession, see Jeffrey S. Passel, D'Vera Cohn and Ana Gonzalez-Barrera, "Net Migration from Mexico Falls to Zero—and Perhaps Less," Pew Research Center: Hispanic Trends, April 23, 2012, http://www.pewhispanic.org/2012/04/23/net-migration-from-mexico-falls-to-zero-and-perhaps-less/. For the figures from 2014–15, see Jens Manuel Krogstad and Mark Hugo Lopez, "Hispanic Population Reaches Record 55 Million, but Growth Has Cooled," Pew Research Center: Hispanic Trends, June 25, 2015, http://www.pewresearch.org/fact-tank/2015/06/25/u-s-hispanic-population-growth-surge-cools/.

For more on the black–Hispanic divide, see Jeffrey M. Jones, "Americans Rate Racial and Ethnic Relations in U.S. Positively," Gallup.com, July 17, 2013, http://www.gallup.com/poll/163535/americans-rate-racial-ethnic-relations-positively.aspx. See also "Where Black and Brown Collide," *Economist*, August 2, 2007, http://www.economist.com/node/9587776.

For racial attacks in Port Richmond, Staten Island, see Andy Humm, "Behind the Hate Crimes on Staten Island," Gothamgazette.com, August 23, 2010, http://www.gothamgazette.com/index.php/civil-rights/583-behind-the-hate-crimes-on-staten-island. For the *New York Post*'s take on the issue, see Steven Long, "The Great Black-Hispanic Split," *New York Post*, January 22, 2008, http://nypost.com/2008/01/22/the-great-black-hispanic-split/.

For walking tours of the Little Mexico neighbourhood in New York City, see http://lasirenanyc.blogspot.ca/p/mexico-walking-tour-la-sirena-27-east-3.html.

For more information on the Deferred Action for Parents of Americans and Lawful Permanent Residents (DAPA) program and Obama's executive actions on immigration, see http://www.uscis.gov/immigrationaction.

For a general picture of how Latinos participate in a discourse that views them as more American than "the Americans," see Arlene Dávila, *Latino Spin*.

For Phoenix as a gateway to America for Indian refugees, see Daniel Gonzalez, "Immigrants from India Surge Across Arizona Border," *Arizona Republic*, September 8, 2013, http://www.azcentral.com/news/politics/articles/20130907immigration-arizona-border-indian.html.

For an overview of Arpaio's legal battles, see Stephen Lemons, "Criminal Enterprise: A Culture of Corruption Pervades Joe Arpaio's Office, Affecting Everyone in Maricopa County," *Phoenix New Times*, June 3, 2015, http://www.phoenixnewtimes.com/news/criminal-enterprise-a-culture-of-corruption-pervades-joe-arpaios-office-affecting-everyone-in-maricopa-county-7383399. For an in-depth look at Arpaio's multiple terms in office and his legacy, see Michael Kiefer, "Sheriff Joe Arpaio Has Always Done It His Way," *Arizona Republic*, September 11, 2015, http://www.azcentral.com/story/news/arizona/investigations/2015/09/11/sheriff-joe-arpaio-legacy/71888720/.

For the murder of Kate Steinle in San Francisco, see Steve Almasy, Pamela Brown and Augie Martin, "Suspect in Killing of San Francisco Woman Had Been Deported Five Times," CNN.com, July 4, 2015, http://www.cnn.com/2015/07/03/us/san-francisco-killing-suspect-immigrant-deported/.

For the ramifications of Kate's Law, see Matt Ford, "The Trouble with Kate's Law," *Atlantic Monthly*, September 6, 2015, http://www.theatlantic.com/politics/archive/2015/09/kates-law-mandatory-sentencing/403990/.

For a defence and overview of respectability politics, see Randall Kennedy, "Lifting as We Climb: A Progressive Defense of Respectability Politics," *Harper's*, October 2015, http://harpers.org/archive/2015/10/lifting-as-we-climb/.

For updates on Puente's campaigns against Arpaio, see http://puenteaz.org. More information on the Center for Neighborhood Leadership's various initiatives can be found at https://www.facebook.com/AzCNL/.

For an analysis of Arizona's immigration laws, including SB 1070, see "Arizona's Immigration Enforcement Laws" on the website of the National Conference of State Legislatures, http://www.ncsl.org/research/immigration/analysis-of-arizonas-immigration-law.aspx.

For information on suicide rates at the Eloy Detention Center, see Megan Jula and Daniel Gonzalez, "Eloy Detention Center: Why So Many Suicides?" *Arizona Republic*, July 29, 2015, http://www.azcentral.com/story/news/arizona/investigations/2015/07/28/eloy-detention-center-immigrant-suicides/30760545/.

For more information on Proposition 200, see Rebekah L. Sanders, "The History of Proposition 200," *Arizona Republic*, June 17, 2013, http://www.azcentral.com/news/politics/articles/20130316proposition-200-history-timeline.html.

For Proposition 300's impact on undocumented students, see Jesse McKinley, "Arizona Law Takes a Toll on Nonresident Students," *New York Times*, January 27, 2008, http://www.nytimes.com/2008/01/27/us/27tuition.html?_r=0.

CHAPTER 11: CANADA: THE WEDGE ISSUE

Project Thread received extensive coverage in the Canadian press. I relied on the following reports from the *Globe and Mail* and the *Toronto Star*: Colin Freeze and Marina Jimenez, "Adjudicator Frees Suspect, Disputes Terrorist Scenario," *Globe and Mail*, August 28, 2003, http://www.theglobeandmail.com/news/national/adjudicator-frees-suspect-disputes-terrorist-scenario/article22500815/; Colin Freeze, "Terror Allegations Termed 'Garbage,'" *Globe and Mail*, August 26, 2003; Michelle Shephard and Sonia Verma, "They Only Arrested the Muhammads," *Toronto Star*, November 30, 2003; and Sonia Verma, "Our Dreams Are Now Dust," *Toronto Star*, February 8, 2004.

For an analysis of how the *Globe and Mail* and the *National Post*, Canada's two national newspapers, covered Project Thread, see Felix Odartey-Wellington, "Racial Profiling and Moral Panic: Operation Thread and the Al-Qaeda Sleeper Cell That Never Was," *Global Media Journal* (Canadian Edition), vol. 2, no. 2 (2009): 25–40, http://www.gmj.uottawa.ca/0902/v2i2_odartey-wellington.pdf. See also Govind Rao, "Inventing Enemies: Project Thread and Canadian 'Security,'" *Canadian Dimension* 38, no. 1 (January/February 2004), https://canadiandimension.com/articles/view/inventing-enemies-project-thread-canadian-security.

For more on the Toronto 18 case, see Michelle Shephard, *Decade of Fear: Reporting from Terrorism's Grey Zone* (Vancouver: Douglas & McIntyre, 2011), and the online series by Isabel Teotonio in the *Toronto Star*, http://www3.thestar.com/static/toronto18/, no date.

For information on security certificates, see the website of Public Safety Canada, http://www.publicsafety.gc.ca/cnt/ntnl-scrt/cntr-trrrsm/scrt-crtfcts-eng.aspx. See also "Security Certificates and Secret Evidence," CBCnews.ca, August 21, 2009, http://www.cbc.ca/news/canada/security-certificates-and-secret-evidence-1.777624.

The analysis of Bill C-51 Charter violations is drawn from Craig Forcese and Kent Roach, *False Security: The Radicalization of Canadian Anti-Terrorism* (Toronto: Irwin Law, 2015).

For the Harper government's treatment of Muslim and Arab-Canadians, see Steven Zhou, "Racism in Stephen Harper's Canada," Jacobinmag.com, December 18, 2014, https://www.jacobinmag.com/2014/12/racism-in-stephen-harpers-canada/, and Davide Mastracci, "Islamophobia Sells in Canada: Harper's Re-election Campaign Is Built on Demonizing Muslims," AlJazeera America, March 2, 2015, http://america.aljazeera.com/opinions/2015/3/islamophobia-sells-in-canada.html. See also Mahdi Darius Nazemroaya, "The Demonization of Arabs, Muslims: The Harper Government Spreads Hate in Canada While It Supports Terror Overseas," Globalresearch.org, March 18, 2015, http://www.globalresearch.ca/the-demonization-of-arabs-muslims-the-harper-government-spreads-hate-in-canada-while-it-supports-terror-overseas/5437409.

For the EKOS poll analysis, see Frank Graves, "Tolerance Under Pressure?" EKOSpolitics.com, March 12, 2015, http://www.ekospolitics.com/index.php/2015/03/tolerance-under-pressure/.

For Jason Kenney's court battle with the CAF, see Debra Black, "Jason Kenney's Decision to Cut Funding to the Canadian Arab Federation Was Reasonable, Court Rules," *Toronto Star*, January 7, 2014, http://www.thestar.com/news/canada/2014/01/07/judge_backs_jason_kenneys_decision_to_cut_funding_to_canadian_arab_federation.html.

For more on the Aga Khan's visit in 2014, see Kim Nursall, "Aga Khan, Prime Minister Stephen Harper Announce $100M Joint Aid Venture," *Toronto Star*, February 28, 2014, http://www.thestar.com/news/gta/2014/02/28/aga_khan_prime_minister_stephen_harper_announce_100m_joint_aid_venture.html.

For the monitoring of the Idle No More movement, see Jorge Barrera, "Aboriginal Affairs Shared Wide Range of Information with Spy Agency to Bolster Idle No More Surveillance: Documents," APTN National News, March 18, 2015, http://aptn.ca/news/2015/03/18/aboriginal-affairs-shared-wide-range-information-spy-agency-bolster-idle-surveillance-documents/.

For Ashley Callingbull-Burnham's comments on the Conservatives' treatment of First Nations, see "New Mrs. Universe Says Tory Government Treats First Nations People 'Like Terrorists,'" CBC News, September 3, 2015, http://www.cbc.ca/news/politics/mrs-universe-conservatives-ashley-callingbull-1.3214214.

For more on the Mohamed Harkat case, visit http://www.justiceforharkat.com/news.php.

I wrote about the first set of Brampton flyers in the context of race and nostalgia. See Kamal Al-Solaylee, "What You Don't See When You Look Back," *Canadian Notes & Queries* 91 (Fall/Winter 2014): 18–20. Details about subsequent flyers come from Angie Seth, "Brampton Hit with Another String of Anti-immigration Flyers," Global News, August 7, 2014, http://globalnews.ca/news/1498130/brampton-hit-with-another-string-of-anti-immigration-flyers/.

For more on Williamson's comments, see "John Williamson Faces Heavy Criticism After 'Whities' Comment," CBC News, March 10, 2015, http://www.cbc.ca/news/canada/new-brunswick/john-williamson-faces-heavy-criticism-after-whities-comment-1.2988674, and Jamie Long, "Harper Urged to Remove MP John Williamson over 'Whities' Comments,' CBC News, March 12, 2015, http://www.cbc.ca/news/politics/harper-urged-to-remove-mp-john-williamson-over-whities-comment-1.2992300.

For the racial makeup of the Liberal caucus, see Mike Blanchfield, "Diverse Liberal Caucus Has 38 of 46 Visible Minorities Elected," *Toronto Star*, November 1, 2015, http://www.thestar.com/news/canada/2015/11/01/diverse-liberal-caucus-has-38-of-the-46-visible-minorities-elected.html.

For the expulsion of Asians from Uganda, see Richard Dowden, "Short-Sighted Demagogue Who Played the Race Card," *Independent*, August 4, 1992, http://www.independent.co.uk/news/world/short-sighted-demagogue-who-played-the-race-card-idi-amin-expelled-the-asians-20-years-ago-richard-1538196.html. See also Marc Lacey, "Once Outcasts, Asians Again Drive Uganda's Economy," *New York Times*, August 17, 2003, http://www.nytimes.com/2003/08/17/world/once-outcasts-asians-again-drive-uganda-s-economy.html.

For allegations about Hamdani's past, see Catherine Solyom, "Hussein Hamdani: Vetted by the Feds, Felled by a Blog," *Montreal Gazette*, May 26, 2015, http://montrealgazette.com/news/local-news/hussein-hamdani-vetted-by-the-feds-felled-by-a-blog.

The 1996 Muslim Students Association publication that got Hamdani into trouble is available on the *Point de Bascule* blog, http://pointdebasculecanada.ca/wp-content/uploads/2013/09/MSA-National-Guide-Islamization-Hamdani-Haddara.pdf.

For Blaney's termination of Hamdani's tenure on the roundtable, see "Suspended Hamilton National Security Adviser Gets Thank You Letter from Feds," Canadian Press/CBC News, August 19, 2015, http://www.cbc.ca/news/canada/hamilton/news/suspended-hamilton-national-security-adviser-gets-thank-you-letter-from-feds-1.3196036.

On the proliferation of anti-Muslim websites (and their funding sources), see Matthew Duss, Yasmine Taeb, Ken Gude and Ken Sofer, "Fear, Inc. 2.0: The

Islamophobia Network's Efforts to Manufacture Hate in America," Center for American Progress, February 2015, https://cdn.americanprogress.org/wp-content/uploads/2015/02/FearInc-report2.11.pdf.

For lessons from the 2015 federal election on Canada's vulnerability to racial incitement, see Erna Paris, "Canada Is Not Immune to the Most Dangerous Tactic in Politics," *Ottawa Citizen*, October 26, 2015, http://ottawacitizen.com/news/politics/canada-is-not-immune-to-the-most-dangerous-tactic-in-politics.